Free Video  **Free Video**

Essential Test Tips Video from Trivium Test Prep

Dear Customer,

Thank you for purchasing from Trivium Test Prep! We're honored to help you prepare for your big exam.

To show our appreciation, we're offering a **FREE** *CHSPE Essential Test Tips* **Video by Trivium Test Prep.*** Our video includes 35 test preparation strategies that will make you successful on the CHSPE. All we ask is that you email us your feedback and describe your experience with our product. Amazing, awful, or just so-so: we want to hear what you have to say!

To receive your **FREE** *CHSPE Essential Test Tips* **Video**, please email us at 5star@ triviumtestprep.com. Include "Free 5 Star" in the subject line and the following information in your email:

1. The title of the product you purchased.
2. Your rating from 1 – 5 (with 5 being the best).
3. Your feedback about the product, including how our materials helped you meet your goals and ways in which we can improve our products.
4. Your full name and shipping address so we can send your **FREE** *CHSPE Essential Test Tips* **Video**.

If you have any questions or concerns please feel free to contact us directly at 5star@ triviumtestprep.com.

Thank you!

– Trivium Test Prep Team

*To get access to the free video please email us at 5star@triviumtestprep.com, and please follow the instructions above.

CHSPE

Preparation Book 2024-2025:

550+ Practice Questions and CHSPE Test Review Study Guide

Jonathan Cox

Table of Contents

Online Resources

Accepted, Inc. includes online resources with the purchase of this study guide to help you fully prepare for your CHSPE exam.

PRACTICE TESTS

In addition to the practice test included in this book, we also offer an online exam. Since many exams today are computer based, practicing your test-taking skills on the computer is a great way to prepare.

REVIEW QUESTIONS

Need more practice? Our review questions use a variety of formats to help you memorize key terms and concepts.

FLASH CARDS

Accepted, Inc.'s flash cards allow you to review important terms easily on your computer or smartphone.

CHEAT SHEETS

Review the core skills you need to master the exam with easy-to-read Cheat Sheets.

FROM STRESS to SUCCESS

Watch "From Stress to Success," a brief but insightful YouTube video that offers the tips, tricks, and secrets experts use to score higher on the exam.

REVIEWS

Leave a review, send us helpful feedback, or sign up for Accepted, Inc. promotions—including free books!

Access these materials at: **www.acceptedinc.com/chspe-online-resources**

Introduction

Congratulations on choosing to take the California High School Proficiency Examination (CHSPE)! By purchasing this book, you've taken an important step on your path to earning your high school–equivalency credential in California.

This guide will provide you with a detailed overview of the CHSPE so that you know exactly what to expect on test day. We'll take you through all the concepts covered on the exam and give you the opportunity to test your knowledge with practice questions. Even if it's been a while since you last took a major test, don't worry; we'll make sure you're more than ready!

What is the CHSPE?

The California High School Proficiency Examination, or CHSPE, is a proficiency test in reading, writing, and mathematics. Candidates who pass the CHSPE are awarded a **CERTIFICATE OF PROFICIENCY** by the California State Board of Education.

By law, the Certificate of Proficiency is equivalent to a high school diploma in the state of California. However, the Certificate of Proficiency may not be substituted for completing four years of high school coursework. Students who wish to go on to college or university studies must contact the admissions office of the school of their choice for details on admissions requirements. The Certificate of Proficiency may not be sufficient for admission in all cases.

What's on the CHSPE?

The CHSPE has two sections: Mathematics and English Language Arts. Candidates are expected to be able to read closely, write clearly and edit and understand standard written English as it is used in context. They must also be able to solve quantitative and algebraic problems, understand geometry and probability, and analyze data. The test includes multiple-choice questions and one essay question.

The English Language Arts section is further divided into two subtests: the Language subtest, which focuses on grammar and mechanics, and includes the written essay; and the Reading subtest, which tests reading comprehension and vocabulary knowledge.

You may take both sections in the same sitting, or you may take them on separate test dates. You may also take the English Language Arts subtests on different test dates. However, you must pay the full fee each time you test, even if you only take one section or subtest.

You will have three hours and thirty minutes to test. You will not be prompted to switch between sections; you must manage your time yourself.

What's on the CHSPE?

MATHEMATICS SECTION

SKILLS ASSESSED	TOPICS	NUMBER OF QUESTIONS
▶ Understand key mathematical concepts ▶ Demonstrate skill and fluency with key math procedures ▶ Understand patterns involving numbers, symbols, and geometric figures ▶ Understand algebraic principles ▶ Interpret data and understand probability ▶ Understand plane and solid figures, spatial reasoning, and coordinate geometry	▶ Number sense and operations ▶ Patterns, relationships, and algebra ▶ Data, statistics, and probability ▶ Geometry and measurement	50

ENGLISH LANGUAGE ARTS SECTION

SKILLS ASSESSED	TOPICS	NUMBER OF QUESTIONS
Language Subtest		
▶ Demonstrate correct grammar, mechanics, and usage (capitalization, punctuation)	Language questions	48
▶ Demonstrate correct sentence structure ▶ Edit and understand the use of standard written English in context ▶ Plan and organize writing ▶ Write clearly and persuasively	Essay	1

ENGLISH LANGUAGE ARTS SECTION (CONTINUED)		
SKILLS ASSESSED	**TOPICS**	**NUMBER OF QUESTIONS**
Reading Subtest		
▶ Read and analyze text closely	Reading comprehension	54
▶ Inference skills ▶ Understand vocabulary (including synonyms and words with multiple meanings, and by using context clues)	Vocabulary	30
Total	**3 hours and 30 minutes**	**182 + 1 essay**

The English Language Arts section contains two subtests: Language and Reading. The Language subtest assesses your knowledge of standard English grammar, mechanics, and sentence structure. Be prepared to analyze sentences, searching for errors in capitalization, punctuation, and usage. You must also read short passages and identify errors in organization and sentence structure. The Reading subtest assesses your ability to understand a range of texts that can be found in both academic and workplace settings. The test includes literary and informational texts. You will be asked to identify details and make logical inferences from—as well as valid claims about—the texts. You will also be asked to define key vocabulary using context clues.

The Mathematics section assesses mastery of key fundamental math concepts. The test also assesses reasoning skills and modes of thinking like estimation, communication and representation, and problem-solving. Prepare for content on patterns, relationships, and algebra; data analysis; geometry and measurement; and operations and number sense. Questions will assess your ability to make sense of complex problems, use logical thinking to find solutions, recognize structure, and look for and express regularity in repeated reasoning. You will also be evaluated on the precision of your mathematics.

A formula sheet will be provided to you for the Mathematics section. You may bring a calculator if you wish. It must be a basic, non-programmable, nonscientific calculator. Acceptable calculators have twenty-five or fewer buttons. They perform only the standard mathematical functions of addition, subtraction, multiplication, and division. Square root, sign change, and percentage features are also acceptable. Check the CHSPE bulletin for the most current information on permissible calculators.

How is the CHSPE Scored?

Each multiple-choice question is worth one raw point. The essay is scored on a scale from one to five. One is the lowest and five is the highest. Two scorers will read and score your essay; your final score is the average of their scores.

Your raw score (the number of multiple-choice questions you answer correctly) is converted into a scaled score. The scaled scores range from 250 to 450.

To pass the Mathematics section, you must earn a score of 350 or higher.

To pass the English Language Arts section, you must pass both the Reading and Language subtests.

- ▶ To pass the Reading subtest, you must earn a score of 350 or higher.
- ▶ To pass the Language subtest, you must earn one of the following combinations of scores on your essay and multiple-choice questions:
- ▶ If you score a 2 or lower on the essay, there is no way to pass the subtest.
- ▶ If you score a 2.5 on the essay, you must score at least 365 on the multiple-choice questions.
- ▶ If you score a 3 on the essay, you must score at least 350 on the multiple-choice questions.
- ▶ If you score a 3.5 or higher on the essay, you must score at least 342 on the multiple-choice questions.

Each test is scored independently, and points from one test cannot affect the point value of another.

There is no guessing penalty on the CHSPE, so you should always guess if you do not know the answer to a question.

You will be able to view your unofficial CHSPE scores at http://www.chspe.net/results/online approximately one month after you test. You will receive your official CHSPE scores by mail approximately five weeks after you test. If you pass both sections of the test, you will also receive your Certificate of Proficiency at that time.

How is the CHSPE Administered?

The CHSPE is a pencil-and-paper test offered at a wide range of sites throughout California. To register for the CHSPE, visit https://www.chspe.net/registration. You may also register by mail using the CHSPE bulletin. Both methods require supporting documentation proving your age, eligibility, and any special accommodation requests, if applicable.

Eligibility is determined by age and status in school. You may prove your eligibility by submitting a copy of your government-issued identification, or by having your school complete documentation. For details, please check https://www.chspe.net/registration/.

Once you register, you will receive an **Admission Ticket**. If you register on the website, you will receive an electronic Admission Ticket. Those who register by mail will receive their Admission Ticket in the mail about three weeks later. Be sure that your name is correctly spelled on your Admission Ticket and that it matches your identification.

You will need to bring your Admission Ticket and your identification to the testing site on test day. Some test centers will require other forms or documentation, so make sure to check with your test center in advance. No pens, pencils, erasers, printed or written materials, electronic devices or calculators are allowed.

A formula reference sheet will be provided. for the math test A calculator is not required, but you may bring a basic calculator that performs only arithmetic functions. Check in advance with your testing center for specific testing guidelines, including restrictions on dress and accessories.

You may take the sections and subtests all on the same day or individually on separate days. There is no required order for completing the test.

The CHSPE is offered three times a year. If you do not pass one subtest, you are not required to retake all of the tests—only the one you failed. You may retake the test as many times as you like.

About This Guide

This guide will help you to master the most important test topics and also develop critical test-taking skills. We have built features into our books to prepare you for your tests and increase your score. Along with a detailed summary of the test's format, content, and scoring, we offer an in-depth overview of the content knowledge required to pass the test. In the review you'll find sidebars that provide interesting information, highlight key concepts, and review content so that you can solidify your understanding of the exam's concepts. You can also test your knowledge with sample questions throughout the text and practice questions that reflect the content and format of the CHSPE. We're pleased you've chosen Accepted, Inc., to be a part of your journey!

CHAPTER ONE

Numbers and Operations

This chapter provides a review of the basic yet critical components of mathematics such as manipulating fractions, comparing numbers, and using units. These concepts will provide the foundation for more complex mathematical operations in later chapters.

Types of Numbers

Numbers are placed in categories based on their properties.

▶ A **NATURAL NUMBER** is greater than 0 and has no decimal or fraction attached. These are also sometimes called counting numbers {1, 2, 3, 4, ...}.

▶ **WHOLE NUMBERS** are natural numbers and the number 0 {0, 1, 2, 3, 4, ...}.

▶ **INTEGERS** include positive and negative natural numbers and 0 {..., –4, –3, –2, –1, 0, 1, 2, 3, 4, ...}.

▶ A **RATIONAL NUMBER** can be represented as a fraction. Any decimal part must terminate or resolve into a repeating pattern. Examples include –12, $-\frac{4}{5}$, 0.36, $7.\overline{7}$, $26\frac{1}{2}$, etc.

▶ An **IRRATIONAL NUMBER** cannot be represented as a fraction. An irrational decimal number never ends and never resolves into a repeating pattern. Examples include $-\sqrt{7}$, π, and 0.34567989135...

▶ A **REAL NUMBER** is a number that can be represented by a point on a number line. Real numbers include all the rational and irrational numbers.

▶ An **IMAGINARY NUMBER** includes the imaginary unit i, where $i = \sqrt{-1}$. Because $i^2 = -1$, imaginary numbers produce a negative value when squared. Examples of imaginary numbers include $-4i$, $0.75i$, $i\sqrt{2}$ and $\frac{8}{3}i$.

▶ A **COMPLEX NUMBER** is in the form $a + bi$, where a and b are real numbers. Examples of complex numbers include $3 + 2i$, $-4 + i$, $\sqrt{3} - i\sqrt[3]{5}$ and $\frac{5}{8} - \frac{7i}{8}$. All imaginary numbers are also complex.

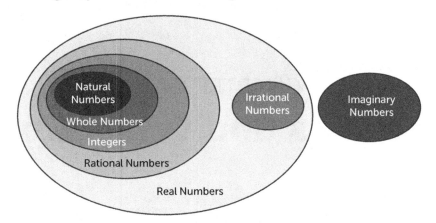

Figure 1.1. Types of Numbers

The **FACTORS** of a natural number are all the numbers that can multiply together to make the number. For example, the factors of 24 are 1, 2, 3, 4, 6, 8, 12, and 24. Every natural number is either prime or composite. A **PRIME NUMBER** is a number that is only divisible by itself and 1. (The number 1 is not considered prime.) Examples of prime numbers are 2, 3, 7, and 29. The number 2 is the only even prime number. A **COMPOSITE NUMBER** has more than two factors. For example, 6 is composite because its factors are 1, 6, 2, and 3. Every composite number can be written as a unique product of prime numbers, called the **PRIME FACTORIZATION** of the number. For example, the prime factorization of 90 is 90 = $2 \times 3^2 \times 5$. All integers are either even or odd. An even number is divisible by 2; an odd number is not.

PROPERTIES of NUMBER SYSTEMS

A system is **CLOSED** under an operation if performing that operation on two elements of the system results in another element of that system. For example, the integers are closed under the operations of addition, subtraction, and multiplication but not division. Adding, subtracting, or multiplying two integers results in another integer. However, dividing two integers could result in a rational number that is not an integer $(-2 \div 3 = \frac{-2}{3})$.

▶ The rational numbers are closed under all four operations (except for division by 0).

▶ The real numbers are closed under all four operations.

▶ The complex numbers are closed under all four operations.

▶ The irrational numbers are NOT closed under ANY of the four operations.

The **COMMUTATIVE PROPERTY** holds for an operation if order does not matter when performing the operation. For example, multiplication is commutative for integers: $(-2)(3) = (3)(-2)$.

The **ASSOCIATIVE PROPERTY** holds for an operation if elements can be regrouped without changing the result. For example, addition is associative for real numbers: $-3 + (-5 + 4) = (-3 + -5) + 4$.

The **DISTRIBUTIVE PROPERTY** of multiplication over addition allows a product of sums to be written as a sum of products: $a(b + c) = ab + ac$. The value a is distributed over the sum $(b + c)$. The acronym FOIL (First, Outer, Inner, Last) is a useful way to remember the distributive property.

When an operation is performed with an **IDENTITY ELEMENT** and another element a, the result is a. The identity element for multiplication on real numbers is 1 ($a \times 1 = a$), and for addition is 0 ($a + 0 = a$).

An operation of a system has an **INVERSE ELEMENT** if applying that operation with the inverse element results in the identity element. For example, the inverse element of a for addition is $-a$ because $a + (-a) = 0$. The inverse element of a for multiplication is $\frac{1}{a}$ because $a \times \frac{1}{a} = 1$.

EXAMPLES

1. Classify the following numbers as natural, whole, integer, rational, or irrational. (The numbers may have more than one classification.)

   [A] 72

   [B] $-\frac{2}{3}$

   [C] $\sqrt{5}$

2. Determine the real and imaginary parts of the following complex numbers.

   [A] 20

   [B] $10 - i$

   [C] $15i$

3. Answer true or false for each statement:

   [A] The natural numbers are closed under subtraction.

   [B] The sum of two irrational numbers is irrational.

   [C] The sum of a rational number and an irrational number is irrational.

4. Answer true or false for each statement:

   [A] The associative property applies for multiplication in the real numbers.

   [B] The commutative property applies to all real numbers and all operations.

OPERATIONS with COMPLEX NUMBERS

Operations with complex numbers are similar to operations with real numbers in that complex numbers can be added, subtracted, multiplied, and divided. When adding or subtracting, the imaginary parts and real parts are combined separately. When multiplying, the distributive property (FOIL) can be applied. Note that multiplying complex numbers often creates the value i^2 which can be simplified to –1.

To divide complex numbers, multiply both the top and bottom of the fraction by the **COMPLEX CONJUGATE** of the divisor (bottom number). The complex conjugate is the complex number with the sign of the imaginary part changed. For example, the complex conjugate of $3 + 4i$ would be $3 - 4i$. Since both the top and the bottom of the fraction are multiplied by the same number, the fraction is really just being multiplied by 1. When simplified, the denominator of the fraction will now be a real number.

EXAMPLES

5. Simplify: $(3 - 2i) - (-2 + 8i)$

6. Simplify: $\dfrac{4i}{(5 - 2i)}$

Scientific Notation

SCIENTIFIC NOTATION is a method of representing very large and small numbers in the form $a \times 10^n$, where a is a value between 1 and 10, and n is a nonzero integer. For example, the number 927,000,000 is written in scientific notation as 9.27×10^8. Multiplying 9.27 by 10 eight times gives 927,000,000. When performing operations with scientific notation, the final answer should be in the form $a \times 10^n$.

When adding and subtracting numbers in scientific notation, the power of 10 must be the same for all numbers. This results in like terms in which the a terms are added or subtracted and the 10^n remains unchanged. When multiplying numbers in scientific notation, multiply the a factors, and then multiply that answer by 10 to the sum of the exponents. For division, divide the a factors and subtract the exponents.

65000000.
7 6 5 4 3 2 1
↓
6.5×10^7

.0000987
-1-2-3-4-5
↓
9.87×10^{-5}

Figure 1.2. Scientific Notation

DID YOU KNOW?
When multiplying numbers in scientific notation, add the exponents. When dividing, subtract the exponents.

EXAMPLES

7. Simplify: $(3.8 \times 10^3) + (4.7 \times 10^2)$

8. Simplify: $(8.1 \times 10^{-5})(1.4 \times 10^7)$

Positive and Negative Numbers

POSITIVE NUMBERS are greater than 0, and NEGATIVE NUMBERS are less than 0. Both positive and negative numbers can be shown on a NUMBER LINE.

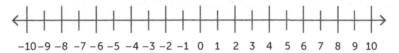

Figure 1.3. Number Line

The ABSOLUTE VALUE of a number is the distance the number is from 0. Since distance is always positive, the absolute value of a number is always positive. The absolute value of a is denoted $|a|$. For example, $|-2| = 2$ since -2 is two units away from 0.

Positive and negative numbers can be added, subtracted, multiplied, and divided. The sign of the resulting number is governed by a specific set of rules shown in the table below.

Table 1.1. Operations with Positive and Negative Numbers			
ADDING REAL NUMBERS		**SUBTRACTING REAL NUMBERS**	
Positive + Positive = Positive	7 + 8 = 15	Negative – Positive = Negative	–7 – 8 = –7 + (–8) = –15
Negative + Negative = Negative	–7 + (–8) = –15	Positive – Negative = Positive	7 – (–8) = 7 + 8 = 15
Negative + Positive OR Positive + Negative = Keep the sign of the number with larger absolute value	–7 + 8 = 1 7 + –8 = –1	Negative – Negative = Change the subtraction to addition and change the sign of the second number; then use addition rules.	–7 – (–8) = –7 + 8 = 1 –8 – (–7) = –8 + 7 = –1
MULTIPLYING REAL NUMBERS		**DIVIDING REAL NUMBERS**	
Positive × Positive = Positive	8 × 4 = 32	Positive ÷ Positive = Positive	8 ÷ 4 = 2
Negative × Negative = Positive	–8 × (–4) = 32	Negative ÷ Negative = Positive	–8 ÷ (–4) = 2
Positive × Negative OR Negative × Positive = Negative	8 × (–4) = –32 –8 × 4 = –32	Positive ÷ Negative OR Negative ÷ Positive = Negative	8 ÷ (–4) = –2 –8 ÷ 4 = –2

9. Add or subtract the following real numbers:

[A] −18 + 12

[B] −3.64 + (−2.18)

[C] 9.37 − 4.25

[D] 86 − (−20)

10. Multiply or divide the following real numbers:

[A] $\left(\frac{10}{3}\right)\left(-\frac{9}{5}\right)$

[B] $\frac{-64}{-10}$

[C] (2.2)(3.3)

[D] −52 ÷ 13

Order of Operations

The ORDER OF OPERATIONS is simply the order in which operations are performed. Multiplication and division, and addition and subtraction, are performed together from left to right. So, performing multiple operations on a set of numbers is a four-step process. **PEMDAS** is a common way to remember the order of operations:

1. **P**arentheses: Calculate expressions inside parentheses, brackets, braces, etc.

2. **E**xponents: Calculate exponents and square roots.

3. **M**ultiplication: Calculate any remaining multiplication and division in order from left to right.

4. **D**ivision: Calculate any remaining multiplication and division in order from left to right.

5. **A**ddition: Calculate any remaining addition and subtraction in order from left to right.

6. **S**ubtraction: Calculate any remaining addition and subtraction in order from left to right.

Always work from left to right within each step when simplifying expressions.

EXAMPLES

11. Simplify: 2(21 − 14) + 6 ÷ (−2) x 3 − 10

12. Simplify: −(3)^2 + 4(5) + (5 − 6)^2 − 8

13. Simplify: $\frac{(7-9)^3 + 8(10-12)}{4^2 - 5^2}$

Units of Measurement

The standard units for the metric and American systems are shown below, along with the prefixes used to express metric units.

Table 1.2. Units and Conversion Factors		
DIMENSION	AMERICAN	SI
length	inch/foot/yard/mile	meter
mass	ounce/pound/ton	gram
volume	cup/pint/quart/gallon	liter
force	pound-force	newton
pressure	pound-force per square inch	pascal
work and energy	cal/British thermal unit	joule
temperature	Fahrenheit	kelvin
charge	faraday	coulomb

Table 1.3. Metric Prefixes		
PREFIX	SYMBOL	MULTIPLICATION FACTOR
tera	T	1,000,000,000,000
giga	G	1,000,000,000
mega	M	1,000,000
kilo	k	1,000
hecto	h	100
deca	da	10
base unit	--	--
deci	d	0.1
centi	c	0.01
milli	m	0.001
micro	μ	0.000001
nano	n	0.000000001
pico	p	0.000000000001

Units can be converted within a single system or between systems. When converting from one unit to another unit, a conversion factor (a numeric multiplier used to convert a value with a unit to another unit) is used. The process of converting between units using a conversion factor is sometimes known as dimensional analysis.

Table 1.4. Conversion Factors	
1 in. = 2.54 cm	1 lb. = 0.454 kg
1 yd. = 0.914 m	1 cal = 4.19 J
1 mi. = 1.61 km	$1°F = \frac{9}{5}°C + 32°C$
1 gal. = 3.785 L	$1 \text{ cm}^3 = 1 \text{ mL}$
1 oz. = 28.35 g	1 hr = 3600 s

EXAMPLES

14. Convert the following measurements in the metric system.

 [A] 4.25 kilometers to meters

 [B] 8 m² to mm²

15. Convert the following measurements in the American system.

 [A] 12 feet to inches

 [B] 7 yd² to ft²

16. Convert the following measurements in the metric system to the American system.

 [A] 23 meters to feet

 [B] 10 m² to yd²

17. Convert the following measurements in the American system to the metric system.

 [A] 8 in³ to milliliters

 [B] 16 kilograms to pounds

Decimals and Fractions
DECIMALS

A DECIMAL is a number that contains a decimal point. A decimal number is an alternative way of writing a fraction. The place value for a decimal includes TENTHS (one place after the decimal), HUNDREDTHS (two places after the decimal), THOUSANDTHS (three places after the decimal), etc.

Table 1.5. Place Values		
1,000,000	10^6	millions
100,000	10^5	hundred thousands
10,000	10^4	ten thousands
1,000	10^3	thousands
100	10^2	hundreds
10	10^1	tens
1	10^0	ones
.		decimal
$\frac{1}{10}$	10^{-1}	tenths
$\frac{1}{100}$	10^{-2}	hundredths
$\frac{1}{1000}$	10^{-3}	thousandths

Decimals can be added, subtracted, multiplied, and divided:

▶ To add or subtract decimals, line up the decimal point and perform the operation, keeping the decimal point in the same place in the answer.

▶ To multiply decimals, first multiply the numbers without the decimal points. Then, sum the number of decimal places to the right of the decimal point in the original numbers and place the decimal point in the answer so that there are that many places to the right of the decimal.

▶ When dividing decimals move the decimal point to the right in order to make the divisor a whole number and move the decimal the same number of places in the dividend. Divide the numbers without regard to the decimal. Then, place the decimal point of the quotient directly above the decimal point of the dividend.

DID YOU KNOW?
To determine which way to move the decimal after multiplying, remember that changing the decimal should always make the final answer smaller.

$$2.5\overline{)10.5}$$

4.2 ← quotient
10.5 ← dividend
↑ divisor

Figure 1.4. Division Terms

EXAMPLES

18. Simplify: 24.38 + 16.51 − 29.87

19. Simplify: (10.4)(18.2)

20. Simplify: 80 ÷ 2.5

FRACTIONS

A **FRACTION** is a number that can be written in the form $\frac{a}{b}$, where b is not equal to 0. The a part of the fraction is the **NUMERATOR** (top number) and the b part of the fraction is the **DENOMINATOR** (bottom number).

If the denominator of a fraction is greater than the numerator, the value of the fraction is less than 1 and it is called a **PROPER FRACTION** (for example, $\frac{3}{5}$ is a proper fraction). In an **IMPROPER FRACTION**, the denominator is less than the numerator and the value of the fraction is greater than 1 ($\frac{8}{3}$ is an improper fraction). An improper fraction can be written as a **MIXED NUMBER**, which has a whole number part and a proper fraction part. Improper fractions can be converted to mixed numbers by dividing the numerator by the denominator, which gives the whole number part, and the remainder becomes the numerator of the proper fraction part. (For example, the improper fraction $\frac{25}{9}$ is equal to mixed number $2\frac{7}{9}$ because 9 divides into 25 two times, with a remainder of 7.)

DID YOU KNOW?

To convert mixed numbers to improper fractions:
$$a\frac{m}{n} = \frac{n \times a + m}{n}$$

Conversely, mixed numbers can be converted to improper fractions. To do so, determine the numerator of the improper fraction by multiplying the denominator by the whole number, and then adding the numerator. The final number is written as the (now larger) numerator over the original denominator.

Fractions with the same denominator can be added or subtracted by simply adding or subtracting the numerators; the denominator will remain unchanged. To add or subtract fractions with different denominators, find the **LEAST COMMON DENOMINATOR (LCD)** of all the fractions. The LCD is the smallest number exactly divisible by each denominator. (For example, the least common denominator of the numbers 2, 3, and 8 is 24.) Once the LCD has been found, each fraction should be written in an equivalent form with the LCD as the denominator.

To multiply fractions, the numerators are multiplied together and denominators are multiplied together. If there are any mixed numbers, they should first be changed to improper fractions. Then, the numerators are multiplied together and the denominators are multiplied together. The fraction can then be reduced if necessary. To divide fractions, multiply the first fraction by the reciprocal of the second.

DID YOU KNOW?

$$\frac{a}{b} + \frac{c}{b} = \frac{a+c}{b}$$
$$\frac{a}{b} \times \frac{c}{d} = \frac{ac}{bd}$$
$$\frac{a}{b} \div \frac{c}{d} = \frac{a}{(b)}\frac{d}{(c)} = \frac{ad}{bc}$$

Any common denominator can be used to add or subtract fractions. The quickest way to find a common denominator of a set of values is simply to multiply all the values together. The result might not be the least common denominator, but it will allow the problem to be worked.

EXAMPLES

21. Simplify: $2\frac{3}{5} + 3\frac{1}{4} - 1\frac{1}{2}$

22. Simplify: $\frac{7}{8} \times 3\frac{1}{3}$

23. Simplify: $4\frac{1}{2} \div \frac{2}{3}$

CONVERTING BETWEEN FRACTIONS and DECIMALS

A fraction is converted to a decimal by using long division until there is no remainder and no pattern of repeating numbers occurs.

A decimal is converted to a fraction using the following steps:

▶ Place the decimal value as the numerator in a fraction with a denominator of 1.

▶ Multiply the fraction by $\frac{10}{10}$ for every digit in the decimal value, so that there is no longer a decimal in the numerator.

▶ Reduce the fraction.

EXAMPLES

24. Write the fraction $\frac{7}{8}$ as a decimal.

25. Write the fraction $\frac{5}{11}$ as a decimal.

26. Write the decimal 0.125 as a fraction.

Rounding and Estimation

ROUNDING is a way of simplifying a complicated number. The result of rounding will be a less precise value with which it is easier to write or perform operations. Rounding is performed to a specific place value, for example the thousands or tenths place.

The rules for rounding are as follows:

1. Underline the place value being rounded to.

2. Locate the digit one place value to the right of the underlined value. If this value is less than 5, then keep the underlined value and replace all digits to the right of the underlined value with 0. If the value to the right of the underlined digit is greater than or equal to 5, then increase the underlined digit by one and replace all digits to the right of it with 0.

ESTIMATION is when numbers are rounded and then an operation is performed. This process can be used when working with large numbers to find a close, but not exact, answer.

DID YOU KNOW?

Estimation can often be used to eliminate answer choices on multiple-choice tests without having to work the problem to completion.

Ratios

A RATIO is a comparison of two numbers and can be represented as $\frac{a}{b}$, $a{:}b$, or a to b. The two numbers represent a constant relationship, not a specific value: for every a number of items in the first group, there will be b number of items in the second. For example, if the ratio of blue to red candies in a bag is 3:5, the bag will contain 3 blue candies for every 5 red candies. So, the bag might contain 3 blue candies and 5 red candies, or it might contain 30 blue candies and 50 red candies, or 36 blue candies and 60 red candies. All of these values are representative of the ratio 3:5 (which is the ratio in its lowest, or simplest, terms).

To find the "whole" when working with ratios, simply add the values in the ratio. For example, if the ratio of boys to girls in a class is 2:3, the "whole" is five: 2 out of every 5 students are boys, and 3 out of every 5 students are girls.

EXAMPLES

29. There are 10 boys and 12 girls in a first-grade class. What is the ratio of boys to the total number of students? What is the ratio of girls to boys?

30. A family spends $600 a month on rent, $400 on utilities, $750 on groceries, and $550 on miscellaneous expenses. What is the ratio of the family's rent to their total expenses?

Proportions

A PROPORTION is an equation which states that two ratios are equal. A proportion is given in the form $\frac{a}{b} = \frac{c}{d}$, where the a and d terms are the extremes and the b and c terms are the means. A proportion is solved using cross-multiplication ($ad = bc$) to create an equation with no fractional components. A proportion must have the same units in both numerators and both denominators.

EXAMPLES

31. Solve the proportion for x: $\frac{3x-5}{2} = \frac{x-8}{3}$.

32. A map is drawn such that 2.5 inches on the map equates to an actual distance of 40 miles. If the distance measured on the map between two cities is 17.25 inches, what is the actual distance between them in miles?

33. A factory knows that 4 out of 1000 parts made will be defective. If in a month there are 125,000 parts made, how many of these parts will be defective?

Percentages

A **PERCENT** (or percentage) means per hundred and is expressed with a percent symbol (%). For example, 54% means 54 out of every 100. A percent can be converted to a decimal by removing the % symbol and moving the decimal point two places to the left, while a decimal can be converted to a percent by moving the decimal point two places to the right and attaching the % sign. A percent can be converted to a fraction by writing the percent as a fraction with 100 as the denominator and reducing. A fraction can be converted to a percent by performing the indicated division, multiplying the result by 100, and attaching the % sign.

The equation for finding percentages has three variables: the part, the whole, and the percent (which is expressed in the equation as a decimal). The equation, as shown below, can be rearranged to solve for any of these variables.

▶ part = whole × percent

▶ percent = $\dfrac{\text{part}}{\text{whole}}$

▶ whole = $\dfrac{\text{part}}{\text{percent}}$

This set of equations can be used to solve percent word problems. All that's needed is to identify the part, whole, and/or percent, and then to plug those values into the appropriate equation and solve.

EXAMPLES

34. Change the following values to the indicated form:

    [A] 18% to a fraction

    [B] $\frac{3}{5}$ to a percent

    [C] 1.125 to a percent

    [D] 84% to a decimal

35. In a school of 650 students, 54% of the students are boys. How many students are girls?

PERCENT CHANGE

DID YOU KNOW?
Key terms associated with percent change problems include *discount*, *sales tax*, and *markup*.

Percent change problems involve a change from an original amount. Often percent change problems appear as word problems that include discounts, growth, or markups. In order to solve percent change problems, it's necessary to identify the percent change (as a decimal), the amount of change, and the original amount. (Keep in mind that one of these will be the value being solved for.) These values can then be plugged into the equations below:

▶ amount of change = original amount × percent change

▶ percent change = $\dfrac{\text{amount of change}}{\text{original amount}}$

▶ original amount = $\dfrac{\text{amount of change}}{\text{percent change}}$

EXAMPLES

36. An HDTV that originally cost $1,500 is on sale for 45% off. What is the sale price for the item?

37. A house was bought in 2000 for $100,000 and sold in 2015 for $120,000. What was the percent growth in the value of the house from 2000 to 2015?

Comparison of Rational Numbers

DID YOU KNOW?
Drawing a number line can help when comparing numbers: the final list should go in order from left to right (least to greatest) or right to left (greatest to least) on the line.

Rational numbers can be ordered from least to greatest (or greatest to least) by placing them in the order in which they fall on a number line. When comparing a set of fractions, it's often easiest to convert each value to a common denominator. Then, it's only necessary to compare the numerators of each fraction.

When working with numbers in multiple forms (for example, a group of fractions and decimals), convert the values so that the set contains only fractions or only decimals. When ordering negative numbers, remember that the negative numbers with the largest absolute values are farthest from 0 and are therefore the smallest numbers. (For example, –75 is smaller than –25.)

EXAMPLES

38. Order the following numbers from greatest to least: $-\frac{2}{3}$, 1.2, 0, –2.1, $\frac{5}{4}$, –1, $\frac{1}{8}$

Exponents and Radicals
EXPONENTS

An expression in the form b^n is in exponential notation where b is the **BASE** and n is an **EXPONENT**. To perform the operation, multiply the base by itself the number of times indicated by the exponent. For example, 2^3 is equal to $2 \times 2 \times 2$ or 8.

	Table 1.6. Operations with Exponents	
RULE	**EXAMPLE**	**EXPLANATION**
$a^0 = 1$	$5^0 = 1$	Any base (except 0) to the 0 power is 1.
$a^{-n} = \frac{1}{a^n}$	$5^{-3} = \frac{1}{5^3}$	A negative exponent becomes positive when moved from numerator to denominator (or vice versa).
$a^m a^n = a^{m+n}$	$5^3 5^4 = 5^{3+4} = 5^7$	Add the exponents to multiply two powers with the same base.
$(a^m)^n = a^{m \times n}$	$(5^3)^4 = 5^{3(4)} = 5^{12}$	Multiply the exponents to raise a power to a power.
$\frac{a^m}{a^n} = a^{m-n}$	$\frac{5^4}{5^3} = 5^{4-3} = 5^1$	Subtract the exponents to divide two powers with the same base.
$(ab)^n = a^n b^n$	$(5 \times 6)^3 = 5^3 6^3$	Apply the exponent to each base to raise a product to a power.
$\left(\frac{a}{b}\right)^n = \frac{a^n}{b^n}$	$\left(\frac{5}{6}\right)^3 = \frac{5^3}{6^3}$	Apply the exponent to each base to raise a quotient to a power.
$\left(\frac{a}{b}\right)^{-n} = \left(\frac{b}{a}\right)^n$	$\left(\frac{5}{6}\right)^{-3} = \left(\frac{6}{5}\right)^3$	Invert the fraction and change the sign of the exponent to raise a fraction to a negative power.
$\frac{a^m}{b^n} = \frac{b^{-n}}{a^{-m}}$	$\frac{5^3}{6^4} = \frac{6^{-4}}{5^{-3}}$	Change the sign of the exponent when moving a number from the numerator to denominator (or vice versa).

EXAMPLES

40. Simplify: $\frac{(10^2)^3}{(10^2)^2}$

41. Simplify: $\frac{(x^{-2}y^2)^2}{x^3 y}$

RADICALS

RADICALS are expressed as $\sqrt[b]{a}$, where b is called the **INDEX** and a is the **RADICAND**. A radical is used to indicate the inverse operation of an exponent: finding the base which can be raised to b to yield a. For example, $\sqrt[3]{125}$ is equal to 5 because $5 \times 5 \times 5$ equals 125. The same operation can be expressed using a fraction exponent, so $\sqrt[b]{a} = a^{\frac{1}{b}}$. Note that when no value is indicated for b, it is assumed to be 2 (square root).

When b is even and a is positive, $\sqrt[b]{a}$ is defined to be the positive real value n such that $nb = a$ (example: $\sqrt{16} = 4$ only, and not –4, even though $(-4)(-4) = 16$). If b is even and a is negative, $\sqrt[b]{a}$ will be a complex number (example: $\sqrt{-9} = 3i$). Finally if b is odd, $\sqrt[b]{a}$ will always be a real number regardless of the sign of a. If a is negative, $\sqrt[b]{a}$ will be negative since a number to an odd power is negative (example: $\sqrt[5]{-32} = -2$ since $(-2)^5 = -32$).

$\sqrt[n]{x}$ is referred to as the nth root of x.

▶ $n = 2$ is the square root

▶ $n = 3$ is the cube root

▶ $n = 4$ is the fourth root

▶ $n = 5$ is the fifth root

The following table of operations with radicals holds for all cases EXCEPT the case where b is even and a is negative (the complex case).

Table 1.7. Operations with Radicals

RULE	EXAMPLE	EXPLANATION
$\sqrt[b]{ac} = \sqrt[b]{a}\,\sqrt[b]{c}$	$\sqrt[3]{81} = \sqrt[3]{27}\,\sqrt[3]{3} = 3\sqrt[3]{3}$	The values under the radical sign can be separated into values that multiply to the original value.
$\sqrt[b]{\dfrac{a}{c}} = \dfrac{\sqrt[b]{a}}{\sqrt[b]{c}}$	$\sqrt{\dfrac{4}{81}} = \dfrac{\sqrt{4}}{\sqrt{81}} = \dfrac{2}{9}$	The b-root of the numerator and denominator can be calculated when there is a fraction under a radical sign.
$\sqrt[b]{a^c} = (\sqrt[b]{a})^c = a^{\frac{c}{b}}$	$\sqrt[3]{6^2} = (\sqrt[3]{6})^2 = 6^{\frac{2}{3}}$	The b-root can be written as a fractional exponent. If there is a power under the radical sign, it will be the numerator of the fraction.
$\dfrac{c}{\sqrt[b]{a}} \times \dfrac{\sqrt[b]{a}}{\sqrt[b]{a}} = \dfrac{c\sqrt[b]{a}}{a}$	$\dfrac{5}{\sqrt{2}}\,\dfrac{\sqrt{2}}{\sqrt{2}} = \dfrac{5\sqrt{2}}{2}$	To rationalize the denominator, multiply the numerator and denominator by the radical in the denominator until the radical has been canceled out.
$\dfrac{c}{b - \sqrt{a}} \times \dfrac{b + \sqrt{a}}{b + \sqrt{a}}$ $= \dfrac{c(b + \sqrt{a})}{b^2 - a}$	$\dfrac{4}{3 - \sqrt{2}}\,\dfrac{3 + \sqrt{2}}{3 + \sqrt{2}}$ $= \dfrac{4(3 + \sqrt{2})}{9 - 2} = \dfrac{12 + 4\sqrt{2}}{7}$	To rationalize the denominator, the numerator and denominator are multiplied by the conjugate of the denominator.

42. Simplify: $\sqrt{48}$

43. Simplify: $\dfrac{6}{\sqrt{8}}$

Factorials

A **FACTORIAL** of a number n is denoted by $n!$ and is equal to $1 \times 2 \times 3 \times 4 \times \ldots \times n$. Both $0!$ and $1!$ are equal to 1 by definition. Fractions containing factorials can often be simplified by crossing out the portions of the factorials that occur in both the numerator and denominator.

EXAMPLES

44. Simplify: $8!$

45. Simplify: $\dfrac{10!}{7!3!}$

Sequences and Series

Sequences can be thought of as a set of numbers (called **TERMS**) with a rule that explains the particular pattern between the terms. The terms of a sequence are separated by commas. There are two types of sequences that will be examined, arithmetic and geometric. The sum of an arithmetic sequence is known as an **ARITHMETIC SERIES**; similarly the sum of a geometric sequence is known as a **GEOMETRIC SERIES**.

ARITHMETIC SEQUENCES

ARITHMETIC GROWTH is constant growth, meaning that the difference between any one term in the series and the next consecutive term will be the same constant. This constant is called the **COMMON DIFFERENCE**. Thus, to list the terms in the sequence, one can just add (or subtract) the same number repeatedly. For example, the series {20, 30, 40, 50} is arithmetic since 10 is added each time to get from one term to the next. One way to represent this sequence is using a **RECURSIVE** definition, which basically says: *next term = current term + common difference*. For this example, the recursive definition would be $a_{n+1} = a_n + 10$ because the *next* term a_{n+1} in the sequence is the current term a_n plus 10. In general, the recursive definition of a series is:

$a_{n+1} = a_n + d$, where d is the common difference.

Often, the objective of arithmetic sequence questions is to find a specific term in the sequence or the sum of a certain series of terms. The formulas to use are:

Table 1.8. Formulas for Arithmetic Sequences and Series	
FINDING THE *N*TH TERM . . .	
$a_n = a_1 + d(n - 1)$ $a_n = a_m + d(n - m)$	d = the common difference of the sequence a_n = the nth term in the sequence n = the number of the term a_m = the mth term in the sequence m = the number of the term a_1 = the first term in the sequence
FINDING THE PARTIAL SUM . . .	
$S_n = \dfrac{n(a_1 + a_n)}{2}$	S_n = sum of the terms through the nth term a_n = the nth term in the sequence n = the number of the term a_1 = the first term in the sequence

EXAMPLES

46. Find the ninth term of the sequence: −57, −40, −23, −6 ...

47. If the twenty-third term in an arithmetic sequence is 820, and the fifth term is 200, find the common difference between each term.

48. Evaluate $\sum_{n=14}^{45} 2n + 10$.

GEOMETRIC SEQUENCES

While an arithmetic sequence has an additive pattern, a **GEOMETRIC SEQUENCE** has a multiplicative pattern. This means that to get from any one term in the sequence to the next term in the sequence, the term is multiplied by a fixed number (called the **COMMON RATIO**). The following sequence is a geometric sequence: {8, 4, 2, 1, .5, .25, .125}. In this case, the multiplier (or common ratio) is $\frac{1}{2}$. The multiplier can be any real number other than 0 or 1. To find the common ratio, simply choose any term in the sequence and divide it by the previous term (this is the ratio of two consecutive terms—thus the name common *ratio*). In the above example, the ratio between the second and third terms is $\frac{2}{4} = \frac{1}{2}$.

Geometric sequences require their own formulas to find the next term and a sum of a specific series.

Table 1.9. Geometric Sequences: Formulas

FINDING THE *N*TH TERM . . .

$a_n = a_1 \times r^{n-1}$ $a_n = a_m \times r^{n-m}$	r = the common ratio of the sequence a_n = the nth term in the sequence n = the number of the term a_m = the mth term in the sequence m = the number of the term a_1 = the first term in the sequence

FINDING THE PARTIAL SUM . . .

$S_n = \dfrac{a_1(1 - r^n)}{1 - r}$	S_n = sum of the terms through the nth term r = the common ratio of the sequence a_n = the nth term in the sequence n = the number of the term a_1 = the first term in the sequence

FINDING THE SUM OF AN INFINITE SERIES . . .

$S_\infty = \dfrac{a_1}{1 - r}$ $(\lvert r \rvert < 1)$	S_∞ = sum of all terms r = the common ratio of the sequence a_1 = the first term in the sequence

The finite sum formula works similarly to the arithmetic sequence sum. However, sometimes the **INFINITE SUM** of the sequence must be found. The sum of an infinite number of terms of a sequence is called a **SERIES**. If the infinite terms of the sequence add up to a finite number, the series is said to **CONVERGE** to that number. If the sum of the terms is infinite, then the series **DIVERGES**. Another way to say this is to ask: is there a limit to the finite sum S_n as n goes to infinity? For geometric series in the form $\sum_{n=1}^{\infty} a \times r^n$, the series converges only when $\lvert r \rvert$ < 1 (or –1 < r < 1). If r is greater than 1, the sum will approach infinity, so the series diverges.

DID YOU KNOW?

Compared to arithmetic growth, geometric growth is much faster. As seen in the formulas used to find a geometric term, geometric growth is exponential, whereas arithmetic growth is linear.

EXAMPLES

49. Find the 8th term in the sequence: {13, 39, 117, 351 . . .}

50. Find the sum of the first 10 terms of this sequence: {–4, 16, –64, 256 . . .}

Answer Key

1. [A] **The number is natural, whole, an integer, and rational.**

   [B] **The fraction is rational.**

   [C] **The number is irrational.** (It cannot be written as a fraction, and written as a decimal is approximately 2.2360679...)

2. A complex number is in the form of $a + bi$, where a is the real part and bi is the imaginary part.

   [A] $20 = 20 + 0i$

   The real part is 20, and there is no imaginary part.

   [B] $10 - i = 10 - 1i$

   The real part is 10, and $-1i$ is the imaginary part.

   [C] $15i = 0 + 15i$

   The real part is 0, and the imaginary part is 15i.

3. [A] **is false.** Subtracting the natural number 7 from 2 results in $2 - 7 = -5$, which is an integer, but not a natural number.

   [B] **is false.** For example, $(5 - 2\sqrt{3}) + (2 + 2\sqrt{3}) = 7$. The sum of two irrational numbers in this example is a whole number, which is not irrational. The sum of a rational number and an irrational number is sometimes rational and sometimes irrational.

   [C] **is true.** Because irrational numbers have decimal parts that are unending and with no pattern, adding a repeating or terminating decimal will still result in an unending decimal without a pattern.

4. [A] **is true.** For all real numbers, $a \times (b \times c) = (a \times b) \times c$. Order of

multiplication does not change the result.

[B] **is false.** The commutative property does not work for subtraction or division on real numbers. For example, $12 - 5 = 7$, but $5 - 12 = -7$, and $10 \div 2 = 5$, but $2 \div 10 = \frac{1}{5}$.

5. $(3 - 2i) - (-2 + 8i)$

   Distribute the -1.

   $= (3 - 2i) - 1(-2 + 8i)$

   $= 3 - 2i + 2 - 8i$

   Combine like terms.

   $\mathbf{= 5 - 10i}$

6. $\dfrac{4i}{(5 - 2i)}$

   Multiply the top and bottom of the fraction by the complex conjugate of $5 + 2i$.

   $= \dfrac{4i}{5 - 2i}\left(\dfrac{5 + 2i}{5 + 2i}\right)$

   $= \dfrac{20i + 8i^2}{25 + 10i - 10i - 4i^2}$

   Simplify the result using the identity $i^2 = -1$.

   $= \dfrac{20i + 8(-1)}{25 + 10i - 10i - 4(-1)}$

   $= \dfrac{20i - 8}{25 + 10i - 10i + 4}$

   Combine like terms.

   $= \dfrac{20i - 8}{29}$

   Write the answer in the form $a + bi$.

   $\mathbf{= -\dfrac{8}{29} + \dfrac{20}{29}i}$

7. $(3.8 \times 10^3) + (4.7 \times 10^2)$

   To add, the exponents of 10 must be the same.

   $3.8 \times 10^3 = 3.8 \times 10 \times 10^2$

   $= 38 \times 10^2$

   Add the a terms together.

$38 \times 10^2 + 4.7 \times 10^2 = 42.7 \times 10^2$

Write the number in proper scientific notation.

$= \mathbf{4.27 \times 10^3}$

8. $(8.1 \times 10^{-5})(1.4 \times 10^7)$

Multiply the *a* factors and add the exponents on the base of 10.

$8.1 \times 1.4 = 11.34$

$-5 + 7 = 2$

$= 11.34 \times 10^2$

Write the number in proper scientific notation.

$= \mathbf{1.134 \times 10^3}$

9. [A] Since $|-18| > |12|$, the answer is negative: $|-18| - |12| = 6$. So the answer is **−6**.

[B] Adding two negative numbers results in a negative number. Add the values: **−5.82**.

[C] The first number is larger than the second, so the final answer is positive: **5.12**.

[D] Change the subtraction to addition, change the sign of the second number, and then add: $86 - (-20) = 86 + (+20) = \mathbf{106}$.

10. [A] Multiply the numerators, multiply the denominators, and simplify: $\frac{-90}{15} = \mathbf{-6}$.

[B] A negative divided by a negative is a positive number: **6.4**.

[C] Multiplying positive numbers gives a positive answer: **7.26**.

[D] Dividing a negative by a positive number gives a negative answer: **−4**.

11. $2(21 - 14) + 6 \div (-2) \times 3 - 10$

Calculate expressions inside parentheses.

$= 2(7) + 6 \div (-2) \times 3 - 10$

There are no exponents or radicals, so perform multiplication and division from left to right.

$= 14 + 6 \div (-2) \times 3 - 10$

$= 14 + (-3) \times 3 - 10$

$= 14 + (-9) - 10$

Perform addition and subtraction from left to right.

$= 5 - 10 = \mathbf{-5}$

12. $-(3)^2 + 4(5) + (5 - 6)^2 - 8$

Calculate expressions inside parentheses.

$= -(3)^2 + 4(5) + (-1)^2 - 8$

Simplify exponents and radicals.

$= -9 + 4(5) + 1 - 8$

Perform multiplication and division from left to right.

$= -9 + 20 + 1 - 8$

Perform addition and subtraction from left to right.

$= 11 + 1 - 8$

$= 12 - 8 = \mathbf{4}$

13. Simplify: $\dfrac{(7 - 9)^3 + 8(10 - 12)}{4^2 - 5^2}$

Calculate expressions inside parentheses.

$= \dfrac{(-2)^3 + 8(-2)}{4^2 - 5^2}$

Simplify exponents and radicals.

$= \dfrac{-8 + (-16)}{16 - 25}$

Perform addition and subtraction from left to right.

$= \dfrac{-24}{-9}$

Simplify.

$= \dfrac{8}{3}$

14. [A] 4.25 km $\left(\frac{1000 \text{ m}}{1 \text{ km}}\right)$ = **4250 m**

[B] $\frac{8 \text{ m}^2}{1} \times \frac{1000 \text{ mm}}{1 \text{ m}} \times \frac{1000 \text{ mm}}{1 \text{ m}}$ = **8,000,000 mm²**

Since the units are square units (m²), multiply by the conversion factor twice, so that both meters cancel.

15. [A] 12 ft$\left(\frac{12 \text{ in}}{1 \text{ ft}}\right)$ = **144 in**

[B] 7 yd²$\left(\frac{3 \text{ ft}^2}{1 \text{ yd}^2}\right)\left(\frac{3 \text{ ft}^2}{1 \text{ yd}^2}\right)$ = **63 ft²**

Since the units are square units (ft²), multiply by the conversion factor twice.

16. [A] 23 m $\left(\frac{3.28 \text{ ft}}{1 \text{ m}}\right)$ = **75.44 ft**

[B] $\frac{10 \text{ m}^2}{1} \times \frac{1.094 \text{ yd}}{1 \text{ m}} \times \frac{1.094 \text{ yd}}{1 \text{ m}}$ = **11.97 yd²**

17. [A] 8 in³ $\left(\frac{16.39 \text{ ml}}{1 \text{ in}^3}\right)$ = **131.12 mL**

[B] 16 kg$\left(\frac{2.2 \text{ lb}}{1 \text{ kg}}\right)$ = **35.2 lb**

18. 24.38 + 16.51 − 29.87

Align the decimals and apply the order of operations left to right.

$$\begin{array}{r} 24.38 \\ + 16.51 \\ \hline = 40.89 \end{array} \quad \rightarrow \quad \begin{array}{r} 40.89 \\ - 29.87 \\ \hline = \mathbf{11.02} \end{array}$$

19. (10.4)(18.2)

Multiply the numbers ignoring the decimals.

104 × 182 = 18,928

The original problem includes two decimal places (one in each number), so move the decimal point in the answer so that there are two places after the decimal point.

18,928 → **189.28**

Estimating is a good way to check the answer: 10.4 ≈ 10, 18.2 ≈ 18, and 10 × 18 = 180.

20. 80 ÷ 2.5

Move both decimals one place to the right (multiply by 10) so that the divisor is a whole number.

80 → 800

2.5 → 25

Divide normally.

800 ÷ 25 = **32**

21. $2\frac{3}{5} + 3\frac{1}{4} - 1\frac{1}{2}$

Change each fraction so it has a denominator of 20, which is the LCD of 5, 4, and 2.

2 + 3 − 1 = 4

$\frac{12}{20} + \frac{5}{20} - \frac{10}{20} = \frac{7}{20}$

Combine to get the final answer (a mixed number).

$\mathbf{4\frac{7}{20}}$

22. $\frac{7}{8} \times 3\frac{1}{3}$

Change the mixed number to an improper fraction.

$3\frac{1}{3} = \frac{10}{3}$

Multiply the numerators together and the denominators together.

$\frac{7}{8}\left(\frac{10}{3}\right) = \frac{7 \times 10}{8 \times 3} = \frac{70}{24}$

Reduce the fraction.

$= \frac{35}{12} = \mathbf{2\frac{11}{12}}$

23. $4\frac{1}{2} \div \frac{2}{3}$

Change the mixed number to an improper fraction.

$4\frac{1}{2} = \frac{9}{2}$

Multiply the first fraction by the reciprocal of the second fraction.

$\frac{9}{2} \div \frac{2}{3} = \frac{9}{2} \times \frac{3}{2} = \frac{27}{4}$

Simplify.

$= 6\frac{3}{4}$

24. Divide the denominator into the numerator using long division.

```
      0.875
   8)7000
    -64↓|
      60
     -56↓
       40
```

25. Dividing using long division yields a repeating decimal.

```
       0.4545
   11)50000
     -44 ↓||
       60 ||
      -55↓|
        50|
       -44↓
         60
```

26. Create a fraction with 0.125 as the numerator and 1 as the denominator.

$= \dfrac{0.125}{1}$

Multiply by $\frac{10}{10}$ three times (one for each numeral after the decimal).

$\dfrac{0.125}{1} \times \dfrac{10}{10} \times \dfrac{10}{10} \times \dfrac{10}{10} = \dfrac{125}{1000}$

Simplify.

$= \dfrac{1}{8}$

Alternatively, recognize that 0.125 is read "one hundred twenty-five thousandths" and can therefore be written in fraction form as $\frac{125}{1000}$.

27. The 8 is in the thousands place, and the number to its right is 4. Because 4 is less than 5, the 8 remains and all numbers to the right become 0.

$138,472 \approx \mathbf{138,000}$

28. Round each value to the thousands place.

$12,341 \approx 12,000$

$8975 \approx 9000$

$9431 \approx 9000$

$10,521 \approx 11,000$

$11,427 \approx 11,000$

Add.

$12,000 + 9000 + 9000 + 11,000 + 11,000 = \mathbf{52,000}$

29. Identify the variables.

number of boys: 10

number of girls: 12

number of students: 22

Write out and simplify the ratio of boys to total students.

number of boys : number of students

$= 10 : 22 = \dfrac{10}{22} = \mathbf{\dfrac{5}{11}}$

Write out and simplify the ratio of girls to boys.

number of girls : number of boys

$= 12 : 10 = \dfrac{12}{10} = \mathbf{\dfrac{6}{5}}$

30. Identify the variables.

rent = 600

utilities = 400

groceries = 750

miscellaneous = 550

total expenses =

$600 + 400 + 750 + 550 = 2300$

Write out and simplify the ratio of rent to total expenses.

rent : total expenses

$= 600 : 2300 = \dfrac{600}{2300} = \mathbf{\dfrac{6}{23}}$

31. $\dfrac{(3x - 5)}{2} = \dfrac{(x - 8)}{3}$

Cross-multiply.

$3(3x - 5) = 2(x - 8)$

Solve the equation for x.

$9x - 15 = 2x - 16$

$7x - 15 = -16$

$7x = -1$

$x = -\dfrac{1}{7}$

32. Write a proportion where x equals the actual distance and each ratio is written as inches : miles.

$\dfrac{2.5}{40} = \dfrac{17.25}{x}$

Cross-multiply and divide to solve for x.

$2.5x = 690$

$x = 276$

The two cities are **276 miles apart**.

33. Write a proportion where x is the number of defective parts made and both ratios are written as defective : total.

$\dfrac{4}{1000} = \dfrac{x}{125,000}$

Cross-multiply and divide to solve for x.

$1000x = 500,000$

$x = 500$

There are **500 defective parts** for the month.

34. [A] The percent is written as a fraction over 100 and reduced:

$\dfrac{18}{100} = \dfrac{9}{50}$

[B] Dividing 3 by 5 gives the value 0.6, which is then multiplied by 100: **60%**.

[C] The decimal point is moved two places to the right:
$1.125 \times 100 = \mathbf{112.5\%}$.

[D] The decimal point is moved two places to the left: $84 \div 100 = \mathbf{0.84}$.

35. Identify the variables.

Percent of students who are girls = 100% − 54% = 46%

percent = 46% = 0.46

whole = 650 students

part = ?

Plug the variables into the appropriate equation.

part = whole × percent

= 0.46 × 650 = 299

There are 299 girls.

36. Identify the variables.

original amount = $1,500

percent change = 45% = 0.45

amount of change = ?

Plug the variables into the appropriate equation.

amount of change = original amount × percent change

= 1500 × 0.45 = 675

To find the new price, subtract the amount of change from the original price.

1500 − 675 = 825

The final price is $825.

37. Identify the variables.

original amount = $100,000

amount of change = 120,000 − 100,000 = 20,000

percent change = ?

Plug the variables into the appropriate equation.

percent change = $\dfrac{\text{amount of change}}{\text{original amount}}$

= $\dfrac{20,000}{100,000}$ = 0.20

To find the percent growth, multiply by 100.

0.20 × 100 = **20%**

38. Change each fraction to a decimal.

$-\dfrac{2}{3} = -0.\overline{66}$

$\dfrac{5}{4} = 1.25$

$\frac{1}{8} = 0.125$

Place the decimals in order from greatest to least.

1.25, 1.2, 0.125, 0, $-0.\overline{66}$, −1, −2.1

Convert back to fractions if the problem requires it.

$\frac{5}{4}$, 1.2, $\frac{1}{8}$, 0, $-\frac{2}{3}$, −1, −2.1

39. Convert each value using the least common denominator of 24.

$\frac{1}{3} = \frac{8}{24}$

$-\frac{5}{6} = -\frac{20}{24}$

$1\frac{1}{8} = \frac{9}{8} = \frac{27}{24}$

$\frac{7}{12} = \frac{14}{24}$

$-\frac{3}{4} = -\frac{18}{24}$

$-\frac{3}{2} = -\frac{36}{24}$

Arrange the fractions in order from least to greatest by comparing the numerators.

$-\frac{36}{24}, -\frac{20}{24}, -\frac{18}{24}, \frac{8}{24}, \frac{14}{24}, \frac{27}{24}$

Put the fractions back in their original form if the problem requires it.

$-\frac{3}{2}, -\frac{5}{6}, -\frac{3}{4}, \frac{1}{3}, \frac{7}{12}, 1\frac{1}{8}$

40. $\frac{(10^2)^3}{(10^2)^2}$

Multiply the exponents raised to a power.

$= \frac{10^6}{10^{-4}}$

Subtract the exponent in the denominator from the one in the numerator.

$= 10^{6 - (-4)}$

Simplify.

$= 10^{10} =$ **10,000,000,000**

41. $\frac{(x^{-2}y^2)^2}{x^3y}$

Multiply the exponents raised to a power.

$= \frac{x^{-4}y^4}{x^3y}$

Subtract the exponent in the denominator from the one in the numerator.

$= x^{-4-3}y^{4-1} = x^{-7}y^3$

Move negative exponents to the denominator.

$= \frac{y^3}{x^7}$

42. $\sqrt{48}$

Determine the largest square number that is a factor of the radicand (48) and write the radicand as a product using that square number as a factor.

$= \sqrt{16 \times 3}$

Apply the rules of radicals to simplify.

$= \sqrt{16}\sqrt{3} =$ **$4\sqrt{3}$**

43. $\frac{6}{\sqrt{8}}$

Apply the rules of radicals to simplify.

$= \frac{6}{\sqrt{4}\sqrt{2}} = \frac{6}{2\sqrt{2}}$

Multiply by $\frac{\sqrt{2}}{\sqrt{2}}$ to rationalize the denominator.

$= \frac{6}{2\sqrt{2}}\left(\frac{\sqrt{2}}{\sqrt{2}}\right) = $ **$\frac{3\sqrt{2}}{2}$**

44. 8!

Expand the factorial and multiply.

$= 8 \times 7 \times 6 \times 5 \times 4 \times 3 \times 2 \times 1$

$= 40,320$

45. $\frac{10!}{7!3!}$

Expand the factorial.

$= \frac{10 \times 9 \times 8 \times 7!}{7! \times 3 \times 2 \times 1}$

Cross out values that occur in both the numerator and denominator.

$= \frac{10 \times 9 \times 8}{3 \times 2 \times 1}$

Multiply and simplify.

$$= \frac{720}{6} = \mathbf{120}$$

46. Identify the variables given.

$a_1 = -57$

$d = -57 - (-40) = 17$

$n = 9$

Plug these values into the formula for the specific term of an arithmetic sequence.

$a_9 = -57 + 17(9 - 1)$

Solve for a_9.

$a_9 = -57 + 17(8)$

$a_9 = -57 + 136$

$\mathbf{a_9 = 79}$

47. Idenfity the variables given.

$a_5 = 200$

$a_{23} = 820$

$n = 23$

$m = 5$

$d = ?$

Plug these values into the equation for using one term to find another in an arithmetic sequence.

$a_n = a_m + d(n - m)$

$820 = 200 + d(23 - 5)$

$620 = d(18)$

$\mathbf{d = 34.\overline{44}}$

48. $\sum_{n=14}^{45} 2n + 10$.

Find the partial sum of the first 45 terms.

$a_1 = 2(1) + 10 = 12$

$n = 45$

$a_n = 2(45) + 10 = 100$

$$S_n = \frac{n(a_1 + a_n)}{2} = \frac{45(12 + 100)}{2} = 2520$$

Find the partial sum of the first 13 terms.

$a_1 = 2(1) + 10 = 12$

$n = 13$

$a_n = 2(13) + 10 = 36$

$$S_n = \frac{n(a_1 + a_n)}{2} = \frac{13(12 + 36)}{2} = 312$$

The sum of the terms between 14 and 45 will be the difference between S_{45} and S_{13}.

$S_{45} - S_{13} = 2520 - 312 = \mathbf{2208}$

49. Identify the variables given.

$a_1 = 13$

$n = 8$

$r = \frac{39}{13} = 3$

Plug these values into the equation to find a specific term in a geometric sequence.

$a_8 = 13 \times 3^{8-1}$

$a_8 = 13 \times 2187 = 28{,}431$

The eighth term of the given sequence is **28,431**.

50. Identify the variables given.

$a_1 = -4$

$n = 10$

$r = \frac{16}{-4} = -4$

Plug these values into the equation for the partial sum of a geometric sequence.

$$S_{10} = \frac{-4(1 - (-4)^{10})}{1 - (-4)}$$

$$= \frac{-4(1 - 1{,}048{,}576)}{5} = \frac{4{,}194{,}300}{5}$$

$$= \mathbf{838{,}860}$$

CHAPTER TWO
Algebra

Algebra, meaning "restoration" in Arabic, is the mathematical method of finding the unknown. The first algebraic book in Egypt was used to figure out complex inheritances that were to be split among many individuals. Today, algebra is just as necessary when dealing with unknown amounts.

Algebraic Expressions

The foundation of algebra is the **VARIABLE**, an unknown number represented by a symbol (usually a letter such as x or a). Variables can be preceded by a **COEFFICIENT**, which is a constant (i.e., a real number) in front of the variable, such as $4x$ or $-2a$. An **ALGEBRAIC EXPRESSION** is any sum, difference, product, or quotient of variables and numbers (for example $3x^2$, $2x + 7y - 1$, and $\frac{5}{x}$ are algebraic expressions). **TERMS** are any quantities that are added or subtracted (for example, the terms of the expression $x^2 - 3x + 5$ are x^2, $3x$, and 5). A **POLYNOMIAL EXPRESSION** is an algebraic expression where all the exponents on the variables are whole numbers. A polynomial with only two terms is known as a **BINOMIAL**, and one with three terms is a **TRINOMIAL**. A **MONOMIAL** has only one term.

EVALUATING EXPRESSIONS is another way of saying "find the numeric value of an expression if the variable is equal to a certain number." To evaluate the expression, simply plug the given value(s) for the variable(s) into the equation and simplify. Remember to use the order of operations when simplifying:

1. Parentheses
2. Exponents
3. Multiplication

DID YOU KNOW?
Simplified expressions are ordered by variable terms alphabetically with highest exponent first then down to constants.

4. Division
5. Addition
6. Subtraction

EXAMPLE

1. If $m = 4$, find the value of the following expression: $5(m - 2)^3 + 3m^2 - \frac{m}{4} - 1$

Operations with Expressions
ADDING and SUBTRACTING

Expressions can be added or subtracted by simply adding and subtracting LIKE TERMS, which are terms with the same variable part (the variables must be the same, with the same exponents on each variable). For example, in the expressions $2x + 3xy - 2z$ and $6y + 2xy$, the like terms are $3xy$ and $2xy$. Adding the two expressions yields the new expression $2x + 5xy - 2z + 6y$. Note that the other terms did not change; they cannot be combined because they have different variables.

EXAMPLE

2. If $a = 12x + 7xy - 9y$ and $b = 8x - 9xz + 7z$, what is $a + b$?

DISTRIBUTING and FACTORING

Distributing and factoring can be seen as two sides of the same coin. **DISTRIBUTION** multiplies each term in the first factor by each term in the second factor to get rid of parentheses. **FACTORING** reverses this process, taking a polynomial in standard form and writing it as a product of two or more factors.

When distributing a monomial through a polynomial, the expression outside the parentheses is multiplied by each term inside the parentheses. Using the rules of exponents, coefficients are multiplied and exponents are added.

When simplifying two polynomials, each term in the first polynomial must be multiplied by each term in the second polynomial. A binomial (two terms) multiplied by a binomial, will require 2 × 2 or 4 multiplications. For the binomial × binomial case, this process is sometimes called **FOIL**, which stands for first, outside, inside, and last. These terms refer to the placement of each term of the expression: multiply the first term in each expression, then the outside terms, then the inside terms, and finally the last terms. A binomial (two terms) multiplied by a trinomial (three terms), will require 2 × 3 or 6 products to simplify. The first term in the first polynomial multiplies each of the three terms in the second polynomial, then the second term in the first polynomial multiplies each of the three terms in the second polynomial. A trinomial (three terms) by a trinomial will require 3 × 3 or 9 products, and so on.

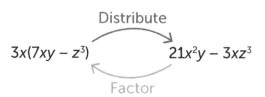

Figure 2.1. Distribution and Factoring

Factoring is the reverse of distributing: the first step is always to remove ("undistribute") the GCF of all the terms, if there is a GCF (besides 1). The GCF is the product of any constants and/or variables that <u>every</u> term shares. (For example, the GCF of $12x^3$, $15x^2$, and $6xy^2$ is $3x$ because $3x$ evenly divides all three terms.) This shared factor can be taken out of each term and moved to the outside of the parentheses, leaving behind a polynomial where each term is the original term divided by the GCF. (The remaining terms for the terms in the example would be $4x^2$, $5x$, and $2y^2$.) It may be possible to factor the polynomial in the parentheses further, depending on the problem.

EXAMPLES

3. Expand the following expression: $5x(x^2 - 2c + 10)$

4. Expand the following expression: $(x^2 - 5)(2x - x^3)$

5. Factor the expression $16z^2 + 48z$

6. Factor the expression $6m^3 + 12m^3n - 9m^2$

FACTORING TRINOMIALS

If the leading coefficient is $a = 1$, the trinomial is in the form $x^2 + bx + c$ and can often be rewritten in the factored form, as a product of two binomials: $(x + m)(x + n)$. Recall that the product of two binomials can be written in expanded form $x^2 + mx + nx + mn$. Equating this expression with $x^2 + bx + c$, the constant term c would have to equal the product mn. Thus, to work backward from the trinomial to the factored form, consider all the numbers m and n that multiply to make c. For example, to factor $x^2 + 8x + 12$, consider all the pairs that multiply to be 12 (12 = 1 × 12 or 2 × 6 or 3 × 4). Choose the pair that will make the coefficient of the middle term (8) when added. In this example 2 and 6 add to 8, so making $m = 2$ and $n = 6$ in the expanded form gives:

$$x^2 + 8x + 12 = x^2 + 2x + 6x + 12$$

$= (x^2 + 2x) + (6x + 12)$	Group the first two terms and the last two terms.

$= x(x + 2) + 6(x + 2)$	Factor the GCF out of each set of parentheses.
$= (x + 6)(x + 2)$	The two terms now have the common factor $(x + 2)$, which can be removed, leaving $(x + 6)$ and the original polynomial is factored.

In general:

$$x^2 + bx + c = x^2 + mx + nx + mn, \text{ where } c = mn \text{ and } b = m + n$$

$= (x^2 + mx) + (nx + mn)$	Group.
$= x(x + m) + n(x + m)$	Factor each group.
$= (x + m)(x + n)$	Factor out the common binomial.

Note that if none of the factors of c add to the value b, then the trinomial cannot be factored, and is called PRIME.

If the leading coefficient is not 1 ($a \neq 1$), first make sure that any common factors among the three terms are factored out. If the a-value is negative, factor out –1 first as well. If the a-value of the new polynomial in the parentheses is still not 1, follow this rule: Identify two values r and s that multiply to be ac and add to be b. Then write the polynomial in this form: $ax^2 + bx + c = ax^2 + rx + sx + c$, and proceed by grouping, factoring, and removing the common binomial as above.

There are a few special factoring cases worth memorizing: difference of squares, binomial squared, and the sum and difference of cubes.

▶ **DIFFERENCE OF SQUARES** (each term is a square and they are subtracted):

▷ $a^2 - b^2 = (a + b)(a - b)$

▷ Note that a SUM of squares is never factorable.

▶ **BINOMIAL SQUARED:** $a^2 + 2ab + b^2 = (a + b)(a + b) = (a + b)^2$

▶ **SUM AND DIFFERENCE OF CUBES:**

▷ $a^3 + b^3 = (a + b)(a^2 - ab + b^2)$

▷ $a^3 - b^3 = (a - b)(a^2 + ab + b^2)$

▷ Note that the second factor in these factorizations will never be able to be factored further.

EXAMPLES

7. Factor: $16x^2 + 52x + 30$

8. Factor: $-21x^2 - x + 10$

Linear Equations

An **EQUATION** states that two expressions are equal to each other. Polynomial equations are categorized by the highest power of the variables they contain: the highest power of any exponent of a linear equation is 1, a quadratic equation has a variable raised to the second power, a cubic equation has a variable raised to the third power, and so on.

SOLVING LINEAR EQUATIONS

Solving an equation means finding the value or values of the variable that make the equation true. To solve a linear equation, it is necessary to manipulate the terms so that the variable being solved for appears alone on one side of the equal sign while everything else in the equation is on the other side.

The way to solve linear equations is to "undo" all the operations that connect numbers to the variable of interest. Follow these steps:

1. Eliminate fractions by multiplying each side by the least common multiple of any denominators.

2. Distribute to eliminate parentheses, braces, and brackets.

3. Combine like terms.

4. Use addition or subtraction to collect all terms containing the variable of interest to one side, and all terms not containing the variable to the other side.

5. Use multiplication or division to remove coefficients from the variable of interest.

Sometimes there are no numeric values in the equation or there are a mix of numerous variables and constants. The goal is to solve the equation for one of the variables in terms of the other variables. In this case, the answer will be an expression involving numbers and letters instead of a numeric value.

EXAMPLES

9. Solve for x: $\dfrac{100(x + 5)}{20} = 1$

10. Solve for x: $2(x + 2)^2 - 2x^2 + 10 = 42$

11. Solve the equation for D: $\dfrac{A(3B + 2D)}{2N} = 5M - 6$

GRAPHS of LINEAR EQUATIONS

The most common way to write a linear equation is the **SLOPE-INTERCEPT FORM**, $y = mx + b$. In this equation, m is the slope, which describes how steep the line is, and b is the *y*-intercept. Slope is often described as "rise over run" because it is calculated as the difference in *y*-values (rise) over the difference in *x*-values (run). The slope of the line is also the rate of change of the dependent variable *y* with respect to the independent variable *x*. The *y*-intercept is the point where the line crosses the *y*-axis, or where *x* equals zero.

DID YOU KNOW?

Use the phrase "Begin, Move" to remember that *b* is the *y*-intercept (where to begin) and *m* is the slope (how the line moves).

To graph a linear equation, identify the *y*-intercept and place that point on the *y*-axis. If the slope is not written as a fraction, make it a fraction by writing it over 1 $\left(\frac{m}{1}\right)$. Then use the slope to count up (or down, if negative) the "rise" part of the slope and over the "run" part of the slope to find a second point. These points can then be connected to draw the line.

To find the equation of a line, identify the *y*-intercept, if possible, on the graph and use two easily identifiable points to find the slope. If the *y*-intercept is not easily identified, identify the slope by choosing easily identifiable points; then choose one point on the graph, plug the point and the slope values into the equation, and solve for the missing value *b*.

▶ standard form: $Ax + By = C$

▶ $m = -\frac{A}{B}$

▶ *x*-intercept = $\frac{C}{A}$

▶ *y*-intercept = $\frac{C}{B}$

DID YOU KNOW?

slope-intercept form:
$y = mx + b$
slope: $m = \frac{y_2 - y_1}{x_2 - x_1}$

Another way to express a linear equation is standard form: $Ax + By = C$. In order to graph equations in this form, it is often easiest to convert them to point-slope form. Alternately, it is easy to find the *x*- or *y*-intercept from this form, and once these two points are known, a line can be drawn through them. To find the *x*-intercept, simply make *y* = 0 and solve for *x*. Similarly, to find the *y*-intercept, make *x* = 0 and solve for *y*.

EXAMPLES

12. What is the equation of the following line?

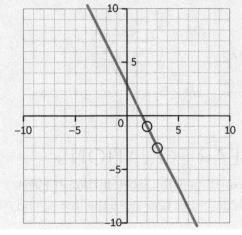

13. What is the slope of the line whose equation is $6x - 2y - 8 = 0$?

14. Write the equation of the line which passes through the points $(-2,5)$ and $(-5,3)$.

15. What is the equation of the following graph?

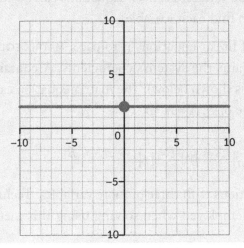

SYSTEMS of LINEAR EQUATIONS

Systems of equations are sets of equations that include two or more variables. These systems can only be solved when there are at least as many equations as there are variables. Systems involve working with more than one equation to solve for more than one variable. For a system of linear equations, the solution to the system is the set of values for the variables that satisfies every equation in the system. Graphically, this will be the point where every line meets. If the lines are parallel (and hence do not intersect), the system will have no solution. If the lines are multiples of each other, meaning they share all coordinates, then the system has infinitely many solutions (because every point on the line is a solution).

DID YOU KNOW?
Plug answers back into both equations to ensure the system has been solved properly.

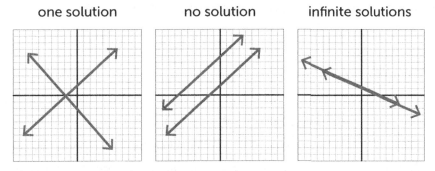

Figure 2.2. Systems of Equations

There are three common methods for solving systems of equations. To perform **SUB-STITUTION**, solve one equation for one variable, and then plug in the resulting expression for that variable in the second equation. This process works best for systems of two equations with two variables where the coefficient of one or more of the variables is 1.

To solve using **ELIMINATION**, add or subtract two equations so that one or more variables are eliminated. It's often necessary to multiply one or both of the equations by a scalar (constant) in order to make the variables cancel. Equations can be added or subtracted as many times as necessary to find each variable.

Yet another way to solve a system of linear equations is to use a **MATRIX EQUATION**. In the matrix equation $AX = B$, A contains the system's coefficients, X contains the variables, and B contains the constants (as shown below). The matrix equation can then be solved by multiplying B by the inverse of A: $X = A^{-1}B$

$$\begin{matrix} ax + by = e \\ cx + dy = f \end{matrix} \rightarrow A = \begin{bmatrix} a & b \\ c & d \end{bmatrix} \quad X = \begin{bmatrix} x \\ y \end{bmatrix} \quad B = \begin{bmatrix} e \\ f \end{bmatrix} \rightarrow AX = B$$

This method can be extended to equations with three or more variables. Technology (such as a graphing calculator) is often employed when solving using this method if more than two variables are involved.

EXAMPLES

16. Solve for x and y:

$2x - 4y = 28$

$4x - 12y = 36$

17. Solve the system for x and y:

$3 = -4x + y$

$16x = 4y + 2$

18. Solve the system of equations:

$6x + 10y = 18$

$4x + 15y = 37$

19. Solve the following system of equations using matrix arithmetic:

$2x - 3y = -5$

$3x - 4y = -8$

BUILDING EQUATIONS

In word problems, it is often necessary to translate a verbal description of a relationship into a mathematical equation. No matter the problem, this process can be done using the same steps:

1. Read the problem carefully and identify what value needs to be solved for.

2. Identify the known and unknown quantities in the problem, and assign the unknown quantities a variable.

3. Create equations using the variables and known quantities.

4. Solve the equations.

5. Check the solution: Does it answer the question asked in the problem? Does it make sense?

EXAMPLES

20. A school is holding a raffle to raise money. There is a $3 entry fee, and each ticket costs $5. If a student paid $28, how many tickets did he buy?

21. Kelly is selling shirts for her school swim team. There are two prices: a student price and a nonstudent price. During the first week of the sale, Kelly raised $84 by selling 10 shirts to students and 4 shirts to nonstudents. She earned $185 in the second week by selling 20 shirts to students and 10 shirts to nonstudents. What is the student price for a shirt?

Linear Inequalities
SOLVING LINEAR INEQUALITIES

An inequality shows the relationship between two expressions, much like an equation. However, the equal sign is replaced with an inequality symbol that expresses the following relationships:

▶ < less than

▶ > greater than

▶ ≤ less than or equal to

▶ ≥ greater than or equal to

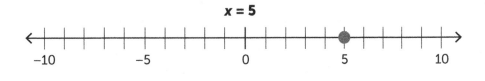

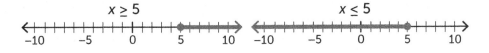

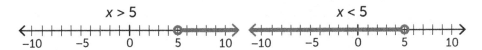

Figure 2.3. Inequalities on a Number Line

Inequalities are read from left to right. For example, the inequality $x \le 8$ would be read as "x is less than or equal to 8," meaning x has a value smaller than or equal to 8. The set of solutions of an inequality can be expressed using a number line. The shaded region on the number line represents the set of all the numbers that make an inequality true. One major difference between equations and inequalities is that equations generally have a finite number of solutions, while inequalities generally have infinitely many solutions (an entire interval on the number line containing infinitely many values).

Linear inequalities can be solved in the same way as linear equations, with one exception. When multiplying or dividing both sides of an inequality by a negative number, the direction of the inequality sign must reverse—"greater than" becomes "less than" and "less than" becomes "greater than."

EXAMPLES

22. Solve for z: $3z + 10 < -z$

23. Solve for x: $2x - 3 > 5(x - 4) - (x - 4)$

COMPOUND INEQUALITIES

Compound inequalities have more than one inequality expression. Solutions of compound inequalities are the sets of all numbers that make *all* the inequalities true. Some compound inequalities may not have any solutions, some will have solutions that contain some part of the number line, and some will have solutions that include the entire number line.

Table 2.1. Unions and Intersections

INEQUALITY	MEANING IN WORDS	NUMBER LINE
$a < x < b$	All values x that are greater than a and less than b	
$a \le x \le b$	All values x that are greater than or equal to a and less than or equal to b	
$x < a$ or $x > b$	All values of x that are less than a or greater than b	
$x \le a$ or $x \ge b$	All values of x that are less than or equal to a or greater than or equal to b	

Compound inequalities can be written, solved, and graphed as two separate inequalities. For compound inequalities in which the word *and* is used, the solution to the compound inequality will be the set of numbers on the number line where both inequalities have solutions (where both are shaded). For compound inequalities where *or* is used, the solution to the compound inequality will be *all* the shaded regions for *either* inequality.

EXAMPLES

24. Solve the compound inequalities: $2x - 4 < -18$ *or* $4(x + 2) > 18$

25. Solve the inequality: $-1 \leq 3(x + 2) - 1 \leq x + 3$

GRAPHING LINEAR INEQUALITIES in TWO VARIABLES

Linear inequalities in two variables can be graphed in much the same way as linear equations. Start by graphing the corresponding equation of a line (temporarily replace the inequality with an equal sign, and then graph). This line creates a boundary line of two half-planes. If the inequality is a "greater/less than," the boundary should not be included and a dotted line is used. A solid line is used to indicate that the boundary should be included in the solution when the inequality is "greater/less than or equal to."

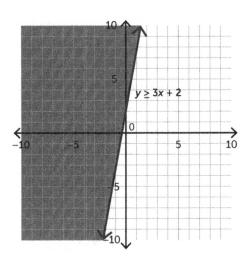

Figure 2.4. Graphing Inequalities

One side of the boundary is the set of all points (x, y) that make the inequality true. This side is shaded to indicate that all these values are solutions. If y is greater than the expression containing x, shade above the line; if it is less than, shade below. A point can also be used to check which side of the line to shade.

A set of two or more linear inequalities is a **SYSTEM OF INEQUALITIES.** Solutions to the system are all the values of the variables that make every inequality in the system true. Systems of inequalities are solved graphically by graphing all the inequalities in the same plane. The region where all the shaded solutions overlap is the solution to the system.

DID YOU KNOW?

A dotted line is used for "greater/less than" because the solution may approach that line, but the coordinates on the line can never be a solution.

EXAMPLES

26. Graph the following inequality: $3x + 6y \leq 12$.

27. Graph the system of inequalities: $-x + y \leq 1, x \geq -1, y > 2x - 4$

28. What is the inequality represented on the graph below?

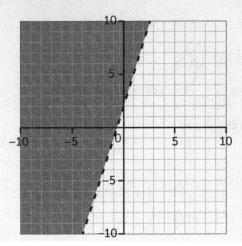

Quadratic Equations

Quadratic equations are degree 2 polynomials; the highest power on the dependent variable is two. While linear functions are represented graphically as lines, the graph of a quadratic function is a **PARABOLA**. The graph of a parabola has three important components. The **VERTEX** is where the graph changes direction. In the parent graph $y = x^2$, the origin $(0, 0)$ is the vertex. The **AXIS OF SYMMETRY** is the vertical line that cuts the graph into two equal halves. The line of symmetry always passes through the vertex. On the parent graph, the y-axis is the axis of symmetry. The **ZEROS** or **ROOTS** of the quadratic are the x-intercepts of the graph.

FORMS of QUADRATIC EQUATIONS

Quadratic equations can be expressed in two forms:

▶ **STANDARD FORM:** $y = ax^2 + bx + c$
  ▷ Axis of symmetry: $x = -\frac{b}{2a}$
  ▷ Vertex: $(-\frac{b}{2a}, f(-\frac{b}{2a}))$
▶ **VERTEX FORM:** $y\ a(x - h)^2 + k$
  ▷ Vertex: (h, k)
  ▷ Axis of symmetry: $x = h$

In both equations, the sign of a determines which direction the parabola opens: if a is positive, then it opens upward; if a is negative, then it opens downward. The wideness or narrowness is also determined by a. If the absolute value of a is less than one (a proper fraction), then the parabola will get wider the closer $|a|$ is to zero. If the absolute value of a is greater than one, then the larger $|a|$ becomes, the narrower the parabola will be.

Equations in vertex form can be converted to standard form by squaring out the $(x - h)^2$ part (using FOIL), distributing the a, adding k, and simplifying the result.

Equations can be converted from standard form to vertex form by **COMPLETING THE SQUARE**. Take an equation in standard form, $y = ax^2 + bc + c$.

1. Move c to the left side of the equation.

2. Divide the entire equation through by a (to make the coefficient of x^2 be 1).

3. Take half of the coefficient of x, square that number, and then add the result to both sides of the equation.

4. Convert the right side of the equation to a perfect binomial squared, $(x + m)^2$.

5. Isolate y to put the equation in proper vertex form.

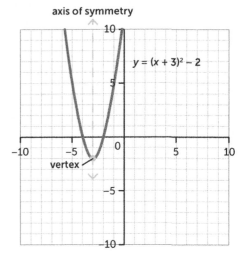

Figure 2.5. Parabola

EXAMPLES

29. What is the line of symmetry for $y = -2(x + 3)^2 + 2$?

30. What is the vertex of the parabola $y = -3x^2 + 24x - 27$?

31. Write $y = -3x^2 + 24x - 27$ in vertex form by completing the square.

SOLVING QUADRATIC EQUATIONS

Solving the quadratic equation $\mathbf{ax^2 + bx + c = 0}$ finds x-intercepts of the parabola (by making $y = 0$). These are also called the **ROOTS** or **ZEROS** of the quadratic function. A quadratic equation may have zero, one, or two real solutions. There are several ways of finding the zeros. One way is to factor the quadratic into a product of two binomials, and then use the zero product property. (If $m \times n = 0$, then either $m = 0$ or $n = 0$.) Another way is to complete the square and square root both sides. One way that works every time is to memorize and use the **QUADRATIC FORMULA**:

$$x = \frac{-b \pm \sqrt{b^2 - 4ac}}{2a}$$

The a, b, and c come from the standard form of quadratic equations above. (Note that to use the quadratic equation, the right-hand side of the equation must be equal to zero.)

The part of the formula under the square root radical ($b^2 - 4ac$) is known as the **DISCRIMINANT**. The discriminant tells how many and what type of roots will result without actually calculating the roots.

DID YOU KNOW?

With all graphing problems, putting the function into the $y =$ window of a graphing calculator will aid the process of elimination when graphs are examined and compared to answer choices with a focus on properties like axis of symmetry, vertices, and roots of formulas.

Table 2.2. Discriminants

If $B^2 - 4AC$ is	There will be	And the parabola
zero	only 1 real root	has its vertex on the x-axis
positive	2 real roots	has two x-intercepts
negative	0 real roots 2 complex roots	has no x-intercepts

EXAMPLES

32. Find the zeros of the quadratic equation: $y = -(x + 3)^2 + 1$.

33. Find the root(s) for: $z^2 - 4z + 4 = 0$

34. Write a quadratic function that has zeros at $x = -3$ and $x = 2$ that passes through the point $(-2,8)$.

GRAPHING QUADRATIC EQUATIONS

The final expected quadratic skills are graphing a quadratic function given its equation and determining the equation of a quadratic function from its graph. The equation's form determines which quantities are easiest to obtain:

Table 2.3. Obtaining Quantities from Quadratic Functions

Name of Form	Equation of Quadratic	Easiest Quantity to Find	How to Find Other Quantities
vertex form	$y = a(x - h)^2 + k$	vertex at (h,k) and axis of symmetry $x = h$	Find zeros by making $y = 0$ and solving for x.
factored form	$y = a(x - m)(x - n)$	x–intercepts at $x = m$ and $x = n$	Find axis of symmetry by averaging m and n: $x = \frac{m+n}{2}$. This is also the x-value of the vertex.
standard form	$y = ax^2 + bx + c$	y–intercept at $(0,c)$	Find axis of symmetry and x-value of the vertex using $x = \frac{-b}{2a}$. Find zeros using quadratic formula.

To graph a quadratic function, first determine if the graph opens up or down by examining the a-value. Then determine the quantity that is easiest to find based on the form given, and find the vertex. Then other values can be found, if necessary, by choosing x-values and finding the corresponding y-values. Using symmetry instantly doubles the number of points that are known.

Given the graph of a parabola, the easiest way to write a quadratic equation is to identify the vertex and insert the h- and k-values into the vertex form of the equation. The a-value can be determined by finding another point the graph goes through, plugging these values in for x and y, and solving for a.

EXAMPLES

35. Graph the quadratic $y = 2(x - 3)^2 + 4$.

36. What is the vertex form of the equation shown on the following graph?

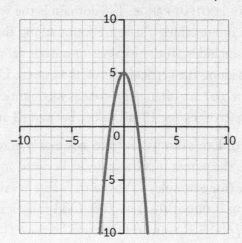

Functions
WORKING with FUNCTIONS

Functions can be thought of as a process: when something is put in, an action (or operation) is performed, and something different comes out. A **FUNCTION** is a relationship between two quantities (for example x and y) in which, for every value of the independent variable (usually x), there is exactly one value of the dependent variable (usually y). Briefly, each input has *exactly one* output. Graphically this means the graph passes the **VERTICAL LINE TEST**: anywhere a vertical line is drawn on the graph, the line hits the curve at exactly one point.

The notation $f(x)$ or $g(t)$, etc., is often used when a function is being considered. This is **FUNCTION NOTATION**. The input value is x and the output value y is written as $y = f(x)$. Thus, $f(2)$ represents the output value (or y value) when $x = 2$, and $f(2) = 5$ means that when $x = 2$ is plugged into the $f(x)$ function, the output (y value) is 5. In other words, $f(2) = 5$ represents the point $(2, 5)$ on the graph of $f(x)$.

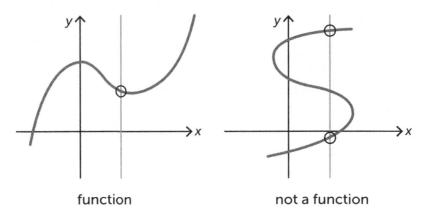

function   not a function

Figure 2.6. Vertical Line Test

Every function has an **INPUT DOMAIN** and **OUTPUT RANGE**. The domain is the set of all the possible x values that can be used as input values (these are found along the horizontal axis on the graph), and the range includes all the y values or output values that result from applying $f(x)$ (these are found along the vertical axis on the graph). Domain and range are usually intervals of numbers and are often expressed as inequalities, such as $x < 2$ (the domain is all values less than 2) or $3 < x < 15$ (all values between 3 and 15).

A function $f(x)$ is **EVEN** if $f(-x) = f(x)$. Even functions have symmetry across the y-axis. An example of an even function is the parent quadratic $y = x^2$, because any value of x (for example, 3) and its opposite $-x$ (for example, -3) have the same y value (for example, $3^2 = 9$ and $(-3)^2 = 9$). A function is **ODD** if $f(-x) = -f(x)$. Odd functions have symmetry about the origin. For example, $f(x) = x^3$ is an odd function because $f(3) = 27$, and $f(-3) = -27$. A function may be even, odd, or neither.

even   odd

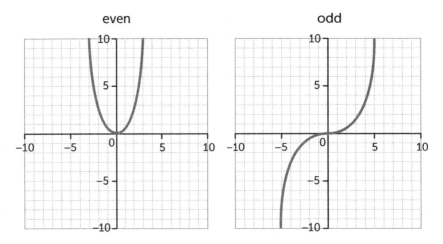

Figure 2.7. Even and Odd Functions

EXAMPLES

37. Evaluate: $f(4)$ if $f(x) = x^3 - 2x + \sqrt{x}$

38. What are the domain and range of the following function?

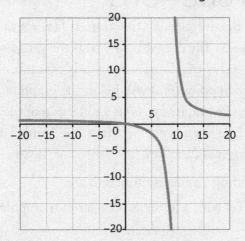

39. What are the domain and the range of the following graph?

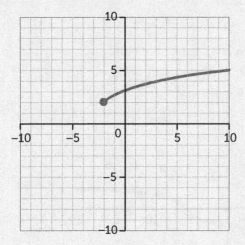

40. Which of the following represents a function?

A)

x	g(x)
0	0
1	1
2	2
1	3

B)

x	f(x)
0	1
0	2
0	3
0	4

C)

t	f(t)
1	1
2	2
3	3
4	4

D)

x	f(x)
0	0
5	1
0	2
5	3

INVERSE FUNCTIONS

INVERSE FUNCTIONS switch the inputs and the outputs of a function. If $f(x) = k$ then the inverse of that function would read $f^{-1}(k) = x$. The domain of $f^{-1}(x)$ is the range of $f(x)$, and the range of $f^{-1}(x)$ is the domain of $f(x)$. If point (a, b) is on the graph of $f(x)$, then point (b, a) will be on the graph of $f^{-1}(x)$. Because of this fact, the graph of $f^{-1}(x)$ is a reflection of the graph of $f(x)$ across the line $y = x$. Inverse functions "undo" all the operations of the original function.

The steps for finding an inverse function are:

1.   Replace $f(x)$ with y to make it easier to manipulate the equation.

2.   Switch the x and y.

3.   Solve for y.

4.   Label the inverse function as $f^{-1}(x) =$.

DID YOU KNOW?

Inverse graphs can be tested by taking any point on one graph and flipping coordinates to see if that new point is on the other curve. For example, the coordinate point (5,−2) is on the function and (−2,5) is a point on its inverse.

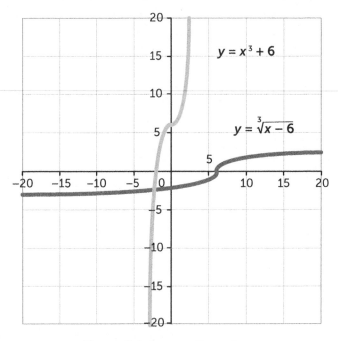

Figure 2.8. Inverse Functions

EXAMPLES

41. What is the inverse of function of $f(x) = 5x + 5$?

42. Find the inverse of the graph of $f(x) = -1 - \frac{1}{5}x$.

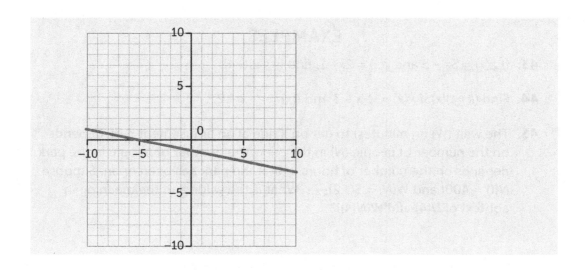

COMPOUND FUNCTIONS

COMPOUND FUNCTIONS take two or more functions and combine them using operations or composition. Functions can be combined using addition, subtraction, multiplication, or division:

- addition: $(f + g)(x) = f(x) + g(x)$
- subtraction: $(f - g)(x) = f(x) - g(x)$
- multiplication: $(fg)(x) = f(x)g(x)$
- division: $\left(\frac{f}{g}\right)(x) = \frac{f(x)}{g(x)}$ (note that $g(x) \neq 0$)

Functions can also be combined using **COMPOSITION**. Composition of functions is indicated by the notation $(f \circ g)(x)$. Note that the $\circ$ symbol does NOT mean multiply. It means take the output of $g(x)$ and make it the input of $f(x)$:

$$(f \circ g)(x) = f(g(x))$$

This equation is read f of g of x, and will be a new function of x. Note that order is important. In general, $f(g(x)) \neq g(f(x))$. They *will* be equal when $f(x)$ and $g(x)$ are inverses of each other, however, as both will simplify to the original input x. This is because performing a function on a value and then using that output as the input to the inverse function should bring you back to the original value.

The domain of a composition function is the set of x values that are in the domain of the "inside" function $g(x)$ such that $g(x)$ is in the domain of the outside function $f(x)$. For example, if $f(x) = \frac{1}{x}$ and $g(x) = \sqrt{x}$, $f(g(x))$ has a domain of $x > 0$ because $g(x)$ has a domain of $x \geq 0$. But when $f(x)$ is applied to the $\sqrt{x}$ function, the composition function becomes $\frac{1}{\sqrt{x}}$ and the value $x = 0$ is no longer allowed because it would result in 0 in the denominator, so the domain must be further restricted.

43. If $z(x) = 3x - 3$ and $y(x) = 2x - 1$, find $(y \circ z)(-4)$.

44. Find $(k \circ t)(x)$ if $k(x) = \frac{1}{2}x - 3$ and $t(x) = \frac{1}{2}x - 2$.

45. The wait (W) (in minutes) to get on a ride at an amusement park depends on the number of people (N) in the park. The number of people in the park depends on the number of hours, t, that the park has been open. Suppose $N(t) = 400t$ and $W(N) = 5(1.2)\frac{N}{100}$. What is the value and the meaning in context of $N(4)$ and $W(N(4))$?

TRANSFORMING FUNCTIONS

Many functions can be graphed using simple transformation of parent functions. Transformations include reflections across axes, vertical and horizontal translations (or shifts), and vertical or horizontal stretches or compressions. The table gives the effect of each transformation to the graph of any function $y = f(x)$.

Table 2.4. Effects of Transformations	
EQUATION	**EFFECT ON GRAPH**
$y = -f(x)$	reflection across the x-axis (vertical reflection)
$y = f(x) + k$	vertical shift up k units ($k > 0$) or down k units ($k < 0$)
$y = kf(x)$	vertical stretch (if $k > 1$) or compression (if $k < 1$)
$y = f(-x)$	reflection across the y-axis (horizontal reflection)
$y = f(x + k)$	horizontal shift right k units ($k < 0$) or left k units ($k > 0$)
$y = f(kx)$	horizontal stretch ($k < 1$) or compression ($k > 1$)

Note that the first three equations have an operation applied to the *outside* of the function $f(x)$ and these all cause *vertical changes* to the graph of the function that are INTUITIVE (for example, adding a value moves it up). The last three equations have an operation applied to the *inside* of the function $f(x)$ and these all cause HORIZONTAL CHANGES to the graph of the function that are COUNTERINTUITIVE (for example, multiplying the x's by a fraction results in stretch, not compression, which would seem more intuitive). It is helpful to group these patterns together to remember how each transformation affects the graph.

EXAMPLES

46. Graph: $y = |x + 1| + 4$

47. Graph: $y = -3|x - 2| + 2$

Answer Key

1. $5(m-2)^3 + 3m^2 - \frac{m}{4} - 1$

Plug the value 4 in for m in the expression.

$= 5(4-2)^3 + 3(4)^2 - \frac{4}{4} - 1$

Calculate all the expressions inside the parentheses.

$= 5(2)^3 + 3(4)^2 - \frac{4}{4} - 1$

Simplify all exponents.

$= 5(8) + 3(16) - \frac{4}{4} - 1$

Perform multiplication and division from left to right.

$= 40 + 48 - 1 - 1$

Perform addition and subtraction from left to right.

= 86

2. The only like terms in both expressions are $12x$ and $8x$, so these two terms will be added, and all other terms will remain the same.

$a + b = (12x + 8x) + 7xy - 9y - 9xz + 7z =$ **$20x + 7xy - 9y - 9xz + 7z$**

3. $5x(x^2 - 2c + 10)$

Distribute and multiply the term outside the parentheses to all three terms inside the parentheses.

$(5x)(x^2) = 5x^3$

$(5x)(-2c) = -10xc$

$(5x)(10) = 50x$

$= 5x^3 - 10xc + 50x$

4. $(x^2 - 5)(2x - x^3)$

Apply FOIL: first, outside, inside, and last.

$(x^2)(2x) = 2x^3$

$(x^2)(-x^3) = -x^5$

$(-5)(2x) = -10x$

$(-5)(-x^3) = 5x^3$

Combine like terms and put them in order.

$= 2x^3 - x^5 - 10x + 5x^3$

$= -x^5 + 7x^3 - 10x$

5. $16z^2 + 48z$

Both terms have a z, and 16 is a common factor of both 16 and 48. So the greatest common factor is $16z$. Factor out the GCF.

$16z^2 + 48z$

$= 16z(z + 3)$

6. $6m^3 + 12m^3n - 9m^2$

All the terms share the factor m^2, and 3 is the greatest common factor of 6, 12, and 9. So, the GCF is $3m^2$.

$= 3m^2(2m + 4mn - 3)$

7. $16x^2 + 52x + 30$

Remove the GCF of 2.

$= 2(8x^2 + 26x + 15)$

To factor the polynomial in the parentheses, calculate $ac = (8)(15) = 120$, and consider all the pairs of numbers that multiply to be 120: 1×120, 2×60, 3×40, 4×30, 5×24, 6×20, 8×15, and 10×12. Of these pairs, choose the pair that adds to the b-value 26 (6 and 20).

$= 2(8x^2 + 6x + 20x + 15)$

Group.

$= 2[(8x^2 + 6x) + (20x + 15)]$

Factor out the GCF of each group.

$= 2[(2x(4x + 3) + 5(4x + 3)]$

Factor out the common binomial.

$= 2[(4x + 3)(2x + 5)]$

$= 2(4x + 3)(2x + 5)$

If there are no values r and s that multiply to be ac and add to be b, then the polynomial is prime and cannot be factored.

8. $-21x^2 - x + 10$

Factor out the negative.

$= -(21x^2 + x - 10)$

Factor the polynomial in the parentheses.

$ac = 210$ and $b = 1$

The numbers 15 and −14 can be multiplied to get 210 and subtracted to get 1.

$= -(21x^2 - 14x + 15x - 10)$

Group.

$= -[(21x^2 - 14x) + (15x - 10)]$

Factor out the GCF of each group.

$= -[7x(3x - 2) + 5(3x - 2)]$

Factor out the common binomial.

$= -(3x - 2)(7x + 5)$

9. $\dfrac{100(x + 5)}{20} = 1$

Multiply both sides by 20 to cancel out the denominator.

$(20)\left(\dfrac{100(x + 5)}{20}\right) = (1)(20)$

$100(x + 5) = 20$

Distribute 100 through the parentheses.

$100x + 500 = 20$

"Undo" the +500 by subtracting 500 on both sides of the equation to isolate the variable term.

$100x = -480$

"Undo" the multiplication by 100 by dividing by 100 on both sides to solve for x.

$x = \dfrac{-480}{100}$

$x = -4.8$

10. $2(x + 2)^2 - 2x^2 + 10 = 42$

Eliminate the exponents on the left side.

$2(x + 2)(x + 2) - 2x^2 + 10 = 42$

Apply FOIL.

$2(x^2 + 4x + 4) - 2x^2 + 10 = 42$

Distribute the 2.

$2x^2 + 8x + 8 - 2x^2 + 10 = 42$

Combine like terms on the left-hand side.

$8x + 18 = 42$

Isolate the variable. "Undo" +18 by subtracting 18 on both sides.

$8x = 24$

"Undo" multiplication by 8 by dividing both sides by 8.

$x = 3$

11. $\dfrac{A(3B + 2D)}{2N} = 5M - 6$

Multiply both sides by $2N$ to clear the fraction, and distribute the A through the parentheses.

$3AB + 2AD = 10MN - 12N$

Isolate the term with the D in it by moving $3AB$ to the other side of the equation.

$2AD = 10MN - 12N - 3AB$

Divide both sides by $2A$ to get D alone on the right-hand side.

$D = \dfrac{(10MN - 12N - 3AB)}{2A}$

12. The y-intercept can be identified on the graph as (0,3).

$b = 3$

To find the slope, choose any two points and plug the values into the slope equation. The two points chosen here are (2,−1) and (3,−3).

$m = \dfrac{(-3) - (-1)}{3 - 2} = \dfrac{-2}{1} = -2$

Replace m with -2 and b with 3 in $y = mx + b$.

$y = -2x + 3$

13. $6x - 2y - 8 = 0$

Rearrange the equation into slope-intercept form by solving the equation for y.

$-2y = -6x + 8$

$y = \frac{-6x + 8}{-2}$

$y = 3x - 4$

The slope is 3, the value attached to x.

$m = 3$

14. $(-2,5)$ and $(-5,3)$

Calculate the slope.

$m = \frac{3 - 5}{(-5) - (-2)} = \frac{-2}{-3} = \frac{2}{3}$

To find b, plug into the equation $y = mx + b$ the slope for m and a set of points for x and y.

$5 = \frac{2}{3}(-2) + b$

$5 = \frac{-4}{3} + b$

$b = \frac{19}{3}$

Replace m and b to find the equation of the line.

$y = \frac{2}{3}x + \frac{19}{3}$

15. The line has a rise of 0 and a run of 1, so the slope is $\frac{0}{1} = 0$. There is no x-intercept. The y-intercept is $(0,2)$, meaning that the b-value in the slope-intercept form is 2.

$y = 0x + 2$, or $y = 2$

16. Solve the system with substitution. Solve one equation for one variable.

$2x - 4y = 28$

$x = 2y + 14$

Plug in the resulting expression for x in the second equation and simplify.

$4x - 12y = 36$

$4(2y + 14) - 12y = 36$

$8y + 56 - 12y = 36$

$-4y = -20$

$y = 5$

Plug the solved variable into either equation to find the second variable.

$2x - 4y = 28$

$2x - 4(5) = 28$

$2x - 20 = 28$

$2x = 48$

$x = 24$

The answer is $y = 5$ and $x = 24$ or **(24,5)**.

17. Isolate the variable in one equation.

$3 = -4x + y$

$y = 4x + 3$

Plug the expression into the second equation.

Both equations have slope 4. This means the graphs of the equations are parallel lines, so no intersection (solution) exists.

$16x = 4y + 2$

$16x = 4(4x + 3) + 2$

$16x = 16x + 12 + 2$

$0 = 14$

No solution exists.

18. Because solving for x or y in either equation will result in messy fractions, this problem is best solved using elimination. The goal is to eliminate one of the variables by making the coefficients in front of one set of variables the same, but with different signs, and then adding both equations.

To eliminate the x's in this problem, find the least common multiple of coefficients 6 and 4. The smallest number that both 6 and 4 divide into evenly is 12. Multiply the top equation by -2, and the bottom equation by 3.

$6x + 10y = 18 \xrightarrow{(-2)} -12x - 20y = -36$

$4x + 15y = 37 \xrightarrow{(3)} 12x + 45y = \underline{111}$

Add the two equations to eliminate the x's.

$25y = 75$

Solve for y.

$y = 3$

Replace y with 3 in either of the original equations.

$6x + 10(3) = 18$

$6x + 30 = 18$

$x = -2$

The solution is **(−2,3)**.

19. Write the system in matrix form, $AX = B$.

$$\begin{bmatrix} 2 & -3 \\ 3 & -4 \end{bmatrix} \begin{bmatrix} x \\ y \end{bmatrix} = \begin{bmatrix} -5 \\ -8 \end{bmatrix}$$

Calculate the inverse of Matrix **A**.

$$\begin{bmatrix} 2 & -3 \\ 3 & -4 \end{bmatrix}^{-1} = \frac{1}{(2)(-4) - (-3)(3)} \begin{bmatrix} -4 & 3 \\ -3 & 2 \end{bmatrix}$$

$$= \begin{bmatrix} -4 & 3 \\ -3 & 2 \end{bmatrix}$$

Multiply **B** by the inverse of **A**.

$$\begin{bmatrix} x \\ y \end{bmatrix} = \begin{bmatrix} -4 & 3 \\ -3 & 2 \end{bmatrix} \begin{bmatrix} -5 \\ -8 \end{bmatrix} = \begin{bmatrix} -4 \\ -1 \end{bmatrix}$$

Match up the 2 × 1 matrices to identify x and y.

$x = -4$

$y = -1$

20. Identify the quantities.

Number of tickets = x

Cost per ticket = 5

Cost for x tickets = $5x$

Total cost = 28

Entry fee = 3

Set up equations. The total cost for x tickets will be equal to the cost for x tickets plus the $3 flat fee.

$5x + 3 = 28$

Solve the equation for x.

$5x + 3 = 28$

$5x = 25$

$x = 5$

The student bought **5 tickets**.

21. Assign variables.

Student price = s

Nonstudent price = n

Create two equations using the number of shirts Kelly sold and the money she earned.

$10s + 4n = 84$

$20s + 10n = 185$

Solve the system of equations using substitution.

$10s + 4n = 84$

$10n = -20s + 185$

$n = -2s + 18.5$

$10s + 4(-2s + 18.5) = 84$

$10s - 8s + 74 = 84$

$2s + 74 = 84$

$2s = 10$

$s = 5$

The student cost for shirts is **$5**.

22. $3z + 10 < -z$

Collect nonvariable terms to one side.

$3z < -z - 10$

Collect variable terms to the other side.

$4z < -10$

Isolate the variable.

$z < -2.5$

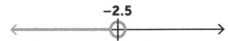

23. $2x - 3 > 5(x - 4) - (x - 4)$

Distribute 5 through the parentheses and −1 through the parentheses.

$2x - 3 > 5x - 20 - x + 4$

Combine like terms.

$2x - 3 > 4x - 16$

Collect x-terms to one side, and constant terms to the other side.

$-2x > -13$

Divide both sides by −2; since dividing by a negative, reverse the direction of the inequality.

$x < 6.5$

24. $2x - 4 < -18$ *or* $4(x + 2) > 18$

Solve each inequality independently.

$2x < -14$ $4x + 8 > 18$

$x < -7$ $4x > 10$

                $x > 2.5$

The solution to the original compound inequality is **the set of all x for which $x < -7$ or $x > 2.5$**.

25. $-1 \leq 3(x + 2) - 1 \leq x + 3$

Break up the compound inequality into two inequalities.

$-1 \leq 3(x + 2) - 1$ *and*
$3(x + 2) - 1 \leq x + 3$

Solve separately.

$-1 \leq 3x + 6 - 1$ $3x + 6 - 1 \leq x + 3$

$-6 \leq 3x$ $2x \leq -2$

$-2 \leq x$ and $x \leq -1$

The only values of x that satisfy *both* inequalities are the values between −2 and −1 (inclusive).

$-2 \leq x \leq -1$

26. Find the x- and y-intercepts.

$3x + 6y \leq 12$

$3(0) + 6y = 12$

$y = 2$

y-intercept: (0,2)

$3x + 6(0) \leq 12$

$x = 4$

x-intercept: (4,0)

Graph the line using the intercepts, and shade below the line.

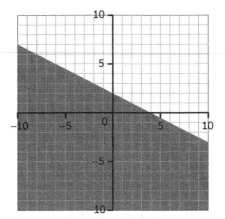

27. To solve the system, graph all three inequalities in the same plane; then identify the area where the three solutions overlap. All

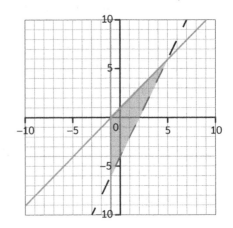

points (x,y) in this area will be solutions to the system since they satisfy all three inequalities.

28. Determine the equation of the boundary line.

y-intercept: $(0,2)$

slope: 3

$y = 3x + 2$

Replace the equal sign with the appropriate inequality: the line is dotted and the shading is above the line, indicating that the symbol should be "greater than." Check a point: for example $(-1,5)$ is a solution since $5 > 3(-1) + 2$.

$y > 3x + 2$

29. This quadratic is given in vertex form, with $h = -3$ and $k = 2$. The vertex of this equation is $(-3,2)$. The line of symmetry is the vertical line that passes through this point. Since the x-value of the point is -3, the line of symmetry is **$x = -3$**.

30. $y = -3x^2 + 24x - 27$

This quadratic equation is in standard form. Use the formula for finding the x-value of the vertex.

$x = -\dfrac{b}{2a}$ where $a = -3$, $b = 24$

$x = -\dfrac{24}{2(-3)} = 4$

Plug $x = 4$ into the original equation to find the corresponding y-value.

$y = -3(4)^2 + 24(4) - 27 = 21$

The vertex is at **$(4,21)$**.

31. $y = -3x^2 + 24x - 27$

Move c to the other side of the equation.

$y + 27 = -3x^2 + 24x$

Divide through by a (-3 in this example).

$\dfrac{y}{-3} - 9 = x^2 - 8x$

Take half of the new b, square it, and add that quantity to both sides: $\frac{1}{2}(-8) = -4$. Squaring it gives $(-4)2 = 16$.

$\dfrac{y}{-3} - 9 + 16 = x^2 - 8x + 16$

Simplify the left side, and write the right side as a binomial squared.

$\dfrac{y}{-3} + 7 = (x - 4)^2$

Subtract 7, and then multiply through by -3 to isolate y.

$y = -3(x - 4)^2 + 21$

32. Method 1: Make $y = 0$; isolate x by square rooting both sides:

Make $y = 0$.

$0 = -(x + 3)^2 + 1$

Subtract 1 from both sides.

$-1 = -(x + 3)^2$

Divide by -1 on both sides.

$1 = (x + 3)^2$

Square root both sides. Don't forget to write plus OR minus 1.

$(x + 3) = \pm 1$

Write two equations using $+1$ and -1.

$(x + 3) = 1$ or $(x + 3) = -1$

Solve both equations. These are the zeros.

$x = -2$ or $x = -4$

Method 2: Convert vertex form to standard form, and then use the quadratic formula.

Put the equation in standard form by distributing and combining like terms.

$y = -(x + 3)^2 + 1$

$y = -(x^2 + 6x + 9) + 1$

$y = -x^2 - 6x - 8$

Find the zeros using the quadratic formula.

$$x = \frac{-b \pm \sqrt{(b^2 - 4ac)}}{2a}$$

$$x = \frac{-(-6) \pm \sqrt{(-6)^2 - 4(-1)(-8)}}{2(-1)}$$

$$x = \frac{6 \pm \sqrt{36 - 32}}{-2}$$

$$x = \frac{6 \pm \sqrt{4}}{-2}$$

$$\boldsymbol{x = -4, -2}$$

33. This polynomial can be factored in the form $(z - 2)(z - 2) = 0$, so the only root is $z = 2$. There is only one x-intercept, and the vertex of the graph is *on* the x-axis.

34. If the quadratic has zeros at $x = -3$ and $x = 2$, then it has factors of $(x + 3)$ and $(x - 2)$. The quadratic function can be written in the factored form $y = a(x + 3)(x - 2)$. To find the a-value, plug in the point $(-2, 8)$ for x and y:

$$8 = a(-2 + 3)(-2 - 2)$$

$$8 = a(-4)$$

$$a = -2$$

The quadratic function is:

$$\boldsymbol{y = -2(x + 3)(x - 2).}$$

35. Start by marking the vertex at $(3, 4)$ and recognizing this parabola opens upward. The line of symmetry is $x = 3$. Now, plug in an easy value for x to get one point on the curve; then use symmetry to find another point. In this case, choose $x = 2$ (one unit to the left of the line of symmetry) and solve for y:

$$y = 2(2 - 3)^2 + 4$$

$$y = 2(1) + 4$$

$$y = 6$$

Thus the point $(2, 6)$ is on the curve. Then use symmetry to find the corresponding point one unit to the right of the line of symmetry, which must also have a

y value of 6. This point is $(4, 6)$. Draw a parabola through the points.

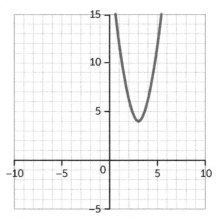

36. Locate the vertex and plug values for h and k into the vertex form of the quadratic equation.

$$(h, k) = (0, 5)$$

$$y = a(x - h)^2 + k$$

$$y = a(x - 0)^2 + 5$$

$$y = ax^2 + 5$$

Choose another point on the graph to plug into this equation to solve for a.

$$(x, y) = (1, 2)$$

$$y = ax^2 + 5$$

$$2 = a(1)^2 + 5$$

$$a = -3$$

Plug a into the vertex form of the equation.

$$\boldsymbol{y = -3x^2 + 5}$$

37. $f(4)$ if $f(x) = x^3 - 2x + \sqrt{x}$

Plug in 4.

$$f(4) = (4)^3 - 2(4) + \sqrt{(4)}$$

Follow the PEMDAS order of operations.

$$= 64 - 8 + 2 = \boldsymbol{58}$$

38. This function has an asymptote at $x = 9$, so is not defined there.

Otherwise, the function is defined for all other values of x.

D: $-\infty < x < 9$ *or* $9 < x < \infty$

Interval notation can also be used to show domain and range. Round brackets indicate that an end value is not included, and square brackets show that it is. The symbol ∪ means *or*, and the symbol ∩ means *and*. For example, the statement $(-\infty, 4) \cup (4, \infty)$ describes the set of all real numbers except 4.

Since the function has a horizontal asymptote at $y = 1$ that it never crosses, the function never takes the value 1, so the range is all real numbers except 1:
R: $-\infty < y < 1$ *or* $1 < y < \infty$.

39. For the domain, this graph goes on to the right to positive infinity. Its leftmost point, however, is $x = -2$. Therefore, its domain is all real numbers equal to or greater than -2, **D**: $-2 \le x < \infty$, or **$[-2, \infty)$**.

The lowest range value is $y = 2$. Although it has a decreasing slope, this function continues to rise. Therefore, the domain is all real numbers greater than 2, **R**: $2 \le y < \infty$ **or $[2, \infty)$**.

40. For a set of numbers to represent a function, every input must generate a unique output. Therefore, if the same input (x) appears more than once in the table, determine if that input has two different outputs. If so, then the table does not represent a function.

A) This table is not a function because input value 1 has two different outputs (1 and 3).

B) Table B is not a function because 0 is the only input and results in four different values.

C) This table shows a function because each input has one output.

D) This table also has one input going to two different values, so it is not a function.

41. Replace $f(x)$ with y.

$y = 5x + 5$

Switch the places of y and x.

$x = 5y + 5$

Solve for y.

$x = 5y + 5$

$x - 5 = 5y$

$y = \frac{x}{5} - 1$

$\boldsymbol{f^{-1}(x) = \frac{x}{5} - 1}$

42. This is a linear graph with some clear coordinates: $(-5,0)$, $(0,-1)$, $(5,-2)$, and $(10,-3)$. This means the inverse function will have coordinate $(0,-5)$, $(-1,0)$, $(-2,5)$, and $(-3,10)$. The inverse function is reflected over the line $y = x$ and is the line $f^{-1}(x) = -5(x + 1)$ below.

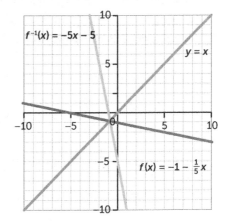

43. $(y \circ z)(-4) = y(z(-4))$

Starting on the inside, evaluate z.

$z(-4)$

$= 3(-4) - 3 = -12 - 3 = -15$

Replace $z(-4)$ with -15, and simplify.

$y(z(-4))$

$= y(-15) = 2(-15) - 1$

$= -30 - 1 = \mathbf{-31}$

44. Replace x in the $k(x)$ function with $(\frac{1}{2}x - 2)$

$(k \circ t)(x) = k(t(x))$

$= k(\frac{1}{2}x - 2) = \frac{1}{2}(\frac{1}{2}x - 2) - 3$

Simplify.

$= \frac{1}{4}x - 1 - 3 = \frac{1}{4}x - 4$

$\mathbf{(k \circ t)(x) = \frac{1}{4x} - 4}$

45. $N(4) = 400(4) = 1600$ and means that 4 hours after the park opens there are 1600 people in the park. $W(N(4)) = W(1600) = 96$ and means that 4 hours after the park opens the wait time is about **96 minutes** for the ride.

46. This function is the absolute value function with a vertical shift up of 4 units (since the 4 is outside the absolute value bars), and a horizontal shift left of 1 unit (since it is inside the bars). The vertex of the graph is at $(-1,4)$ and the line $x = -1$ is an axis of symmetry.

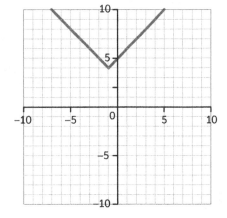

47. The negative sign in front of the absolute value means the graph will be reflected across the x-axis, so it will open down. The 3 causes a vertical stretch of the function, which results in a narrower graph. The basic curve is shifted 2 units right (since the −2 is an inside change) and 2 units up (since the +2 is an outside change), so the vertex is at $(2,2)$.

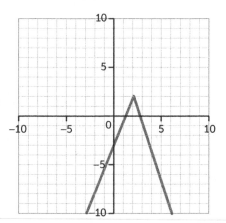

CHAPTER THREE
Geometry

Properties of Shapes
BASIC DEFINITIONS

The basic figures from which many other geometric shapes are built are points, lines, and planes. A **POINT** is a location in a plane. It has no size or shape, but is represented by a dot. It is labeled using a capital letter.

A **LINE** is a one-dimensional collection of points that extends infinitely in both directions. At least two points are needed to define a line, and any points that lie on the same line are **COLINEAR**. Lines are represented by two points, such as *A* and *B*, and the line symbol: ($\overleftrightarrow{AB}$). Two lines on the same plane will intersect unless they are **PARALLEL**, meaning they have the same slope. Lines that intersect at a 90 degree angle are **PERPENDICULAR**.

A **LINE SEGMENT** has two endpoints and a finite length. The length of a segment, called the measure of the segment, is the distance from *A* to *B*. A line segment is a subset of a line, and is also denoted with two points, but with a segment symbol: $\overline{AB}$). The **MIDPOINT** of a line segment is the point at which the segment is divided into two equal parts. A line, segment, or plane that passes through the midpoint of a segment is called a **BISECTOR** of the segment, since it cuts the segment into two equal segments.

A **RAY** has one endpoint and extends indefinitely in one direction. It is defined by its endpoint, followed by any other point on the ray: $\overrightarrow{AB}$. It is important that the first letter represents the endpoint. A ray is sometimes called a half line.

A **PLANE** is a flat sheet that extends indefinitely in two directions (like an infinite sheet of paper). A plane is a two-dimensional (2D) figure. A plane can always be defined through any three noncollinear points in three-dimensional (3D) space. A plane is named using any three points that are in the plane (for example, plane *ABC*). Any points lying in the same plane are said to be **COPLANAR**. When two planes intersect, the intersection is a line.

Term	Dimensions	Graphic	Symbol
Table 3.1. Basic Geometric Figures			
point	zero	●	$\cdot A$
line segment	one	A — B	$\overline{AB}$
ray	one	A — B →	$\overrightarrow{AB}$
line	one	A — B →	$\overleftrightarrow{AB}$
plane	two	M	Plane M

EXAMPLE

1. Which points and lines are not contained in plane M in the diagram below?

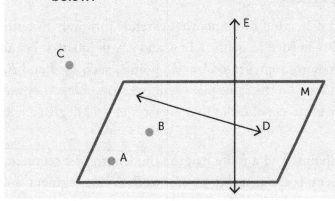

ANGLES

ANGLES are formed when two rays share a common endpoint. They are named using three letters, with the vertex point in the middle (for example $\angle ABC$, where B is the vertex). They can also be labeled with a number or named by their vertex alone (if it is clear to do so). Angles are also classified based on their angle measure. A **RIGHT ANGLE** has a measure of exactly 90°. **ACUTE ANGLES** have measures that are less than 90°, and **OBTUSE ANGLES** have measures that are greater than 90°.

Any two angles that add to make 90° are called **COMPLEMENTARY ANGLES**. A 30° angle would be complementary to a 60° angle.

SUPPLEMENTARY ANGLES add up to 180°. A supplementary angle to a 60° angle would be a 120° angle; likewise, 60° is the SUPPLEMENT of 120°. The complement and supplement of any angle must always be positive. For example, a 140 degree has no complement. Angles that are next to each other and share a common ray are called ADJACENT ANGLES. Angles that are adjacent and supplementary are called a LINEAR PAIR of angles. Their nonshared rays form a line (thus the *linear* pair). Note that angles that are supplementary do not need to be adjacent; their measures simply need to add to 180°.

VERTICAL ANGLES are formed when two lines intersect. Four angles will be formed; the vertex of each angle is at the intersection point of the lines. The vertical angles across from each other will be equal in measure. The angles adjacent to each other will be linear pairs and therefore supplementary.

A ray, line, or segment that divides an angle into two equal angles is called an ANGLE BISECTOR.

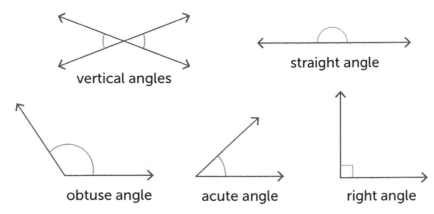

Figure 3.1. Types of Angles

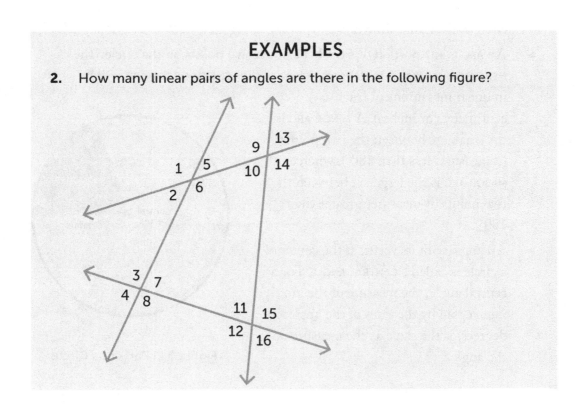

EXAMPLES

2. How many linear pairs of angles are there in the following figure?

CIRCLES

A CIRCLE is the set of all the points in a plane that are the same distance from a fixed point called the CENTER. The distance from the center to any point on the circle is the RADIUS of the circle. The distance around the circle (the perimeter) is called the CIRCUMFERENCE.

The ratio of a circle's circumference to its diameter is a constant value called pi (π), an irrational number which is commonly rounded to 3.14. The formula to find a circle's circumference is $C = 2\pi r$. The formula to find the enclosed area of a circle is $A = \pi r^2$.

Circles have a number of unique parts and properties:

▶ The DIAMETER is the largest measurement across a circle. It passes through the circle's center, extending from one side of the circle to the other. The measure of the diameter is twice the measure of the radius.

▶ A line that cuts across a circle and touches it twice is called a SECANT line. The part of a secant line that lies within a circle is called a CHORD. Two chords within a circle are of equal length if they are the same distance from the center.

▶ A line that touches a circle or any curve at one point is TANGENT to the circle or the curve. These lines are always exterior to the circle. A line tangent to a circle and a radius drawn to the point of tangency meet at a right angle (90°).

▶ An ARC is any portion of a circle between two points on the circle. The MEASURE of an arc is in degrees, whereas the LENGTH OF THE ARC will be in linear measurement (such as centimeters or inches). A MINOR ARC is the small arc between the two points (it measures less than 180°), whereas a MAJOR ARC is the large arc between the two points (it measures greater than 180°).

▶ An angle with its vertex at the center of a circle is called a CENTRAL ANGLE. For a central angle, the measure of the arc intercepted by the sides of the angle (in degrees) is the same as the measure of the angle.

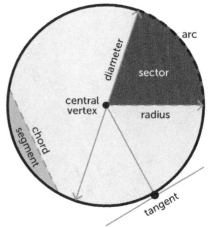

Figure 3.2. Parts of a Circle

▶ A **SECTOR** is the part of a circle *and* its interior that is inside the rays of a central angle (its shape is like a slice of pie).

	Area of Sector	Length of an Arc
Degrees	$A = \dfrac{\theta}{360°} \times \pi r^2$	$s = \dfrac{\theta}{360°} \times 2\pi r$
Radians	$A = \dfrac{1}{2}\pi^2\theta$	$s = r\theta$

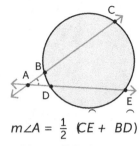

$$m\angle A = \tfrac{1}{2}\,\overset{\frown}{(CE} + \overset{\frown}{BD)}$$

Figure 3.3. Angles Outside a Circle

▶ An **INSCRIBED ANGLE** has a vertex on the circle and is formed by two chords that share that vertex point. The angle measure of an inscribed angle is one-half the angle measure of the central angle with the same endpoints on the circle.

▶ A **CIRCUMSCRIBED ANGLE** has rays tangent to the circle. The angle lies outside of the circle.

▶ Any angle outside the circle, whether formed by two tangent lines, two secant lines, or a tangent line and a secant line, is equal to half the difference of the intercepted arcs.

▶ Angles are formed within a circle when two chords intersect in the circle. The measure of the smaller angle formed is half the sum of the two smaller arc measures (in degrees). Likewise, the larger angle is half the sum of the two larger arc measures.

▶ If a chord intersects a line tangent to the circle, the angle formed by this intersection measures one half the measurement of the intercepted arc (in degrees).

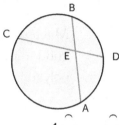

$$m\angle E = \tfrac{1}{2}(\overset{\frown}{AC} + \overset{\frown}{BD})$$

Figure 3.4. Intersecting Chords

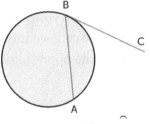

$$m\angle ABC = \tfrac{1}{2}m\overset{\frown}{AB}$$

Figure 3.5. Intersecting Chord and Tangent

EXAMPLES

4. Find the area of the sector *NHS* of the circle below with center at *H*:

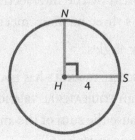

5. In the circle below with center *O*, the minor arc *ACB* measures 5 feet. What is the measurement of *m∠AOB*?

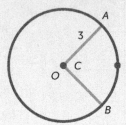

TRIANGLES

Much of geometry is concerned with triangles as they are commonly used shapes. A good understanding of triangles allows decomposition of other shapes (specifically polygons) into triangles for study.

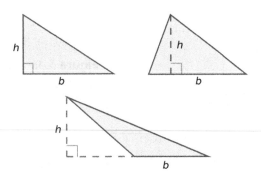

Figure 3.6. Finding the Base and Height of Triangles

Triangles have three sides, and the three interior angles always sum to 180°. The formula for the area of a triangle is $A = \frac{1}{2} bh$ or one-half the product of the base and height (or altitude) of the triangle.

Some important segments in a triangle include the angle bisector, the altitude, and the median. The **ANGLE BISECTOR** extends from the side opposite an angle to bisect that angle. The **ALTITUDE** is the shortest distance from a vertex of the triangle to the line containing the base side opposite that vertex. It is perpendicular to that line and can occur on the outside of the triangle. The **MEDIAN** extends from an angle to bisect the opposite side.

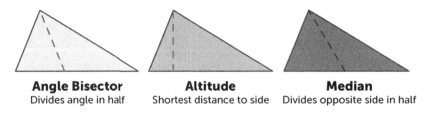

Angle Bisector
Divides angle in half

Altitude
Shortest distance to side

Median
Divides opposite side in half

Figure 3.7. Critical Segments in a Triangle

Triangles have two "centers." The **ORTHOCENTER** is formed by the intersection of a triangle's three altitudes. The **CENTROID** is where a triangle's three medians meet.

Triangles can be classified in two ways: by sides and by angles.

A **SCALENE TRIANGLE** has no equal sides or angles. An **ISOSCELES TRIANGLE** has two equal sides and two equal angles, often called **BASE ANGLES**. In an **EQUILATERAL TRIANGLE**, all three sides are equal as are all three angles. Moreover, because the sum of the angles of a triangle is always 180°, each angle of an equilateral triangle must be 60°.

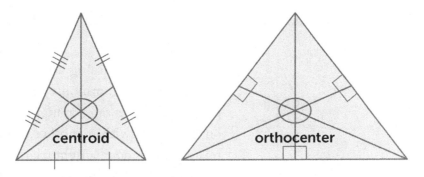

Figure 3.8. Centroid and Orthocenter of a Triangle

A **RIGHT TRIANGLE** has one right angle (90°) and two acute angles. An **ACUTE TRIANGLE** has three acute angles (all angles are less than 90°). An **OBTUSE TRIANGLE** has one obtuse angle (more than 90°) and two acute angles.

Triangles Based on Sides

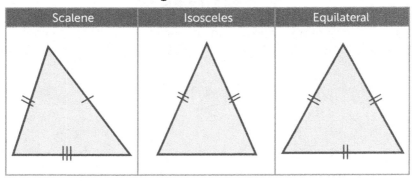

Triangles Based on Angles

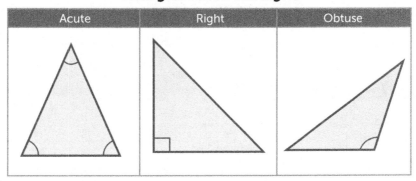

Figure 3.9. Types of Triangles

For any triangle, the side opposite the largest angle will have the longest length, while the side opposite the smallest angle will have the shortest length. The **TRIANGLE INEQUALITY THEOREM** states that the sum of any two sides of a triangle must be greater than the third side. If this inequality does not hold, then a triangle cannot be formed. A consequence of this theorem is the **THIRD-SIDE RULE**: if b and c are two sides of a triangle, then the measure of the third side a must be between

DID YOU KNOW?

Trigonometric functions can be employed to find missing sides and angles of a triangle.

the sum of the other two sides and the difference of the other two sides: $c - b < a < c + b$.

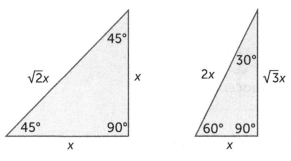

Figure 3.10. Special Right Triangles

Solving for missing angles or sides of a triangle is a common type of triangle problem. Often a right triangle will come up on its own or within another triangle. The relationship among a right triangle's sides is known as the **PYTHAGOREAN THEOREM:** $a^2 + b^2 = c^2$, where c is the hypotenuse and is across from the 90° angle. Right triangles with angle measurements of 90° – 45° – 45° and 90° – 60° – 30° are known as "special" right triangles and have specific relationships between their sides and angles.

EXAMPLES

6. What are the minimum and maximum values of x to the nearest hundredth?

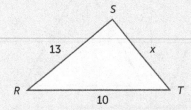

7. Given the diagram, if $XZ = 100$, $WZ = 80$, and $XU = 70$, then $WY = ?$

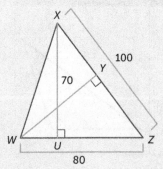

8. Examine and classify each of the following triangles:

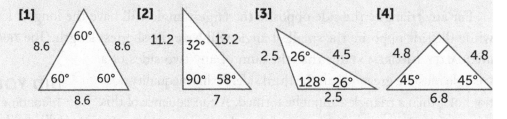

QUADRILATERALS

All closed, four-sided shapes are **QUADRILATERALS**. The sum of all internal angles in a quadrilateral is always 360°. (Think of drawing a diagonal to create two triangles. Since each triangle contains 180°, two triangles, and therefore the quadrilateral, must contain 360°.) The **AREA OF ANY QUADRILATERAL** is $A = bh$, where b is the base and h is the height (or altitude).

A **PARALLELOGRAM** is a quadrilateral with two pairs of parallel sides. A rectangle is a parallelogram with two pairs of equal sides and four right angles. A **KITE** also has two pairs of equal sides, but its equal sides are consecutive. Both a **SQUARE** and a **RHOMBUS** have four equal sides. A square has four right angles, while a rhombus has a pair of acute opposite angles and a pair of obtuse opposite angles. A **TRAPEZOID** has exactly one pair of parallel sides.

Table 3.2 Properties of Parallelograms		
TERM	**SHAPE**	**PROPERTIES**
Parallelogram		Opposite sides are parallel. Consecutive angles are supplementary. Opposite angles are equal. Opposite sides are equal. Diagonals bisect each other.
Rectangle		All parallelogram properties hold. Diagonals are congruent *and* bisect each other. All angles are right angles.
Square		All rectangle properties hold. All four sides are equal. Diagonals bisect angles. Diagonals intersect at right angles and bisect each other.
Kite		One pair of opposite angles is equal. Two pairs of consecutive sides are equal. Diagonals meet at right angles.
Rhombus		All four sides are equal. Diagonals bisect angles. Diagonals intersect at right angles and bisect each other.
Trapezoid		One pair of sides is parallel. Bases have different lengths. Isosceles trapezoids have a pair of equal sides (and base angles).

9. In parallelogram *ABCD*, the measure of angle *m* is is *m*° = 260°. What is the measure of *n*°?

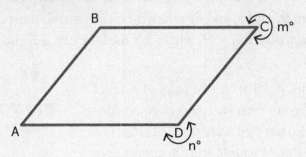

10. A rectangular section of a football field has dimensions of *x* and *y* and an area of 1000 square feet. Three additional lines drawn vertically divide the section into four smaller rectangular areas as seen in the diagram below. If all the lines shown need to be painted, calculate the total number of linear feet, in terms of *x*, to be painted.

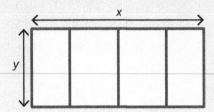

POLYGONS

Any closed shape made up of three or more line segments is a polygon. In addition to triangles and quadrilaterals, **HEXAGONS** and **OCTAGONS** are two common polygons.

DID YOU KNOW?
Breaking an irregular polygon down into triangles and quadrilaterals helps in finding its area.

The two polygons depicted in Figure 3.11 are **REGULAR POLYGONS**, meaning that they are equilateral (all sides having equal lengths) and equiangular (all angles having equal measurements). Angles inside a polygon are **INTERIOR ANGLES**, whereas those formed by one side of the polygon and a line extending outside the polygon are **EXTERIOR ANGLES:**

The sum of all the exterior angles of a polygon is always 360°. Dividing 360° by the number of a polygon's sides finds the measure of the polygon's exterior angles.

To determine the sum of a polygon's interior angles, choose one vertex and draw diagonals from that

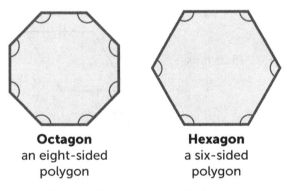

Octagon
an eight-sided
polygon

Hexagon
a six-sided
polygon

Figure 3.11. Common Polygons

vertex to each of the other vertices, decomposing the polygon into multiple triangles. For example, an octagon has six triangles within it, and therefore the sum of the interior angles is $6 \times 180°$ = 1080°. In general, the formula for finding the sum of the angles in a polygon is *sum of angles* = $(n - 2) \times 180°$, where *n* is the number of sides of the polygon.

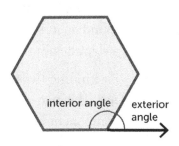

Figure 3.12. Interior and Exterior Angles

To find the measure of a single interior angle in a regular polygon, simply divide the sum of the interior angles by the number of angles (which is the same as the number of sides). So, in the octagon example, each angle is $\frac{1080}{8}$ = 135°.

In general, the formula to find the measure of a regular polygon's interior angles is: *interior angle* = $\frac{(n-2)}{n} \times 180°$ where *n* is the number of sides of the polygon.

To find the area of a polygon, it is helpful to know the perimeter of the polygon (*p*), and the **APOTHEM** (*a*). The apothem is the shortest (perpendicular) distance from the polygon's center to one of the sides of the polygon. The formula for the area is: *area* = $\frac{ap}{2}$.

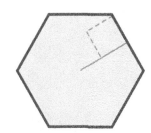

Figure 3.13. Apothem in a Hexagon

Finally, there is no universal way to find the perimeter of a polygon (when the side length is not given). Often, breaking the polygon down into triangles and adding the base of each triangle all the way around the polygon is the easiest way to calculate the perimeter.

EXAMPLES

11. What is the measure of an exterior angle and an interior angle of a regular 400-gon?

12. The circle and hexagon below both share center point *T*. The hexagon is entirely inscribed in the circle. The circle's radius is 5. What is the area of the shaded area?

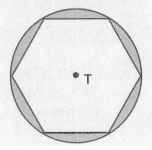

Three-Dimensional Shapes

THREE-DIMENSIONAL SHAPES have depth in addition to width and length. **VOLUME** is expressed as the number of cubic units any solid can hold—that is, what it takes to fill it up. **SURFACE AREA** is the sum of the areas of the two-dimensional figures that are found on its surface. Some three-dimensional shapes also have a unique property called a slant height (ℓ), which is the distance from the base to the apex along a lateral face.

Finding the surface area of a three-dimensional solid can be made easier by using a **NET**. This two-dimensional "flattened" version of a three-dimensional shape shows the component parts that comprise the surface of the solid.

	Table 3.3. Three-Dimensional Shapes and Formulas		
TERM	**SHAPE**	**FORMULA**	
Prism		$V = Bh$ $SA = 2lw + 2wh + 2lh$ $d^2 = a^2 + b^2 + c^2$	B = area of base h = height l = length w = width d = longest diagonal
Cube		$V = s^3$ $SA = 6s^2$	s = cube edge
Sphere		$V = \frac{4}{3}\pi r^3$ $SA = 4\pi r^2$	r = radius
Cylinder		$V = Bh = \pi r^2 h$ $SA = 2\pi r^2 + 2\pi rh$	B = area of base h = height r = radius
Cone		$V = \frac{1}{3}\pi r^2 h$ $SA = \pi r^2 + \pi rl$	r = radius h = height l = slant height
Pyramid		$V = \frac{1}{3}Bh$ $SA = B + \frac{1}{2}(p)l$	B = area of base h = height p = perimeter l = slant height

EXAMPLES

13. A sphere has a radius *z*. If that radius is increased by *t*, by how much is the surface area increased? Write the answer in terms of *z* and *t*.

14. A cube with volume 27 cubic meters is inscribed within a sphere such that all of the cube's vertices touch the sphere. What is the length of the sphere's radius?

Answer Key
EXAMPLES

1. Points *A* and *B* and line *D* are all on plane *M*. Point *C* is above the plane, and line *E* cuts through the plane and thus does not lie on plane *M*. The point at which line *E* intersects plane *M* is on plane *M* but the line as a whole is not.

2. Any two adjacent angles that are supplementary are linear pairs, so there are 16 linear pairs in the figure ($\angle 1$ and $\angle 5$, $\angle 2$ and $\angle 6$, $\angle 5$ and $\angle 6$, $\angle 2$ and $\angle 1$, and so on).

3. Set up a system of equations.

$\angle M + \angle N = 180°$

$\angle M = 2\angle N - 30°$

Use substitution to solve for $\angle N$.

$\angle M + \angle N = 180°$

$(2\angle N - 30°) + \angle N = 180°$

$3\angle N - 30° = 180°$

$3\angle N = 210°$

$\angle N = \mathbf{70°}$

Solve for $\angle M$ using the original equation.

$\angle M + \angle N = 180°$

$\angle M + 70° = 180°$

$\angle M = \mathbf{110°}$

4. Identify the important parts of the circle.

$r = 4$

$\angle NHS = 90°$

Plug these values into the formula for the area of a sector.

$A = \frac{\theta}{360°} \times \pi r^2$

$= \frac{90}{360} \times \pi(4)^2 = \frac{1}{4} \times 16\pi$

$= \mathbf{4\pi}$

5. Identify the important parts of the circle.

$r = 3$

length of $\overline{ACB} = 5$

Plug these values into the formula for the length of an arc and solve for θ.

$s = \frac{\theta}{360°} \times 2\pi r$

$5 = \frac{\theta}{360°} \times 2\pi(3)$

$\frac{5}{6\pi} = \frac{\theta}{360°}$

$\theta = 95.5°$

$\boldsymbol{m\angle AOB = 95.5°}$

6. The sum of two sides is 23 and their difference is 3. To connect the two other sides and enclose a space, *x* must be less than the sum and greater than the difference (that is, $3 < x < 23$). Therefore, **x's minimum value to the nearest hundredth is 3.01 and its maximum value is 22.99.**

7. $WZ = b_1 = 80$

$XU = h_1 = 70$

$XZ = b_2 = 100$

$WY = h_2 = ?$

The given values can be used to write two equations for the area of $\triangle WXZ$ with two sets of bases and heights.

$A = \frac{1}{2}bh$

$A_1 = \frac{1}{2}(80)(70) = 2800$

$A_2 = \frac{1}{2}(100)(h_2)$

Set the two equations equal to each other and solve for *WY*.

$2800 = \frac{1}{2}(100)(h_2)$

$h_2 = 56$

WY = 56

8. **Triangle 1 is an equilateral triangle** (all 3 sides are equal, and all 3 angles are equal)

    Triangle 2 is a scalene, right triangle (all 3 sides are different, and there is a 90° angle)

    Triangle 3 is an obtuse, isosceles triangle (there are 2 equal sides and, consequently, 2 equal angles)

    Triangle 4 is a right, isosceles triangle (there are 2 equal sides and a 90° angle)

9. Find $\angle C$ using the fact that the sum of $\angle C$ and m is 360°.

    $260° + m\angle C = 360°$

    $m\angle C = 100°$

    Solve for $\angle D$ using the fact that consecutive interior angles in a quadrilateral are supplementary.

    $m\angle C + m\angle D = 180°$

    $100° + m\angle D = 180°$

    $m\angle D = 80°$

    Solve for n by subtracting $m\angle D$ from 360°.

    $m\angle D + n = 360°$

    n = 280°

10. Find equations for the area of the field and length of the lines to be painted (L) in terms of x and y.

    $A = 1000 = xy$

    $L = 2x + 5y$

    Substitute to find L in terms of x.

    $y = \frac{1000}{x}$

    $L = 2x + 5y$

    $L = 2x + 5(\frac{1000}{x})$

    $L = 2x + \frac{5000}{x}$

11. The sum of the exterior angles is 360°. Dividing this sum by 400 gives $\frac{360°}{400} = $ **0.9°**. Since an interior angle is supplementary to an exterior angle, all the interior angles have measure $180 - 0.9 = $ **179.1°**. Alternately, using the formula for calculating the interior angle gives the same result:

    $interior\ angle = \frac{400 - 2}{400} \times 180°$

    $= 179.1°$

12. The area of the shaded region will be the area of the circle minus the area of the hexagon. Use the radius to find the area of the circle.

    $A_c = \pi r^2 = \pi(5)^2 = 25\pi$

    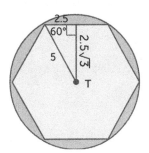

    To find the area of the hexagon, draw a right triangle from the vertex, and use special right triangles to find the hexagon's apothem. Then, use the apothem to calculate the area.

    $a = 2.5\sqrt{3}$

    $A_H = \frac{ap}{2} = \frac{(2.5\sqrt{3})(30)}{2} = 64.95$

    Subtract the area of the hexagon from the circle to find the area of the shaded region.

    $= A_c - A_H$

    $= 25\pi - 2.5\sqrt{3}$

    ≈ 13.59

13. Write the equation for the area of the original sphere.

    $SA_1 = 4\pi z^2$

Write the equation for the area of the new sphere.

$SA_2 = 4\pi(z + t)^2$

$= 4\pi(z^2 + 2zt + t^2)$

$= 4\pi z^2 + 8\pi zt + 4\pi t^2$

To find the difference between the two, subtract the original from the increased surface area:

$A_2 - A_1 = 4\pi z^2 + 8\pi zt + 4\pi t^2 - 4\pi z^2$

$\mathbf{= 4\pi t^2 + 8\pi zt}$

14. Since the cube's volume is 27, each side length is equal to $\sqrt[3]{27} = 3$. The long diagonal distance from one of the cube's vertices to its opposite vertex will provide the sphere's diameter:

$d = \sqrt{3^2 + 3^2 + 3^2} = \sqrt{27} = 5.2$

Half of this length is the radius, which is **2.6 meters**.

CHAPTER FOUR
Statistics and Probability

Describing Sets of Data
MEASURES of CENTRAL TENDENCY

Measures of central tendency help identify the center, or most typical, value within a data set. There are three such central tendencies that describe the "center" of the data in different ways. The **MEAN** is the arithmetic average and is found by dividing the sum of all measurements by the number of measurements. The mean of a population is written as μ and the mean of a sample is written as $\bar{x}$.

$$\text{population mean} = \mu = \frac{x_1 + x_2 + ...xN}{N} = \frac{\Sigma x}{N}$$

$$\text{sample mean} = \bar{x} = \frac{x_1 + x_2 + ...xn}{n} = \frac{\Sigma x}{n}$$

The data points are represented by x's with subscripts; the sum is denoted using the Greek letter sigma (Σ); N is the number of data points in the entire population; and n is the number of data points in a sample set.

The **MEDIAN** divides the measurements into two equal halves. The median is the measurement right in the middle of an odd set of measurements or the average of the two middle numbers in an even data set. When calculating the median, it is important to order the data values from least to greatest before attempting to locate the middle value. The **MODE** is simply the measurement that occurs most often. There can be many modes in a data set, or no mode. Since measures of central tendency describe a *center* of the data, all three of these measures will be between the lowest and highest data values (inclusive).

DID YOU KNOW?

When the same value is added to each term in a set, the mean increases by that value and the standard deviation is unchanged.

When each term in a set is multiplied by the same value, both the mean and standard deviation will also be multiplied by that value.

Unusually large or small values, called OUTLIERS, will affect the mean of a sample more than the mode. If there is a high outlier, the mean will be greater than the median; if there is a low outlier, the mean will be lower than the median. When outliers are present, the median is a better measure of the data's center than the mean because the median will be closer to the terms in the data set.

EXAMPLES

1. What is the mean of the following data set? {1000, 0.1, 10, 1}

2. What is the median of the following data set? {1000, 10, 1, 0.1}

3. Josey has an average of 81 on four equally weighted tests she has taken in her statistics class. She wants to determine what grade she must receive on her fifth test so that her mean is 83, which will give her a B in the course, but she does not remember her other scores. What grade must she receive on her fifth test?

MEASURES of VARIATION

The values in a data set can be very close together (close to the mean), or very spread out. This is called the SPREAD or DISPERSION of the data. There are a few MEASURES OF VARIATION (or MEASURES OF DISPERSION) that quantify the spread within a data set. RANGE is the difference between the largest and smallest data points in a set:

$$R = largest\ data\ point - smallest\ data\ point$$

Notice range depends on only two data points (the two extremes). Sometimes these data points are outliers; regardless, for a large data set, relying on only two data points is not an exact tool.

The understanding of the data set can be improved by calculating QUARTILES. To calculate quartiles, first arrange the data in ascending order and find the set's median (also called quartile 2 or Q2). Then find the median of the lower half of the data, called quartile 1 (Q1), and the median of the upper half of the data, called quartile 3 (Q3). These three points divide the data into four equal groups of data (thus the word *quartile*). Each quartile contains 25% of the data.

INTERQUARTILE RANGE (IQR) provides a more reliable range that is not as affected by extremes. IQR is the difference between the third quartile data point and the first quartile data point and gives the spread of the middle 50% of the data:

$$IQR = Q_3 - Q_1$$

The VARIANCE of a data set is simply the square of the standard variation:

$$V = \sigma^2 = \frac{1}{N} \sum_{i=1}^{N} (x_i - \mu)^2$$

Variance measures how narrowly or widely the data points are distributed. A variance of zero means every data point is the same; a large variance means the data is widely spread out.

EXAMPLE

4. What are the range and interquartile range of the following set? {3, 9, 49, 64, 81, 100, 121, 144, 169}

Graphs, Charts, and Tables
PIE CHARTS

A pie chart simply states the proportion of each category within the whole. To construct a pie chart, the categories of a data set must be determined. The frequency of each category must be found and that frequency converted to a percent of the total. To draw the pie chart, determine the angle of each slice by multiplying the percentage by 360°.

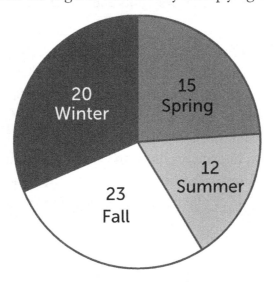

Figure 4.1. Pie Chart

EXAMPLE

5. A firm is screening applicants for a job by education-level attainment. There are 125 individuals in the pool: 5 have a doctorate, 20 have a master's degree, 40 have a bachelor's degree, 30 have an associate's degree, and 30 have a high school degree. Construct a pie chart showing the highest level of education attained by the applicants.

SCATTER PLOTS

A scatter plot is displayed in the first quadrant of the *xy*-plane where all numbers are positive. Data points are plotted as ordered pairs, with one variable along the horizontal axis and the other along the vertical axis. Scatter plots can show if there is a correlation between two variables. There is a **POSITIVE CORRELATION** (expressed as a positive slope) if increasing one variable appears to result in an increase in the other variable. A **NEGATIVE CORRELATION** (expressed as a negative slope) occurs when an increase in one variable causes a decrease in the other. If the scatter plot shows no discernible pattern, then there is no correlation (a zero, mixed, or indiscernible slope).

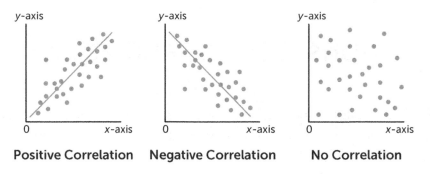

Figure 4.2. Scatter Plots and Correlation

Calculators or other software can be used to find the linear regression equation, which describes the general shape of the data. Graphing this equation produces the regression line, or line of best fit. The equation's **CORRELATION COEFFICIENT** (*r*) can be used to determine how closely the equation fits the data. The value of *r* is between –1 and 1. The closer *r* is to 1 (if the line has a positive slope) or –1 (if the line has a negative slope), the better the regression line fits the data. The closer the *r* value is to 0, the weaker the correlation between the line and the data. Generally, if the absolute value of the correlation coefficient is 0.8 or higher, then it is considered to be a strong correlation, while an |*r*| value of less than 0.5 is considered a weak correlation.

To determine which curve is the "best fit" for a set of data, **RESIDUALS** are calculated. The calculator automatically calculates and saves these values to a list called RESID. These values are all the differences between the actual *y*-value of data points and the *y*-value calculated by the best-fit line or curve for that *x*-value. These values can be plotted on an *xy*-plane to produce a **RESIDUAL PLOT**. The residual plot helps determine if a line is the best model for the data. Residual points that are randomly dispersed above and below the horizontal indicate that a linear model is appropriate, while a *u* shape or upside-down *u* shape indicates a nonlinear model would be more appropriate.

Once a best-fit line is established, it can be used to estimate output values given an input value within the domain of the data. For a short extension outside that domain, reasonable predictions may be possible. However, the further from the domain of the data the line is extended, the greater the reduction in the accuracy of the prediction.

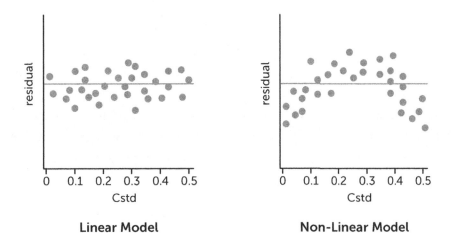

Figure 4.3. Residual Plots

It is important to note here that just because two variables have a strong positive or negative correlation, it cannot necessarily be inferred that those two quantities have a *causal* relationship—that is, that one variable changing *causes* the other quantity to change. There are often other factors that play into their relationship. For example, a positive correlation can be found between the number of ice cream sales and the number of shark attacks at a beach. It would be incorrect to say that selling more ice cream *causes* an increase in shark attacks. It is much more likely that on hot days more ice cream is sold, and many more people are swimming, so one of them is more likely to get attacked by a shark. Confusing correlation and causation is one of the most common statistical errors people make.

DID YOU KNOW?

A graphing calculator can provide the regression line, *r* value, and residuals list.

EXAMPLE

6. Based on the scatter plot on the following page, where the *x*-axis represents hours spent studying per week and the *y*-axis represents the average percent grade on exams during the school year, is there a correlation between the amount of studying for a test and test results?

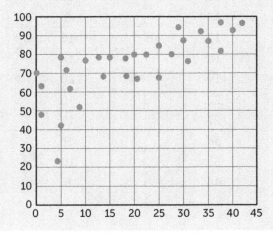

LINE GRAPHS

Line graphs are used to display a relationship between two variables, such as change over time. Like scatter plots, line graphs exist in quadrant I of the *xy*-plane. Line graphs are constructed by graphing each point and connecting each point to the next consecutive point by a line. To create a line graph, it may be necessary to consolidate data into single bivariate data points. Thus, a line graph is a function, with each *x*-value having exactly one *y*-value, whereas a scatter plot may have multiple *y*-values for one *x*-value.

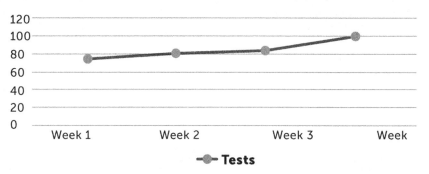

Figure 4.4. Line Graph

EXAMPLE

7. Create a line graph based on the following survey values, where the first column represents an individual's age and the other represents that individual's reported happiness level on a 20-point scale (0 being the least happy that person has been and 20 being the happiest). Then interpret the resulting graph to determine whether the following statement is true or false: *On average, middle-aged people are less happy than young or older people are.*

Age	Happiness	Age (continued)	Happiness (continued)
12	16	33	10
13	15	44	8
20	18	55	10
15	12	80	10
40	5	15	13
17	17	40	8
18	18	17	15
19	15	18	17
42	7	19	20
70	17	22	16
45	10	27	15
60	12	36	9
63	15	33	10
22	14	44	6
27	15		

BAR GRAPHS

Bar graphs compare differences between categories or changes over a time. The data is grouped into categories or ranges and represented by rectangles. A bar graph's rectangles can be vertical or horizontal, depending on whether the dependent variable is placed on the *x*- or *y*-axis. Instead of the *xy*-plane, however, one axis is made up of categories (or ranges) instead of a numeric scale. Bar graphs are useful because the differences between categories are easy to see: the height or length of each bar shows the value for each category.

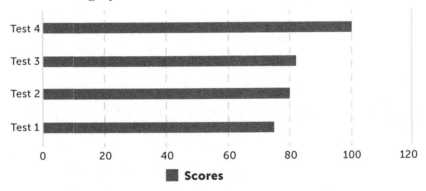

Figure 4.5. Bar Graph

EXAMPLE

8. A company X had a profit of $10,000 in 2010, $12,000 in 2011, $15,600 in 2012, and $20,280 in 2013. Create a bar graph displaying the profit from each of these four years.

STEM-and-LEAF PLOTS

Stem-and-leaf plots are ways of organizing large amounts of data by grouping it into classes. All data points are broken into two parts: a stem and a leaf. For instance, the number 512 might be broken into a stem of 5 and a leaf of 12. All data in the 500 range would appear in the same row (this group of data is a class). Usually a simple key is provided to explain how the data is being represented. For instance, $5|12 = 512$ would show that the stems are representing hundreds. The advantage of this display is that it shows general density and shape of the data in a compact display, yet all original data points are preserved and available. It is also easy to find medians and quartiles from this display.

STEM	LEAF
0	5
1	6, 7
2	8, 3, 6
3	4, 5, 9, 5, 5, 8, 5
4	7, 7, 7, 8
5	5, 4
6	0

Figure 4.6. Stem-and-Leaf Plot

9. The table gives the weights of wrestlers (in pounds) for a certain competition. What is the mean, median, and IQR of the data?

2	05, 22, 40, 53
3	07, 22, 29, 45, 89, 96, 98
4	10, 25, 34
6	21

Key: 2|05 = 205 pounds

FREQUENCY TABLES and HISTOGRAMS

The frequency of a particular data point is the number of times that data point occurs. Constructing a frequency table requires that the data or data classes be arranged in ascending order in one column and the frequency in another column.

A histogram is a graphical representation of a frequency table used to compare frequencies. A histogram is constructed in quadrant I of the *xy*-plane, with data in each equal-width class presented as a bar and the height of each bar representing the frequency of that class. Unlike bar graphs, histograms cannot have gaps between bars. A histogram is used to determine the distribution of data among the classes.

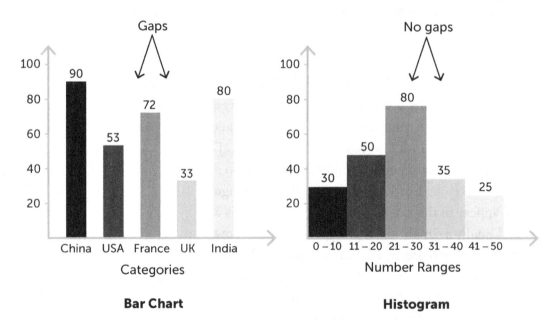

Figure 4.7. Bar Chart vs. Histogram

Histograms can be symmetrical, skewed left or right, or multimodal (data spread around). Note that SKEWED LEFT means the peak of the data is on the *right*, with a tail to the left, while SKEWED RIGHT means the peak is on the *left*, with a tail to the right. This seems counterintuitive to many; the "left" or "right" always refers to the tail of the data. This is because a long tail to the right, for example, means there are high outlier values that are skewing the data to the right.

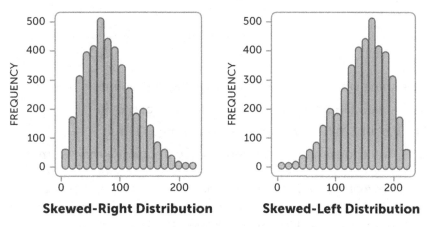

Figure 4.8. Histrograms

A TWO-WAY FREQUENCY TABLE compares CATEGORICAL DATA (data in more than one category) of two related variables (bivariate data). Two-way frequency tables are also called CONTINGENCY TABLES and are often used to analyze survey results. One category is displayed along the top of the table and the other category down along the side. Rows and columns are added and the sums appear at the end of the row or column. The sum of all the row data must equal the sum of all the column data.

From a two-way frequency table, the JOINT RELATIVE FREQUENCY of a particular category can be calculated by taking the number in the row and column of the categories in question and dividing by the total number surveyed. This gives the percent of the total in that particular category. Sometimes the CONDITIONAL RELATIVE FREQUENCY is of interest. In this case, calculate the relative frequency confined to a single row or column.

Students by Grade and Gender					
	9TH GRADE	10TH GRADE	11TH GRADE	12TH GRADE	TOTAL
Male	57	63	75	61	256
Female	54	42	71	60	227
Total	111	105	146	121	483

Figure 4.9. Two-Way Frequency Table

10. Cineflix movie theater polled its moviegoers on a weeknight to determine their favorite type of movie. The results are in the two-way frequency table below.

Moviegoers	Comedy	Action	Horror	Totals
Male	15	24	21	60
Female	8	18	17	43
Totals	23	42	38	103

Determine whether each of the following statements is true or false.

A) Action films are the most popular type of movie

B) About 1 in 5 moviegoers prefers comedy films

C) Men choose the horror genre more frequently than women do

11. A café owner tracked the number of customers he had over a twelve-hour period in the following frequency table. Display the data in a histogram and determine what kind of distribution there is in the data.

Time	Number of Customers
6 a.m. – 8 a.m.	5
8 a.m. – 9 a.m.	6
9 a.m. – 10 a.m.	5
10 a.m. – 12 p.m.	23
12 p.m. – 2 p.m.	24
2 p.m. – 4 p.m.	9
4 p.m. – 6 p.m.	4

Probability

Probability describes how likely something is to happen. In probability, an **EVENT** is the single result of a trial, and an **OUTCOME** is a possible event that results from a trial. The collection of all possible outcomes for a particular trial is called the **SAMPLE SPACE**. For example, when rolling a die, the sample space is the numbers 1 – 6. Rolling a single number, such as 4, would be a single event.

COUNTING PRINCIPLES

Counting principles are methods used to find the number of possible outcomes for a given situation. The **FUNDAMENTAL COUNTING PRINCIPLE** states that, for a series of independent events, the number of outcomes can be found by multiplying the number of possible outcomes for each event. For example, if a die is rolled (6 possible outcomes) and a coin is tossed (2 possible outcomes), there are 6 × 2 = 12 total possible outcomes.

Combinations and permutations describe how many ways a number of objects taken from a group can be arranged. The number of objects in the group is written n, and the number of objects to be arranged is represented by r (or k). In a **COMBINATION**, the order of the selections does not matter because every available slot to be filled is the same. Examples of combinations include:

- picking 3 people from a group of 12 to form a committee (220 possible committees)

- picking 3 pizza toppings from 10 options (120 possible pizzas)

In a **PERMUTATION**, the order of the selection matters, meaning each available slot is different. Examples of permutations include:

- handing out gold, silver, and bronze medals in a race with 100 participants (970,200 possible combinations)

- selecting a president, vice-president, secretary, and treasurer from among a committee of 12 people (11,880 possible combinations)

Die	Coin	
6	× 2	= 12 outcomes

	H	1H, 1T
1	T	2H, 2T
2	H	3H, 3T
	T	4H, 4T
3	H	5H, 5T
	T	6H, 6T
4	H	
	T	
5	H	
	T	
6	H	
	T	

Figure 4.10. Fundamental Counting Principle

The formulas for the both calculations are similar. The only difference—the $r!$ in the denominator of a combination—accounts for redundant outcomes. Note that both permutations and combinations can be written in several different shortened notations.

$$\text{Permutation: } P(n, r) = {_nP_r} = \frac{n!}{(n-r)!}$$

$$\text{Combination: } C(n, r) = {_nC_r} = \left(\frac{n}{r}\right) = \frac{n!}{(n-r)!r!}$$

EXAMPLES

12. A personal assistant is struggling to pick a shirt, tie, and cufflink set that go together. If his client has 70 shirts, 2 ties, and 5 cufflinks, how many possible combinations does he have to consider?

13. If there are 20 applicants for 3 open positions, in how many different ways can a team of 3 be hired?

14. Calculate the number of unique permutations that can be made with five of the letters in the word *pickle*.

15. Find the number of permutations that can be made out of all the letters in the word *cheese*.

PROBABILITY of a SINGLE EVENT

The probability of a single event occurring is the number of outcomes in which that event occurs (called **FAVORABLE EVENTS**) divided by the number of items in the sample space (total possible outcomes):

$$P\,(\text{an event}) = \frac{\textit{number of favorable outcomes}}{\textit{total number of possible outcomes}}$$

The probability of any event occurring will always be a fraction or decimal between 0 and 1. It may also be expressed as a percent. An event with 0 probability will never occur and an event with a probability of 1 is certain to occur. The probability of an event not occurring is referred to as that event's **COMPLEMENT**. The sum of an event's probability and the probability of that event's complement will always be 1.

EXAMPLES

16. What is the probability that an even number results when a six-sided die is rolled? What is the probability the die lands on 5?

17. Only 20 tickets were issued in a raffle. If someone were to buy 6 tickets, what is the probability that person would not win the raffle?

18. A bag contains 26 tiles representing the 26 letters of the English alphabet. If 3 tiles are drawn from the bag without replacement, what is the probability that all 3 will be consonants?

Answer Key

1. Use the equation to find the mean of a sample:
   $$\frac{1000 + 0.1 + 10 + 1}{4} = \mathbf{252.78}$$

2. Since there are an even number of data points in the set, the median will be the mean of the two middle numbers. Order the numbers from least to greatest: 0.1, 1, 10, and 1000. The two middle numbers are 1 and 10, and their mean is:
   $$\frac{1 + 10}{2} = \mathbf{5.5}$$

3. Even though Josey does not know her test scores, she knows her average. Therefore it can be assumed that each test score was 81, since four scores of 81 would average to 81. To find the score, x, that she needs use the equation for the mean of a sample:
   $$\frac{4(81) + x}{5} = 83$$
   $$324 + x = 415$$
   $$\mathbf{x = 91}$$

4. Use the equation for range.

   R = largest point − smallest point = $169 - 3 = \mathbf{166}$

   Place the terms in numerical order and identify Q1, Q2, and Q3.

   3

   9

   $\rightarrow$ Q1 = $\frac{49 + 9}{2}$ = 29

   49

   64

   81 $\rightarrow$ Q2

   100

   121

   $\rightarrow$ Q3 = $\frac{121 + 144}{2}$ = 132.5

   144

   169

   Find the IQR by subtracting Q1 from Q3.

   IQR = Q3 − Q1 = 132.5 − 29 = **103.5**

5. Create a frequency table to find the percentages and angle measurement for each category.

Category	Frequency	Percent	Angle Measure
High School	30	24%	86.4
Associate's	30	24%	86.4
Bachelor's	40	32%	115.2
Master's	20	16%	57.6
Doctorate	5	4%	14.4

   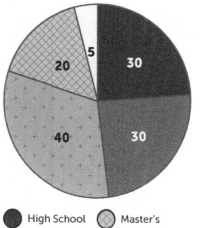

    High School   Master's

   Associate's   Doctorate

    Bachelor's

6. There is a somewhat weak positive correlation. As the number of hours spent studying increases, the average percent grade also generally increases.

7. To construct a line graph, the data must be ordered into consolidated categories by averaging the data

of people who have the same age so that the data is one-to-one. For example, there are 2 twenty-two-year-olds who are reporting. Their average happiness level is 15. When all the data has been consolidated and ordered from least to greatest, the table and graph below can be presented.

Age	Happiness
12	16
13	15
15	12.5
17	16
18	17.5
19	17.5
20	18
22	15
27	15
33	10
36	10.5
40	6.5
42	7
44	7
45	10
55	10
60	12
63	15
70	17
80	10

Average Happiness Rating Versus Age

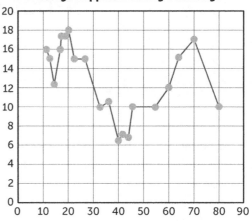

The statement that, on average, middle-aged people are less happy than young or older people appears to be true. According to the graph, people in their thirties, forties, and fifties are less happy than people in their teens, twenties, sixties, and seventies.

8. Place years on the independent axis, and profit on the dependent axis, and then draw a box showing the profit for each year.

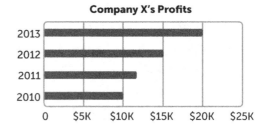

Company X's Profits

9. Find the mean using the equation for the population mean.

$$\mu = \frac{\Sigma x}{N} = \frac{5296}{15} = \textbf{353.1 lbs.}$$

Find the median and IQR by counting the leaves and identifying Q1, Q2, and Q3.

Q1 = 253

Q2 = 345

Q3 = 410

IQR = 410 − 253 = 157

The median is 345 lbs. The IQR is 157 lbs.

10. **A) True.** More people (42) chose action movies than comedy (23) or horror (38).

    B) True. Find the ratio of total number of people who prefer comedy to total number of people. $\frac{23}{103}$ = 0.22; 1 in 5 is 20%, so 22% is about the same.

    C) False. The percentage of men who choose horror is less than the percentage of women who do.

    part = number of men who prefer horror =21

    whole = number of men surveyed = 60

    percent = $\frac{part}{whole}$ = $\frac{21}{60}$

    = 0.35 = 35%

    part = number of women who prefer horror =17

    whole = number of women surveyed = 43

    percent = $\frac{part}{whole}$ = $\frac{17}{43}$

    = 0.40 = 40%

11. Since time is the independent variable, it is on the x-axis and the number of customers is on the y-axis. For the histogram to correctly display data continuously, categories on the x-axis must be equal 2-hour segments. The 8 a.m. − 9 a.m. and 9 a.m. − 10 a.m. categories must be combined for a total of 11 customers in that time period. Although not perfectly symmetrical, the amount of customers peaks in the middle and

    is therefore considered symmetrical.

    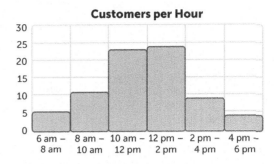
    Customers per Hour

12. Multiply the number of outcomes for each individual event:

    (70)(2)(5) = **700 outfits**

13. The order of the items doesn't matter, so use the formula for combinations:

    $C(n,r) = \frac{n!}{(n-r)!r!}$

    $C(20,3) = \frac{20!}{(20-3)!3!}$

    $= \frac{20!}{(17!\ 3!)} = \frac{(20)(19)(18)}{3!}$

    = **1140 possible teams**

14. To find the number of unique permutations of 5 letters in pickle, use the permutation formula:

    $P(n,r) = \frac{n!}{(n-r)!}$

    $P(6,5) = \frac{6!}{(6-5)!} = \frac{720}{1} = \textbf{720}$

15. The letter *e* repeats 3 times in the word *cheese*, meaning some permutations of the 6 letters will be indistinguishable from others. The number of permutations must be divided by the number of ways the three e's can be arranged to account for these redundant outcomes:

    total number of permutations

    $= \frac{\text{number of ways of arranging 6 letters}}{\text{number of ways of arranging 3 letters}}$

    $= \frac{6!}{3!} = 6 \times 5 \times 4 = \textbf{120}$

16. P(rolling even)

$= \dfrac{\text{number of favorable outcomes}}{\text{total number of possible outcomes}}$

$= \dfrac{3}{6} = \mathbf{\dfrac{1}{2}}$

P(rolling 5)

$= \dfrac{\text{number of favorable\ outcomes}}{\text{total number of possible outcomes}}$

$= \mathbf{\dfrac{1}{6}}$

17. P(not winning)

$= \dfrac{\text{number of favorable\ outcomes}}{\text{total number of possible outcomes}}$

$= \dfrac{14}{20} = \dfrac{7}{10}$ or

P(not winning) $= 1 - P$(winning) $=$

$1 - \dfrac{6}{20} = \dfrac{14}{20} = \mathbf{\dfrac{7}{10}}$

18. $P = \dfrac{\text{number of favorable outcomes}}{\text{total number of possible outcomes}}$

$= \dfrac{\text{number of 3-consonant combinations}}{\text{number of 3-tile combinations}}$

$= \dfrac{_{21}C_3}{_{26}C_3} = \dfrac{1330}{2600} = 0.51 = \mathbf{51\%}$

CHAPTER FIVE
Reading and Vocabulary

The Reading subtest of the English-Language Arts section of the CHSPE contains two types of questions: reading comprehension and vocabulary. To do well on reading comprehension questions on the CHSPE, you should be able to identify explicit details in a text, draw inferences about the text, grasp the author's intent, and understand the main idea of a text. There are fifty-four reading comprehension questions and thirty vocabulary questions on the Reading subtest.

The Main Idea

The main idea of a text describes the author's main topic and general concept; it also generalizes the author's point of view about a subject. It is contained within and throughout the text. The reader can find the main idea by considering how the main topic is addressed throughout a passage. On reading questions, you are expected not only to identify the main idea but also to be able to differentiate it from a text's theme and to summarize the main idea clearly and concisely. For instance, you might be asked to pick an answer choice that best summarizes the main idea of a passage.

The main idea is closely connected to topic sentences and how they are supported in a text. Questions may deal with finding topic sentences, summarizing a text's ideas, or locating supporting details. The sections and practice examples that follow detail the distinctions between these aspects of text.

DID YOU KNOW?
The author's perspective on the subject of the text and how he or she has framed the argument or story hints at the main idea. For example, if the author framed the story with a description, image, or short anecdote, he or she is hinting at a particular idea or point of view.

IDENTIFYING the MAIN IDEA

To identify the main idea, first identify the topic. The difference between these two things is simple: the **TOPIC** is the overall subject matter of a passage; the **MAIN IDEA** is what the author wants to say about that topic. The main idea covers the author's direct perspective about a topic, as distinct from the **THEME**, which is a generally true idea that the reader might derive from a text. Most of the time, fiction has a theme, whereas non-fiction has a main idea. This is the case because in a nonfiction text, the author speaks more directly to the audience about a topic—his or her perspective is more visible. For example, the following passage conveys the topic as well as what the author wants to communicate about that topic.

> The "shark mania" of recent years can be largely pinned on the sensationalistic media surrounding the animals: from the release of *Jaws* in 1975 to the week of ultra-hyped shark feeding frenzies and "worst shark attacks" countdowns known as *Shark Week*, popular culture both demonizes and fetishizes sharks until the public cannot get enough. Swimmers and beachgoers may look nervously for the telltale fin skimming the surface, but the reality is that shark bites are extremely rare and they are almost never unprovoked. Sharks attack people at very predictable times and for very predictable reasons. Rough surf, poor visibility, or a swimmer sending visual and physical signals that mimic a shark's normal prey are just a few examples.
>
> Of course, some places are just more dangerous to swim. Shark attack "hot spots," such as the coasts of Florida, South Africa, and New Zealand try a variety of solutions to protect tourists and surfers. Some beaches employ "shark nets," meant to keep sharks away from the beach, though these are controversial because they frequently trap other forms of marine life as well. Other beaches use spotters in helicopters and boats to alert beach officials when there are sharks in the area. In addition, there is an array of products that claim to offer personal protection from sharks, ranging from wetsuits in different colors to devices that broadcast electrical signals in an attempt to confuse the sharks' sensory organs. At the end of the day, though, beaches like these remain dangerous, and swimmers must assume the risk every time they paddle out from shore.

The author of this passage has a clear topic: sharks and their relationship with humans. In order to identify the main idea of the passage, the reader must ask, What does the author want to say about this topic? What is the reader meant to think or understand?

DID YOU KNOW?
Readers should identify the topic of a text and pay attention to how the details about it relate to one another. A passage may discuss, for example, topic similarities, characteristics, causes, and/ or effects.

The author makes sure to provide information about several different aspects of the relationship between sharks and humans, and points out that humans must respect sharks as dangerous marine animals, without sensationalizing the risk of attack. The reader can figure this out by looking at the various pieces of information the author includes as well as the similarities between them. The passage describes sensationalistic media, then talks about how officials and governments try to protect beaches, and ends with the observation that people must take personal responsibility. These details clarify what the author's main idea is: thanks to safety precautions and their natural behavior, sharks are not as dangerous as they are portrayed to be. Summarizing that main idea by focusing on the connection between the different details helps the reader draw a conclusion.

EXAMPLES

The art of the twentieth and twenty-first centuries demonstrates several aspects of modern social advancement. A primary example is the advent of technology: new technologies have developed new avenues for art making, and the globalization brought about by the internet has both diversified the art world and brought it together simultaneously. Even as artists are able to engage in a global conversation about the categories and characteristics of art, creating a more uniform understanding, they can now express themselves in a diversity of ways for a diversity of audiences. The result has been a rapid change in how art is made and consumed.

1. This passage is primarily concerned with
    A) the importance of art in the twenty-first century.
    B) the use of art to communicate overarching ideals to diverse communities.
    C) the importance of technology to art criticism.
    D) the change in understanding and creation of art in the modern period.

2. Which of the following best describes the main idea of the passage?
    A) Modern advances in technology have diversified art making and connected artists to distant places and ideas.
    B) Diversity in modern art is making it harder for art viewers to understand and talk about that art.
    C) The use of technology to discuss art allows us to create standards for what art should be.
    D) Art-making before the invention of technology such as the internet was disorganized and poorly understood.

TOPIC and SUMMARY SENTENCES

Identifying the main idea requires understanding the structure of a piece of writing. In a short passage of one or two paragraphs, the topic and summary sentences quickly relate what the paragraphs are about and what conclusions the author wants the reader to draw. These sentences function as bookends to a paragraph or passage, telling readers what to think and keeping the passage tied tightly together.

Generally, the TOPIC SENTENCE is the first, or very near the first, sentence in a paragraph. It is a general statement that introduces the topic, clearly and specifically directing the reader to access any previous experience with that topic.

The SUMMARY SENTENCE, on the other hand, frequently—but not always!—comes at the end of a paragraph or passage, because it wraps up all the ideas presented. This sentence provides an understanding of what the author wants to say about the topic and what conclusions to draw about it. While a topic sentence acts as an introduction to a topic, allowing the reader to activate his or her own ideas and experiences, the summary statement asks the reader to accept the author's ideas about that topic. Because of this, a summary sentence helps the reader quickly identify a piece's main idea.

DID YOU KNOW?
A summary is a very brief restatement of the most important parts of an argument or text. Building a summary begins with the most important idea in a text. A longer summary also includes supporting details. The text of a summary should be much shorter than the original.

EXAMPLES

There is nowhere more beautiful and interesting than California. With glimmering azure seas, fertile green plains, endless deserts, and majestic mountains, California offers every landscape. Hikers can explore the wilderness in Yosemite National Park, where a variety of plants and animals make their home. Farmers grow almonds, apricots, cotton, tomatoes, and more in the Central Valley that winds through the middle of the state. Skiers enjoy the slopes and backcountry of the Sierra Nevada and Lake Tahoe areas. In the desert of Death Valley, temperatures rise well over one hundred degrees Fahrenheit. And of course, California's famous beaches stretch from the Mexican border to Oregon. Furthermore, California features some of America's most important cities. In the south, Los Angeles is home to the movie industry and Hollywood. Farther north, the San Francisco Bay Area includes Silicon Valley, where the US tech industry is based. Both places are centers of commercial activity. In fact, California is the most populous state in the country. There is no shortage of things to do or sights to see!

3. Which of the following best explains the general idea and focus indicated by the topic sentence?

    A) The diversity of California's landscape allows agriculture to flourish, and the most important crops will be detailed.

    B) California is beautiful and diverse; the reader will read on to find out what makes it so interesting.

    C) California is a peaceful place; its people live with a sense of predictability and the state is prosperous.

    D) The incredible geography of California is the reason it is a rural state, and the reader can expect a discussion of the countryside.

4. Which of the following best states what the author wants the reader to understand after reading the summary sentence?
- **A)** Tourists should see everything in California when they visit.
- **B)** The cities of California are interesting, but the rural parts are better.
- **C)** The resources of California are nearly exhausted.
- **D)** California is an inspiring and exciting place.

Supporting Details

Between a topic sentence and a summary sentence, the rest of a paragraph is built with **SUPPORTING DETAILS**. Supporting details come in many forms; the purpose of the passage dictates the type of details that will support the main idea. A persuasive passage may use facts and data or detail specific reasons for the author's opinion. An informative passage will primarily use facts about the topic to support the main idea. Even a narrative passage will have supporting details—specific things the author says to develop the story and characters.

The most important aspect of supporting details is exactly what it sounds like: they support the main idea. Examining the various supporting details and how they work with one another will reveal how the author views a topic and what the main idea of the passage is. Supporting details are key to understanding a passage.

Supporting details can often be found in texts by looking for **SIGNAL WORDS**—transitions that explain to the reader how one sentence or idea is connected to another. Signal words can add information, provide counterarguments, create organization in a passage, or draw conclusions. Some common signal words and phrases include *in particular, in addition, besides, contrastingly, therefore,* and *because.*

EXAMPLE

Increasingly, companies are turning to subcontracting services rather than hiring full-time employees. This provides companies with advantages like greater flexibility, reduced legal responsibility to employees, and lower possibility of unionization within the company. However, this has led to increasing confusion and uncertainty over the legal definition of employment. Courts have grappled with questions about the hiring company's responsibility in maintaining fair labor practices. Companies argue that they delegate that authority to subcontractors, while unions and other worker advocate groups argue that companies still have a legal obligation to the workers who contribute to their business.

5. According to the passage, why do companies use subcontractors?

Hiring subcontractors

A) costs less money than hiring full-time employees.

B) increases the need for unionization of employees.

C) reduces the company's legal responsibilities.

D) gives the company greater control over worker's hours.

The Author's Purpose

The author of a passage sets out with a specific goal in mind: to communicate a particular idea to an audience. The **AUTHOR'S PURPOSE** is determined by asking why the author wants the reader to understand the passage's main idea. There are four basic purposes to which an author can write: narrative, expository, technical, and persuasive. Within each of these general purposes, the author may direct the audience to take a clear action or respond in a certain way.

The purpose for which an author writes a passage is also connected to the structure of that text. In a **NARRATIVE**, the author seeks to tell a story, often to illustrate a theme or idea the reader needs to consider. In a narrative, the author uses characteristics of storytelling, such as chronological order, characters, and a defined setting, and these characteristics communicate the author's theme or main idea.

In an **EXPOSITORY** passage, on the other hand, the author simply seeks to explain an idea or topic to the reader. The main idea will probably be a factual statement or a direct assertion of a broadly held opinion. Expository writing can come in many forms, but one essential feature is a fair and balanced representation of a topic. The author may explore one detailed aspect or a broad range of characteristics, but he or she mainly seeks to prompt a decision from the reader.

Similarly, in **TECHNICAL** writing, the author's purpose is to explain specific processes, techniques, or equipment in order for the reader to use that process or equipment to obtain a desired result. Writing like this employs chronological or spatial structures, specialized vocabulary, and imperative or directive language.

DID YOU KNOW?
Reading persuasive text requires an awareness of what the author believes about the topic.

In **PERSUASIVE** writing, the author actively seeks to convince the reader to accept an opinion or belief. Much like expository writing, persuasive writing is presented in many organizational forms.

EXAMPLE

University of California, Berkeley, researchers decided to tackle an age-old problem: why shoelaces come untied. They recorded the shoelaces of a volunteer walking on a treadmill by attaching devices to record the acceleration, or g-force, experienced by the knot. The results were surprising. A shoelace knot experiences more g-force from a person walking than any rollercoaster can generate. However, if the person simply stomped or swung their feet—the two movements that make up a walker's stride—the g-force was not enough to undo the knots.

6. What is the purpose of this passage?
    A) to confirm if shoelaces always come undone
    B) to compare the force of treadmills and rollercoasters
    C) to persuade readers to tie their shoes tighter
    D) to describe the results of an experiment on shoelaces

Organization and Text Structures

It's important to analyze the organization and structure of informational texts, as these details can provide valuable insight into the author's purpose and the overall meaning of a text. Several common structures are used in informative texts, and understanding these structures will help readers quickly make sense of new texts. Texts may be organized in one of the following ways:

▶ **CHRONOLOGICAL** texts describe events in the order they occurred.

▶ **PROBLEM-SOLUTION** texts begin by describing a problem and then offer a possible solution to the issue.

▶ **CAUSE-EFFECT** is a text structure that shows a causal chain of events or ideas.

▶ **GENERAL-TO-SPECIFIC** is a text structure that describes a general topic then provides details about a specific aspect of that topic.

▶ **COMPARE-CONTRAST** texts give the similarities and differences between two things.

Authors choose the organizational structure of their text according to their purpose. For example, an author who hopes to convince people to begin recycling might begin by talking about the problems that are caused by excessive waste and end by offering recycling as a reasonable solution. On the other hand, the author might choose to use a chronological structure for an article whose purpose is to give an impartial history of recycling.

EXAMPLE

For thirteen years, a spacecraft called *Cassini* was on an exploratory mission to Saturn. The spacecraft was designed not to return but to end its journey by diving into Saturn's atmosphere. This dramatic ending provided scientists with unprecedented information about Saturn's atmosphere and its magnetic and gravitational fields. First, however, *Cassini* passed Saturn's largest moon, Titan, where it recorded data on Titan's curious methane lakes, gathering information about potential seasons on the planet-sized moon. Then it passed through the unexplored region between Saturn itself and its famous rings. Scientists hope to learn how old the rings are and to directly examine the particles that make them up. *Cassini*'s mission ended in 2017, but researchers have new questions for future exploration.

7. Which of the following best describes the organization of this passage?
   A) general-to-specific
   B) compare-contrast
   C) chronological
   D) problem-solution

The Audience

The structure, purpose, main idea, and language of a text all converge on one target: the intended AUDIENCE. An author makes decisions about every aspect of a piece of writing based on that audience, and readers can evaluate the writing by considering who the author is writing for. By considering the probable reactions of an intended audience, readers can determine many things:

▶ whether they are part of that intended audience

▶ the author's purpose for using specific techniques or devices

▶ the biases of the author and how they appear in the writing

▶ how the author uses rhetorical strategies.

DID YOU KNOW?
When reading a persuasive text, students should maintain awareness of what the author believes about the topic.

The audience for a text can be identified by careful analysis of the text. First, the reader considers who most likely cares about the topic and main idea of the text: who would want or need to know about this topic? The audience may be SPECIFIC (e.g., biologists who study sharks) or more GENERAL (e.g., people with an interest in marine life).

Next, consider the language of the text. The author tailors language to appeal to the intended audience, so the reader can determine from the language who the author is speaking to. A FORMAL style is used in business and academic settings and can make the author seem more credible. Characteristics of a formal style include:

▶ third person perspective (i.e., no use of *I* or *you*)

▶ no use of slang or clichés

▶ follows a clear structure (e.g., an introduction, a body, and a conclusion)

▶ technically correct grammar and sentence structure

▶ objective language

An **INFORMAL** style is used to appeal to readers in a more casual setting, such as a magazine or blog. Using an informal style may make the author seem less credible, but it can help create an emotional connection with the audience. Characteristics of informal writing include:

▶ use of first or second person (e.g., *I* or *you*)

▶ use of slang or casual language

▶ follows an unusual or flexible structure

▶ bends the rules of grammar

▶ appeals to audience's emotions

EXAMPLE

What do you do with plastic bottles? Do you throw them away, or do you recycle or reuse them? As landfills continue to fill up, there will eventually be no place to put our trash. If you recycle or reuse bottles, you will help reduce waste and turn something old into a creative masterpiece!

8. Which of the following BEST describes the intended audience for this passage?

A) a formal audience of engineering professionals

B) an audience of English language learners

C) a general audience that includes children

D) a group of scientists at an environmental conference

Evaluating Arguments

An author selects details to help support the main idea. The reader must then evaluate these details for relevance and consistency. Though the author generally includes details that support the text's main idea, it's up to the reader to decide whether those details are convincing.

Readers should be able to differentiate between facts and opinions in order to more effectively analyze supporting details. **FACTS** are based in truth and can usually be proven. They are pieces of information that have been confirmed or validated. An opinion is a judgment, belief, or viewpoint that is not based on evidence. **OPINIONS** are often stated in descriptive, subjective language that is difficult to define or prove. While opinions can be included in informative texts, they are often of little impact unless they are supported by some kind of evidence.

QUICK REVIEW
Which of the following phrases would be associated with opinions? *for example, studies have shown, I believe, in fact, it's possible that*

Sometimes, the author's **BIAS**—an inclination towards a particular belief—causes the author to leave out details that do not directly support the main idea or that support an opposite idea. The reader has to be able to notice not only what the author says but also what the author leaves out. Discovering the author's bias and how the supporting details reveal that bias is also key to understanding a text.

Writers will often use specific techniques, or **RHETORICAL STRATEGIES**, to build an argument. Readers can identify these strategies in order to clearly understand what an author wants them to believe, how the author's perspective and purpose may lead to bias, and whether the passage includes any logical fallacies.

Common rhetorical strategies include the appeals to ethos, logos, and pathos. An author uses these to build trust with the reader, explain the logical points of his or her argument, and convince the reader that his or her opinion is the best option.

An **ETHOS (ETHICAL) APPEAL** uses balanced, fair language and seeks to build a trusting relationship between the author and the reader. An author might explain her or his credentials, include the reader in an argument, or offer concessions to an opposing argument.

QUICK REVIEW
Consider how different audiences would react to the same text.

A **LOGOS (LOGICAL) APPEAL** builds on that trust by providing facts and support for the author's opinion, explaining the argument with clear connections and reasoning. At this point, the reader should beware of logical fallacies that connect unconnected ideas and build arguments on incorrect premises. With a logical appeal, an author strives to convince the reader to accept an opinion or belief by demonstrating that not only is it the most logical option but that it also satisfies her or his emotional reaction to a topic.

A **PATHOS (EMOTIONAL) APPEAL** does not depend on reasonable connections between ideas; rather, it seeks to remind the reader, through imagery, strong language, and personal connections, that the author's argument aligns with her or his best interests.

EXAMPLE

Exercise is critical for healthy development in children. Today in the United States, there is an epidemic of poor childhood health; many of these children will face further illnesses in adulthood that are due to poor diet and lack of exercise now. This is a problem for all Americans, especially with the rising cost of health care.

It is vital that school systems and parents encourage children to engage in a minimum of thirty minutes of cardiovascular exercise each day, mildly increasing their heart rate for a sustained period. This is proven to decrease the likelihood of developmental diabetes, obesity, and a multitude of other health problems. Also, children need a proper diet, rich in fruits and vegetables, so they can develop physically and learn healthy eating habits early on.

9. Which of the following statements from the passage is a fact, not an opinion?

A) Fruits and vegetables are the best way to help children be healthy.

B) Children today are lazier than they were in previous generations.

C) The risk of diabetes in children is reduced by physical activity.

D) Children should engage in thirty minutes of exercise a day.

Drawing Conclusions

Reading text begins with making sense of the explicit meanings of information or a narrative. Understanding occurs as the reader draws conclusions and makes logical inferences. First, the reader considers the details or facts. He or she then comes to a **CONCLUSION**—the next logical point in the thought sequence. For example, in a Hemingway story, an old man sits alone in a cafe. A young waiter says that the cafe is closing, but the old man continues to drink. The waiter starts closing up, and the old man signals for a refill. Based on these details, the reader might conclude that the old man has not understood the young waiter's desire for him to leave.

An inference is distinguished from a conclusion drawn. An **INFERENCE** is an assumption the reader makes based on details in the text as well as his or her own knowledge. It is more of an educated guess that extends the literal meaning of a text. Inferences begin with the given details; however, the reader uses the facts to determine additional information. What the reader already knows informs what is being suggested by the details of decisions or situations in the text. Returning to the example of the Hemingway story, the reader might *infer* that the old man is lonely, enjoys being in the cafe, and therefore is reluctant to leave.

When reading fictional text, inferring character motivations is essential. The actions of the characters move the plot forward; a series of events is understood by making sense of why the characters did what they did. Hemingway includes contrasting details as the young waiter and an older waiter discuss the old man. The older waiter sympathizes with the old man; both men have no one at home and experience a sense of emptiness in life, which motivates them to seek the cafe.

Another aspect of understanding text is connecting it to other texts. Readers may connect the Hemingway story about the old man in the cafe to other Hemingway stories about individuals struggling to deal with loss and loneliness in a dignified way.

DID YOU KNOW?
When considering a character's motivations, the reader should ask what the character wants to achieve, what the character will get by accomplishing this, and what the character seems to value the most.

DID YOU KNOW?
Conclusions are drawn by thinking about how the author wants the reader to feel. A group of carefully selected facts can cause the reader to feel a certain way.

They can extend their initial connections to people they know or their personal experiences. When readers read a persuasive text, they often connect the arguments made to counterarguments and opposing evidence of which they are aware. They use these connections to infer meaning.

EXAMPLE

After World War I, political and social forces pushed for a return to normalcy in the United States. The result was disengagement from the larger world and increased focus on American economic growth and personal enjoyment. Caught in the middle were American writers, raised on the values of the prewar world and frustrated with what they viewed as the superficiality and materialism of postwar American culture. Many of them fled to Paris, where they became known as the "lost generation," creating a trove of literary works criticizing their home culture and delving into their own feelings of alienation.

10. Which conclusion about the effects of war is most likely true, according to the passage?

A) War served as an inspiration for literary works.

B) It was difficult to stabilize countries after war occurred.

C) Writers were torn between supporting war and their own ideals.

D) Individual responsibility and global awareness declined after the war.

Tone and Mood

The **TONE** of a passage describes the author's attitude toward the topic. In general, the author's tone can be described as positive, negative, or neutral. The **MOOD** is the pervasive feeling or atmosphere in a passage that provokes specific emotions in the reader. Put simply, tone is how the author feels about the topic. Mood is how the reader feels about the text.

DICTION, or word choice, helps determine mood and tone in a passage. Many readers make the mistake using the author's ideas alone to determine tone; a much better practice is to look at specific words and try to identify a pattern in the emotion they evoke. Does the writer choose positive words like *ambitious* and *confident*? Or does he describe those concepts with negative words like *greedy* and *overbearing*? The first writer's tone might be described as admiring, while the more negative tone would be disapproving.

When looking at tone, it's important to examine not just the literal definition of words. Every word has not only a literal meaning but also a **CONNOTATIVE MEANING**, which relies on the common emotions and experiences an audience might associate with that word. The following words are all synonyms: *dog, puppy, cur, mutt,* *canine, pet.* Two of these words—*dog* and *canine*—are neutral words, without strong associations or emotions. Two others—*pet* and *puppy*—have positive associations. The last two—*cur* and *mutt*—have negative associations. A passage that uses one pair of these words versus another pair activates the positive or negative reactions of the audience.

Table 5.1. Words That Describe Tone

POSITIVE	NEUTRAL	NEGATIVE
admiring	casual	angry
approving	detached	annoyed
celebratory	formal	belligerent
earnest	impartial	bitter
encouraging	informal	condescending
excited	objective	confused
funny	questioning	cynical
hopeful	unconcerned	depressed
humorous		disrespectful
nostalgic		embarrassed
optimistic		fearful
playful		gloomy
poignant		melancholy
proud		mournful
relaxed		pessimistic
respectful		skeptical
sentimental		solemn
silly		suspicious
sympathetic		unsympathetic

EXAMPLES

Day had broken cold and grey, exceedingly cold and grey, when the man turned aside from the main Yukon trail and climbed the high earth-bank, where a dim and little-travelled trail led eastward through the fat spruce timberland. It was a steep bank, and he paused for breath at the top, excusing the act to himself by looking at his watch. It was nine o'clock. There was no sun nor hint of sun, though there was not a cloud in the sky. It was a clear day, and yet there seemed an intangible pall over the face of things, a subtle gloom that made the day dark, and that was due to the absence of sun. This fact did not worry the man. He was used to the lack of sun. It had been days since he had seen the sun, and he knew that a few more days must pass before that cheerful orb, due south, would just peep above the sky-line and dip immediately from view.

—from "To Build a Fire" by Jack London

11. Which of the following best describes the mood of the passage?

   A) exciting and adventurous

   B) unhappy and anxious

   C) bleak but accepting

   D) grim yet hopeful

12. The connotation of the words *intangible pall* is

   A) a death-like covering.

   B) a sense of familiarity.

   C) a feeling of communal strength.

   D) an understanding of the struggle ahead.

Figurative Language

Figures of speech are expressions that are understood to have a nonliteral meaning. Rather than stating their ideas directly, authors use FIGURATIVE LANGUAGE to suggest meaning by speaking of a subject as if it were something else. For example, when Shakespeare says, "All the world's a stage,/ And all men and women merely players," he is speaking of the world as if it is a stage. Since the world is not literally a stage, the reader has to ask how the two are similar and what Shakespeare might be implying about the world through this comparison. Figures of speech extend the meaning of words by engaging the reader's imagination and adding emphasis to different aspects of their subject.

A METAPHOR is a type of figurative language that describes something that may be unfamiliar to the reader (the topic) by referring to it as though it were something else that is more familiar to the reader (the vehicle). A metaphor stands in as a synonym, interchangeable with its corresponding topic. As the reader reflects on the similarities between the topic and the vehicle, he or she forms a clearer understanding of the topic. For example, in Shakespeare's *Romeo and Juliet*, Romeo says that "Juliet is the sun." By making this comparison, Romeo is comparing Juliet's energy to the brightness of the sun, which is familiar to readers.

A SIMILE is a type of figurative language that directly points to similarities between two things. As with a metaphor, the author uses a familiar vehicle to express an idea about a less familiar topic. Unlike a metaphor, however, a simile does not replace the object with a figurative description; it compares the vehicle and topic using "like," "as," or similar words. For example, in his poem "The Rime of the Ancient Mariner," Coleridge describes his ship as "idle as a painted ship/ Upon a painted ocean." He speaks about the boat as if it were painted (unlike Romeo above, who says explicitly that Juliet is the sun itself). The reader understands that paintings do not move, so Coleridge uses this comparison to show the reader that the ship in the poem is completely motionless.

IMAGERY is vivid description that appeals to the reader's sense of sight, sound, smell, taste, or touch. This type of figurative language allows readers to experience through their senses what is being described; as readers use their imaginations to visualize or recall sensory experience, they are drawn into the scene of the story or poem.

HYPERBOLE is an overstatement, an exaggeration intended to achieve a particular effect. Hyperbole can create humor or add emphasis to a text by drawing the reader's attention to a particular idea. For example, a character might say he or she is "so hungry, [he or she] could eat a horse." Though the character probably cannot literally eat a horse, the reader understands that he or she is extremely hungry.

PERSONIFICATION is a type of figurative language in which human characteristics are attributed to objects, abstract ideas, natural forces, or animals. For example, if a writer refers to "murmuring pine trees," he or she is attributing to the pine trees the human ability of murmuring. The writer is using the familiar vehicle of the sound of murmuring to help the reader understand the sound pine trees make in the wind.

SYMBOLISM is a literary device in which the author uses a concrete object, action, or character to represent an abstract idea. The significance of the symbol reaches beyond the object's ordinary meaning. Familiar symbols are roses representing beauty, light representing truth, and darkness representing evil. As readers notice an author's use of symbolism, they begin to make connections and to formulate ideas about what the author is suggesting.

An ALLUSION, not to be confused with illusion, is a reference to a historical person or event, a fictional character or event, a mythological or religious character or event, or an artist or artistic work. When a reader recognizes an allusion, he or she may make associations that contribute to his or her understanding of the text. For example, if a character is described as having a "Mona Lisa smile," an instant image will arise in the minds of most readers. Because allusions can be difficult to recognize, especially for young readers whose experiences are limited, teachers must provide instruction in how to recognize, research, and interpret unfamiliar references.

CLICHÉS are common sayings that lack originality but are familiar and relatable to an audience. Though clichés are not necessarily beneficial to the author who is trying to write a wholly original work, they can be helpful for a writer who is attempting to show that he or she can relate to the audience.

DIALECT and SLANG are linguistic qualities that an author might incorporate into his or her writing in order to develop characters or setting. A character's dialect may reveal where he or she is from, while the slang he or she uses may be an indication of social, economic, and educational status.

IRONY comes in different forms. VERBAL IRONY is used when a character or narrator says something that is the opposite of what he or she means. SITUATIONAL IRONY occurs when something happens that contradicts what the audience expected to happen.

DRAMATIC IRONY occurs when the audience knows about something of which a character or characters are not aware.

EXAMPLE

Alfie closed his eyes and took several deep breaths. He was trying to ignore the sounds of the crowd, but even he had to admit that it was hard not to notice the tension in the stadium. He could feel 50,000 sets of eyes burning through his skin—this crowd expected perfection from him. He took another breath and opened his eyes, setting his sights on the soccer ball resting peacefully in the grass. One shot, just one last shot, between his team and the championship. He didn't look up at the goalie, who was jumping nervously on the goal line just a few yards away. Afterward, he would swear he didn't remember anything between the referee's whistle and the thunderous roar of the crowd.

13. Which of the following best describes the meaning of the phrase "[h]e could feel 50,000 sets of eyes burning through his skin"?

  A) The 50,000 people in the stadium were trying to hurt Alfie.

  B) Alfie felt uncomfortable and exposed in front of so many people.

  C) Alfie felt immense pressure from the 50,000 people watching him.

  D) The people in the stadium are warning Alfie that the field is on fire.

Graphic Sources of Information

Informational texts on the CHSPE may be accompanied by graphic sources of information, including graphs, diagrams, or photographs. There's no simple set of rules for handling these questions, but many of the same strategies that are used for other figures and for text passages are applicable.

Always start with the **TITLE** of a figure—it will provide information that is likely crucial to understanding the figure. An anatomical diagram might have a title such as *Lobes of the Brain* that tells the viewer that the diagram will likely show the names and locations of the brain's lobes. Similarly, a graph may have a title like *Number of Customers per Month*, which describes the information in the graph.

Also make sure to examine any **LABELS**, legends, or scales provided with the figure. Graphs, for example, should always include labels on the axes that describe what's shown on each axis, and a flowchart will have arrows indicating an ordered sequence.

Many of the strategies needed to interpret traditional reading passages can also be used for graphic representations of information, particularly those that may be text heavy. When looking at a photograph or advertisement, it will help to identify:

▶ the purpose of the author

▶ the intended audience

- ▶ rhetorical strategies designed to influence the viewer
- ▶ the main idea of the image

A flyer for a local bake sale, for example, may be designed to appeal to the viewer's emotions by including pictures of local schoolchildren. Similarly, a computer advertisement meant to appeal to corporate buyers would probably use more formal language than one aimed at teenagers.

EXAMPLE

As you can see from the graph, my babysitting business has been really successful. The year started with a busy couple of months—several snows combined with a large number of requests for Valentine's Day services boosted our sales quite a bit. The spring months have admittedly been a bit slow, but we're hoping for a big summer once school gets out. Several clients have already put in requests for our services!

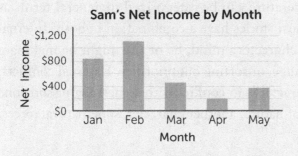

Sam's Net Income by Month

14. Based on the information in the graph, how much more did Sam's Babysitting Service bring in during February than during April?

A) $200

B) $900

C) $1100

D) $1300

Elements of Fiction

FICTION is a prose genre, made up of narratives whose details are not based in truth but are instead the creation of the author. Just as artists have the tools of color and shape to communicate ideas, so have writers their literary tools. These tools include point of view, plot, setting, character, tone, and figurative language. Each of these elements contributes to the overall idea that is developed in the text and, as such, can provide valuable insight into the theme of the work.

POINT OF VIEW is the perspective from which the action in a story is told. By carefully selecting a particular point of view, writers are able to control what their readers know.

Most literature is written in either first person or third person point of view. With the **FIRST PERSON POINT OF VIEW**, the action is narrated by a character within the story, which can make it feel more believable and authentic to the reader. However, as a result of the first person point of view, the reader's knowledge and understanding are constrained by what the narrator notices and influenced by what the narrator thinks and values.

An author may, on the other hand, choose to tell the story from the **THIRD PERSON POINT OF VIEW**. A third person narrator is a voice outside the action of the story, an observer who shares what he or she knows, sees, or hears with the reader. A third person narrator might be **FULLY OMNISCIENT** (able to see into the minds of the characters and share what they are thinking and feeling), **PARTIALLY OMNISCIENT** (able to see into the minds of just one or a few characters), or **LIMITED** (unable to see into the minds of any of the characters and only able to share what can be seen and heard).

PLOT STRUCTURE is the way the author arranges the events of a narrative. In a conventional plot line, the story is structured around a central conflict, a struggle between two opposing forces. Conflicts in literature can be categorized in general terms as either internal or external, though most stories have a combination of both. Internal conflicts take place inside the main character's mind; he or she might be making a difficult decision, struggling with change, or sorting out priorities. External conflicts, on the other hand, occur when a character is in conflict with something or someone in the external world—the elements of nature, another character, supernatural forces, destiny, or society.

In a traditional plot structure, the author begins with **EXPOSITION**: important background information about the setting, the characters, and the current state of the world. Following the exposition, an **INCITING INCIDENT** introduces the antagonist and establishes the conflict. As the story progresses, the conflict becomes more complicated and tension increases, moving the story toward a **CLIMAX** or turning point, in which the conflict reaches a crisis point. Finally, there is a **RESOLUTION** to the conflict, followed by falling actions, events that move the characters away from the conflict and into a new life.

SETTING is the geographical and chronological location of events in a story. When considering setting, readers should examine how characters interact with their surroundings, how they are influenced by the societal expectations of that time and place, and how the location and time period impact the development of the story. Often, setting can seem inseparable from plot; therefore, a helpful question for beginning the discussion of setting is, How would this story change if it were set in a different time or place?

CHARACTER DEVELOPMENT is the process an author uses to create characters that are complex and, to some degree, believable. One way authors develop their characters is directly: they tell the reader explicitly what the character is like by describing traits and assigning values. Sometimes, authors might include the thoughts and feelings of the characters themselves, offering readers even more insight. Authors can also develop their characters indirectly by revealing their actions and interactions with others, sometimes including what one character says or thinks about another and allowing the reader to draw his or her own conclusions. Most authors use a combination of direct and indirect characterization; this ensures that readers know what they need to know while also providing opportunities for reflection and interpretation.

EXAMPLE

15. Which passage below from *A Mystery of Heroism* by Stephen Crane best demonstrates the third person omniscient point of view?

A) In the midst of it all Smith and Ferguson, two privates of A Company, were engaged in a heated discussion, which involved the greatest questions of the national existence.

B) An officer screamed out an order so violently that his voice broke and ended the sentence in a falsetto shriek.

C) The officer's face was grimy and perspiring, and his uniform was tousled as if he had been in direct grapple with an enemy. He smiled grimly when the men stared at him.

D) No, it could not be true. He was not a hero. Heroes had no shames in their lives, and, as for him, he remembered borrowing fifteen dollars from a friend and promising to pay it back the next day, and then avoiding that friend for ten months.

Vocabulary

The Reading subtest will also ask you to provide definitions or intended meanings of words within sentences. There are thirty vocabulary questions on the Reading subtest. You may have never encountered some of these words before the test, but there are tricks you can use to figure out what they mean.

CONTEXT CLUES

One of the most fundamental vocabulary skills is using the context in which a word is used to determine its meaning. Your ability to read sentences carefully is extremely useful when it comes to understanding new vocabulary words.

Vocabulary questions on the CHSPE often include **SENTENCE CONTEXT CLUES** within the sentence that contains the word. There are several clues that can help you understand the context, and therefore the meaning of a word:

RESTATEMENT CLUES state the definition of the word in the sentence. The definition is often set apart from the rest of the sentence by a comma, parentheses, or a colon.

Teachers often prefer teaching students with <u>intrinsic motivation: these students have an internal desire to learn.</u>

The meaning of *intrinsic* is restated as *internal*.

CONTRAST CLUES include the opposite meaning of a word. Words like *but, on the other hand*, and *however* are tip-offs that a sentence contains a contrast clue.

> Janet was destitute after she lost her job, <u>but</u> her wealthy sister helped her get back on her feet.

Destitute is contrasted with *wealthy*, so the definition of destitute is "poor."

POSITIVE/NEGATIVE CLUES tell you whether a word has a positive or negative meaning.

> The film was lauded by critics as <u>stunning</u>, and <u>was nominated for several awards</u>.

The positive descriptions *stunning* and *nominated for several awards* suggest that *lauded* has a positive meaning.

EXAMPLES

Select the answer that most closely matches the definition of the underlined word as it is used in the sentence.

16. The dog was <u>dauntless</u> in the face of danger, braving the fire to save the girl trapped inside the building.

   A) difficult

   B) fearless

   C) imaginative

   D) startled

17. Beth did not spend any time preparing for the test, but Tyrone kept a <u>rigorous</u> study schedule.

   A) strict

   B) loose

   C) boring

   D) strange

ANALYZING WORDS

As you know, determining the meaning of a word can be more complicated than just looking in a dictionary. A word might have more than one **DENOTATION**, or definition. The definition the author intends can only be judged by looking at the surrounding text. For example, the word *quack* can refer to the sound a duck makes or to a person who publicly pretends to have a qualification which they do not actually possess.

As discussed above, a word may also have different **CONNOTATIONS**, which are the implied meanings and emotions a word evokes in the reader. For example, a cubicle is simply a walled desk in an office, but for many the word implies a constrictive, uninspiring workplace. Connotations can vary greatly between cultures and even between individuals.

EXAMPLE

Select the answer that most closely matches the definition of the underlined word or phrase as it is used in the sentence.

18. The nurse looked at the patient's eyes and determined from his uneven pupils that brain damage was possible.

- **A)** part of the eye
- **B)** young student
- **C)** walking pace
- **D)** breathing sounds

WORD STRUCTURE

You are not expected to know every word in the English language for your test; rather, you will need to use deductive reasoning to find the best definition of the word in question. Many words can be broken down into three main parts to help determine their meaning:

> prefix – root – suffix

ROOTS are the building blocks of all words. Every word is either a root itself or has a root. The root is what is left when you strip away the prefixes and suffixes from a word. For example, in the word *unclear*, if you take away the prefix *un–*, you have the root *clear*.

Roots are not always recognizable words, because they often come from Latin or Greek words, such as *nat*, a Latin root meaning born. The word *native*, which means a person born in a referenced place, comes from this root; so does the word *prenatal*, meaning *before birth*. It is important to keep in mind, however, that roots do not always match the original definitions of words, and they can have several different spellings.

PREFIXES are elements added to the beginning of a word, and **SUFFIXES** are elements added to the end of the word; together they are known as affixes. They carry assigned meanings and can be attached to a word to completely change the word's meaning or to enhance the word's original meaning.

Let's use the word *prefix* itself as an example: *fix* means to place something securely and *pre–* means before. Therefore, *prefix* means to place something before or in front of. Now let's look at a suffix: in the

QUICK REVIEW

Can you figure out the definitions of the following words using their parts? Ambidextrous, anthropology, diagram, egocentric, hemisphere, homicide, metamorphosis, nonsense, portable, rewind, submarine, triangle, unicycle word *feminism*, *femin* is a root which means female. The suffix *–ism* means act, practice, or process. Thus, *feminism* is the process of establishing equal rights for women.

Although you cannot determine the meaning of a word from a prefix or suffix alone, you can use this knowledge to eliminate answer choices. Understanding whether the word is positive or negative can give you the partial meaning of the word.

\multicolumn{3}{c}{Table 5.2. Common Roots}		
ROOT	DEFINITION	EXAMPLE
ast(er)	star	asteroid, astronomy
audi	hear	audience, audible
auto	self	automatic, autograph
bene	good	beneficent, benign
bio	life	biology, biorhythm
cap	take	capture
ced	yield	secede
chrono	time	chronometer, chronic
corp	body	corporeal
crac or crat	rule	autocrat
demo	people	democracy
dict	say	dictionary, dictation
duc	lead or make	ductile, produce
gen	give birth	generation, genetics
geo	earth	geography, geometry
grad	step	graduate
graph	write	graphical, autograph
ject	throw	eject
jur or jus	law	justice, jurisdiction
juven	young	juvenile
log or logue	thought	logic, logarithm
luc	light	lucidity
man	hand	manual
mand	order	remand
mis	send	transmission
mono	one	monotone

Root	Definition	Example
omni	all	omnivore
path	feel	sympathy
phil	love	philanthropy
phon	sound	phonograph
port	carry	export
qui	rest	quiet
scrib or script	write	scribe, transcript
sense or sent	feel	sentiment
tele	far away	telephone
terr	earth	terrace
uni	single	unicode
vac	empty	vacant
vid or vis	see	video, vision

Table 5.3. Common Prefixes		
Prefix	Definition	Example
a– (also an–)	not, without; to, toward; of, completely	atheist, anemic, aside, aback, anew, abashed
ante–	before, preceding	antecedent, anteroom
anti–	opposing, against	antibiotic, anticlimax
belli–	warlike, combative	belligerent, antebellum
com– (also co–, col–, con–, cor–)	with, jointly, completely	combat, cooperate, collide, confide, correspond
dis– (also di–)	negation, removal	disadvantage, disbar
en– (also em–)	put into or on; bring into the condition of; intensify	engulf, embrace
hypo–	under	hypoglycemic, hypodermic
in– (also il–, im–, ir–)	not, without; in, into, toward, inside	infertile, impossible, illegal, irregular, influence, include
intra–	inside, within	intravenous, intrapersonal
out–	surpassing, exceeding; external, away from	outperform, outdoor
over–	excessively, completely; upper, outer, over, above	overconfident, overcast

Table 5.3. Common Prefixes (continued)

Prefix	Definition	Example
pre–	before	precondition, preadolescent, prelude
re–	again	reapply, remake
semi–	half, partly	semicircle, semiconscious
syn– (also sym–)	in union, acting together	synthesis, symbiotic
trans–	across, beyond	transdermal
trans–	into a different state	translate
under–	beneath, below; not enough	underarm, undersecretary, underdeveloped

EXAMPLES

Select the answer that most closely matches the definition of the underlined word as it is used in the sentence.

19. The <u>bellicose</u> dog will be sent to training school next week.

    A) misbehaved

    B) friendly

    C) scared

    D) aggressive

20. The new menu <u>rejuvenated</u> the restaurant and made it one of the most popular spots in town.

    A) established

    B) invigorated

    C) improved

    D) motivated

Answer Key

1. **D) is correct.** The art of the modern period reflects the new technologies and globalization possible through the internet.

2. **A) is correct.** According to the text, technology and the internet have "diversified the art world and brought it together simultaneously."

3. **B) is correct.** This option indicates both the main idea and what the reader will focus on while reading.

4. **D) is correct.** The phrase "no shortage of things to do or sights to see" suggests the writer is enthusiastic about the many interesting activities possible in California. There is no indication that the writer should do everything, though, or that one part is better than another.

5. **C) is correct.** The passage states that hiring subcontractors provides the advantage of "reduced legal responsibility to employees."

6. **D) is correct.** The text provides details on the experiment as well as its results.

7. **C) is correct.** The passage describes the journey of *Cassini* in chronological order: it passed by Titan, went through the region between Saturn and its rings, and ended its mission in 2017.

8. **C) is correct.** The informal tone and direct address of this passage suggest that the author is writing for a general audience that may include children. For instance, turning bottles into an art project could be a good activity for children.

9. **C) is correct.** Choice C is a simple fact stated by the author. It is introduced by the word *proven* to indicate that it is supported by evidence.

10. **D) is correct.** After the war, in the US there was a lack of focus on the world and greater focus on personal comforts, which writers viewed as superficiality and materialism.

11. **C) is correct.** The day is described as "cold and grey" with an "intangible pall," which creates a bleak mood. However, the man himself "did not worry" and knew that only "a few more days must pass" before he would see the sun again, suggesting he has accepted his circumstances.

12. **A) is correct.** Within the context of the sentence "It was a clear day, and yet there seemed an intangible pall over the face of things, a subtle gloom that made the day dark," the words *gloom* and *dark* are suggestive of death; the phrase *over the face* suggests a covering.

13. **C) is correct.** The metaphor implies that Alfie felt pressure from the people watching him to perform well. There is no indication that he is threatened physically.

14. **B) is correct.** In February the service earned $1100, and in April it earned $200. The difference between the two months is $900.

15. **D) is correct.** The narrator is reporting the thoughts of the character, as the character's memory about not acting heroic in the past is revealed. The other choices only include descriptions of the characters words or actions.

16. **B) is correct.** Demonstrating bravery in the face of danger would be *fearless*. The restatement clue (*braving*) tells you exactly what the word means.

17. **A) is correct.** The word *but* tells us that Tyrone studied in a different way from Beth, which means it is a contrast clue. If Beth did not study hard, then Tyrone did. The best answer, therefore, is choice A.

18. **A) is correct.** Only choice A matches both the definition of the word and context of the sentence. Choice B is an alternative definition for pupil, but does not make sense in the sentence. Both C and D could be correct in the context of the sentence, but neither is a definition of pupil.

19. **D) is correct.** The prefix *belli–*, which means "warlike," can be used to confirm that "aggressive" is the right answer.

20. **B) is correct.** All the answer choices could make sense in the context of the sentence, so it is necessary to use word structure to find the definition. The root *juven* means young and the prefix *re–* means again, so *rejuvenate* means to be made young again. The answer choice with the most similar meaning is *invigorated*, which means to give something energy.

CHAPTER SIX

Language: Grammar and Sentence Structure

The Language subtest of the English-Language Arts section of the CHSPE will test your understanding of the basic rules of grammar, mechanics, and expression. You will be asked to identify and correct errors in capitalization, punctuation, and usage. To do so correctly, you must know the basic rules of grammar, mechanics, and sentence structure. There are forty-eight multiple-choice questions and one writing task (essay).

Parts of Speech

The **PARTS OF SPEECH** are the building blocks of sentences, paragraphs, and entire texts. Grammarians have typically defined eight parts of speech—nouns, pronouns, verbs, adverbs, adjectives, conjunctions, prepositions, and interjections—all of which play unique roles in the context of a sentence. Thus, a fundamental understanding of the parts of speech is necessary for comprehending basic sentence construction.

Though some words fall easily into one category or another, many words can function as different parts of speech based on their usage within a sentence.

NOUNS and PRONOUNS

NOUNS are the words that describe people, places, things, and ideas. Most often, nouns fill the position of subject or object within a sentence. Nouns have several subcategories: common nouns (*chair, car, house*), proper nouns (*Julie, David*), noncountable nouns (*money, water*), and countable nouns (*dollars, cubes*), among others. There is much crossover among these subcategories (for example, *chair* is common and countable), and other subcategories do exist.

PRONOUNS replace nouns in a sentence or paragraph, allowing a writer to achieve a smooth flow throughout a text by avoiding unnecessary repetition. While there are countless nouns in the English language, there are only a few types of pronouns. The ones important for the CHSPE follow:

PERSONAL PRONOUNS act as subjects or objects in a sentence.

> She received a letter; I gave the letter to her.

POSSESSIVE PRONOUNS indicate possession.

> The apartment is hers, but the furniture is mine.

REFLEXIVE or INTENSIVE PRONOUNS intensify a noun or reflect back on a noun.

> I made the dessert myself.

INDEFINITE PRONOUNS simply replace nouns to avoid unnecessary repetition.

> Several came to the party to see both.

Table 6.1. Personal, Possessive, and Reflexive Pronouns

CASE	FIRST PERSON		SECOND PERSON		THIRD PERSON	
	Singular	Plural	Singular	Plural	Singular	Plural
Subject	I	we	you	you (all)	he, she, it	they
Object	me	us	you	you (all)	him, her, it	them
Possessive	mine	ours	yours	yours	his, hers, its	theirs
Reflexive/ intensive	myself	ourselves	yourself	yourselves	himself, herself, itself	themselves

EXAMPLES

1. What purpose do nouns usually serve in a sentence?
   A) They indicate possession.
   B) They act as subject or object.
   C) They intensify other nouns.
   D) They clarify when an action occurs.

2. Which pronoun best completes the sentence?
   _____ baked the cookies ourselves and ate most of them.
   A) She
   B) Her
   C) I
   D) We

VERBS

VERBS express action (*run, jump, play*) or state of being (*is, seems*). Verbs that describe action are ACTION VERBS, and those that describe being are LINKING VERBS.

> ACTION: My brother <u>plays</u> tennis.
> LINKING: He <u>is</u> the best player on the team.

Verbs are conjugated to indicate PERSON, which refers to the point of view of the sentence. First person is the speaker (*I, we*); second person is the person being addressed (*you*); and third person is outside the conversation (*they, them*). Verbs are also conjugated to match the NUMBER (singular or plural) of their subject. HELPING VERBS (*to be, to have, to do*) are used to conjugate verbs. An unconjugated verb is called an INFINITIVE and includes the word *to* in front (*to be, to break*).

PARTICIPLES are verb forms lacking number and person. The PAST PARTICIPLE is usually formed by adding the suffix *–ed* to the verb stem (*type* becomes *typed*; *drop* becomes *dropped*). The PRESENT PARTICIPLE is always formed by adding the suffix *–ing* to the verb stem (*typing, dropping*). Participles are used in verb conjugation to indicate the state of an action (*she is going; we had waited*).

Participles also act in *participial phrases* that act as descriptors in sentences:

> <u>Seated</u> politely, Ron listened to his friend's boring story.
> Maya petted the <u>sleeping</u> cat.

When a present participle acts as a noun, it is called a GERUND. In the following sentence, *running* is a noun and serving as the subject of the sentence:

> <u>Running</u> is my favorite form of exercise.

A common error in sentence structure is the *dangling participle*: when a participial phrase is disconnected from the word or phrase it modifies.

> INCORRECT: <u>Discussing the state of the nation</u>, I listened to the president's speech.

Here, the president, not the narrator, is discussing the state of the nation; the narrator is simply *listening*. However, the participial phrase "Discussing the state of the nation" is disconnected from the word it modifies, *president*. Thus it is *dangling* in the sentence—a dangling participle.

To fix a dangling particle, rearrange the sentence so that the modifying phrase is next to the word it modifies.

> CORRECT: I listened to the president's speech
> <u>discussing the state of the nation</u>.

Table 6.2. Verb Conjugation (Present Tense)

Person	Singular	Plural
First person	I give	we give
Second person	you give	you (all) give
Third person	he/she/it/ gives	they give

Verbs are also conjugated to indicate TENSE, or when the action has happened. Actions can happen in the past, present, or future. Tense also describes over how long a period the action took place:

► **SIMPLE** verbs describe something that happened once or general truths.

► **CONTINUOUS** verbs describe an ongoing action.

► **PERFECT** verbs describe repeated actions or actions that started in the past and have been completed.

► **PERFECT CONTINUOUS** verbs describe actions that started in the past and are continuing.

Table 6.3. Verb Tenses

Tense	Past	Present	Future
Simple	I gave her a gift yesterday.	I give her a gift every day.	I will give her a gift on her birthday.
Continuous	I was giving her a gift when you got here.	I am giving her a gift; come in!	I will be giving her a gift at dinner.
Perfect	I had given her a gift before you got there.	I have given her a gift already.	I will have given her a gift by midnight.
Perfect continuous	Her friends had been giving her gifts all night when I arrived.	I have been giving her gifts every year for nine years.	I will have been giving her gifts on holidays for ten years next year.

Verbs that follow the standard rules of conjugation are called **REGULAR** verbs. **IRREGULAR** verbs do not follow these rules, and their conjugations must be memorized. Some examples of irregular verbs are given in Table 6.4.

Table 6.4. Irregular Verbs

Present	Past	Has/Have/Had
am	was	been
do	did	done
see	saw	seen
write	wrote	written

Present	Past	Has/Have/Had
break	broke	broken
grow	grew	grown
speak	spoke	spoken
begin	began	begun
run	ran	run
buy	bought	bought

TRANSITIVE VERBS take a **DIRECT OBJECT**, which receives the action of the verb. Intransitive verbs have no object. The person or thing that receives the direct object is the **INDIRECT OBJECT**.

> **TRANSITIVE**: Alex gave the ball to his brother.
> (The *ball* is the direct object; *his* brother is the indirect object.)
> **INTRANSITIVE**: She jumped over the fence.

EXAMPLES

3. Which verb phrase best completes the sentence?

   By this time tomorrow, we _____ in New York.

   A) will have arrived

   B) have arrived

   C) arrive

   D) was arriving

4. Identify the direct object in the following sentence:

   My friends brought me a package of souvenirs from their trip to Spain.

   A) friends

   B) me

   C) package

   D) trip

ADJECTIVES and ADVERBS

ADJECTIVES modify or describe nouns and pronouns. In English, adjectives are usually placed before the word being modified, although they can also appear after a linking verb such as *is* or *smells*.

> The beautiful blue jade necklace will go perfectly with my dress.
> I think that lasagna smells delicious.

When multiple adjectives are used, they should be listed in the following order:

1. Determiners: articles (*a, an,* and *the*), possessive adjectives (e.g., *my, her*), and descriptors of quantity (e.g., *three, several*)
2. Opinions: modifiers that imply a value (e.g., *beautiful, perfect, ugly*)
3. Size: descriptions of size (e.g., *small, massive*)
4. Age: descriptions of age (e.g., *young, five-year-old*)
5. Shape: descriptions of appearance or character (e.g., *smooth, loud*)
6. Color: descriptions of color (e.g., *blue, dark*)
7. Origin: modifiers that describe where something came from (e.g., *American, homemade*)
8. Material: modifiers that describe what something is made from (e.g., *cotton, metallic*)
9. Purpose: adjectives that function as part of the noun to describe its purpose (e.g., sewing *machine,* rocking *chair*)

ADVERBS, which are often formed by adding the suffix *–ly*, modify any word or set of words that is not a noun or pronoun. They can modify verbs, adjectives, other adverbs, phrases, or clauses.

> He quickly ran to the house next door. (*Quickly* modifies the verb *ran.*)
> Her very effective speech earned her a promotion. (*Very* modifies the adjective *effective.*)
> Finally, the table was set and dinner was ready. (*Finally* modifies the clause *the table was set and dinner was ready.*)

DID YOU KNOW?
Adjectives answer the questions *what kind, how many,* or *which one?*
Adverbs answer the questions *how, when, where, why,* or *to what extent?*

COMPARATIVE adjectives and adverbs compare two items. For most one- or two-syllable words, the suffix *–er* is added to make it comparative; the word may be followed by *than.*

SUPERLATIVE adjectives and adverbs compare three or more items. Most one- or two-syllable words are made superlative by adding a suffix, *–est.*

> Comparative: My brother is taller than my sister.
> Superlative: My brother is the tallest of my five siblings.

Longer adjectives and adverbs must be preceded by *more* to form the comparative and *most* to form the superlative.

> Comparative: My bed at home is more comfortable than the one at the hotel.
> Superlative: The bed in your guestroom is the most comfortable bed I've ever slept in!

Some adjectives and adverbs form irregular comparatives and superlatives (see Table 6.5.).

> Comparative: The weather is bad today, but it was <u>worse</u> yesterday.
> Superlative: The <u>worst</u> day this week was Monday, when it rained.

Table 6.5. Irregular Comparative and Superlative Adjectives and Adverbs

ADJECTIVE/ADVERB	COMPARATIVE	SUPERLATIVE
much	more	most
bad	worse	worst
good	better	best
little	less	least
far	further/farther	furthest/farthest

EXAMPLES

5. Which of the following sentences is CORRECTLY constructed?

A) Between my mom and dad, my father is the oldest.

B) I ran less than usual today.

C) Henry's cat is more fatter than mine.

D) After taking medicine, she felt worser.

6. Which is the adverb in the following sentence?

He carelessly sped around the flashing yellow light.

A) flashing

B) yellow

C) around

D) carelessly

CONJUNCTIONS

CONJUNCTIONS join words into phrases, clauses, and sentences. The *coordinating conjunctions* (FANBOYS) join two independent clauses: **F**or, **A**nd, **N**or, **B**ut, **O**r, **Y**et, **S**o.

> Marta went to the pool, <u>and</u> Alex decided to go shopping.
> Aisha didn't want to eat tacos for dinner, <u>so</u> she picked up a pizza
> on her way home.

Subordinating conjunctions join dependent clauses to the independent clauses to which they are related.

> We chose that restaurant <u>because</u> Juan loves pizza.

Table 6.6. Subordinating Conjunctions	
Time	after, as, as long as, as soon as, before, since, until, when, whenever, while
Manner	as, as if, as though
Cause	because
Condition	although, as long as, even if, even though, if, provided that, though, unless, while
Purpose	in order that, so that, that
Comparison	as, than

EXAMPLES

7. The following sentence contains an error. How should it be rewritten?

   He liked to cook and baking was his specialty.

   A) He liked to cook, and baking was his specialty.

   B) He liked to cook so baking was his specialty.

   C) He liked to cook; and baking was his specialty.

   D) He liked to cook, baking was his specialty.

8. Identify the underlined part of speech in the following sentence:

   Anne and Peter drank their coffee languidly <u>while</u> they read the paper.

   A) subordinating conjunction

   B) coordinating conjunction

   C) irregular verb

   D) adverb

PREPOSITIONS

PREPOSITIONS set up relationships in time (*after the party*) or space (*under the cushions*) within a sentence. A preposition will always function as part of a prepositional phrase—the preposition along with the object of the preposition.

Table 6.7. Common Prepositions			
PREPOSITIONS			
about	by	off	toward
among	despite	on	under
around	down	onto	underneath
at	during	out	until
before	except	outside	up

PREPOSITIONS			
behind	for	over	upon
below	from	past	with
beneath	in	since	within
beside	into	through	
between	near	till	
beyond	of	to	

COMPOUND PREPOSITIONS			
according to	because of	in place of	on account of
as of	by means of	in respect to	out of
as well as	in addition to	in spite of	prior to
aside from	in front of	instead of	with regard to

EXAMPLE

9. Identify the prepositional phrase in the following sentence.

   John and Carol must drive through the tunnel, but Carol is claustrophobic.

   A) must drive

   B) through the tunnel

   C) drive through

   D) but Carol is

INTERJECTIONS

INTERJECTIONS have no grammatical attachment to the sentence itself other than to add expressions of emotion. These parts of speech may be punctuated with commas or exclamation points and may fall anywhere within the sentence.

Ouch! He stepped on my toe.

EXAMPLE

10. Identify the interjection in the following sentence.

    "Come here! Look! Our team won the Super Bowl! Yay!"

    A) Come here!

    B) Our team won

    C) Look!

    D) Yay!

Constructing Sentences
PHRASES

A **PHRASE** is a group of words that communicates a partial idea and lacks either a subject or a predicate. Several phrases may be strung together, one after another, to add detail and interest to a sentence.

Phrases are categorized based on the main word in the phrase. A **PREPOSITIONAL PHRASE** begins with a preposition and ends with an object of the preposition; a **VERB PHRASE** is composed of the main verb along with its helping verbs; and a **NOUN PHRASE** consists of a noun and its modifiers.

> **PREPOSITIONAL PHRASE:** The dog is hiding <u>under the porch</u>.
> **VERB PHRASE:** The chef <u>wanted to cook</u> a different dish.
> **NOUN PHRASE:** <u>The big, red barn</u> rests beside <u>the vacant chicken house</u>.

An **APPOSITIVE PHRASE** is a particular type of noun phrase that renames the word or group of words that precedes it. Appositive phrases usually follow the noun they describe and are set apart by commas.

> **APPOSITIVE PHRASE:** My dad, <u>a clock maker</u>, loved antiques.

VERBAL PHRASES begin with a word that would normally act as a verb but is instead filling another role within the sentence. These phrases can act as nouns, adjectives, or adverbs.

> **NOUN:** <u>To become a doctor</u> had always been her goal.
> **ADJECTIVE:** <u>Enjoying the stars that filled the sky</u>, Ben lingered outside for quite a while.

EXAMPLE

11. Identify the type of phrase underlined in the following sentence:

<u>Dodging traffic,</u> Rachel drove to work on back roads.

A) prepositional phrase

B) noun phrase

C) verb phrase

D) verbal phrase

CLAUSES and TYPES of SENTENCES

CLAUSES contain both a subject and a predicate. They can be either independent or dependent. An **INDEPENDENT** (or main) **CLAUSE** can stand alone as its own sentence:

> The dog ate her homework.

Dependent (or subordinate) clauses cannot stand alone as their own sentences. They start with a subordinating conjunction, relative pronoun, or relative adjective, which will make them sound incomplete:

> <u>Because</u> the dog ate her homework

Table 6.8. Words That Begin Dependent Clauses	
SUBORDINATING CONJUNCTIONS	RELATIVE PRONOUNS AND ADJECTIVES
after, before, once, since, until, when, whenever, while, as, because, in order that, so, so that, that, if, even if, provided that, unless, although, even though, though, whereas, where, wherever, than, whether	who, whoever, whom, whomever, whose, which, that, when, where, why, how

Sentences can be classified based on the number and type of clauses they contain. A SIMPLE SENTENCE will have only one independent clause and no dependent clauses. The sentence may contain phrases, complements, and modifiers, but it will comprise only one independent clause, one complete idea.

> The cat ran under the porch.

A COMPOUND SENTENCE has two or more independent clauses and no dependent clauses.

> The cat ran under the porch, and the dog ran after him.

A COMPLEX SENTENCE has only one independent clause and one or more dependent clauses.

> The cat, who is scared of the dog, ran under the porch.

A COMPOUND-COMPLEX SENTENCE has two or more independent clauses and one or more dependent clauses.

> The cat, who is scared of the dog, ran under the porch, and the dog ran after him.

Table 6.9. Sentence Structure and Clauses		
SENTENCE STRUCTURE	INDEPENDENT CLAUSES	DEPENDENT CLAUSES
Simple	1	0
Compound	2 +	0
Complex	1	1 +
Compound-complex	2 +	1 +

12. Which of the following is a compound sentence?

A) The turtle swam slowly around the pond.

B) Alligators generally lie still, but they can move with lightning speed.

C) Mice are most likely to come out at night after other animals have gone to sleep.

D) Squirrels, to prepare for winter, gather and hide seeds and nuts underground.

PUNCTUATION

Terminal punctuation marks are used to end sentences. The **PERIOD** (.) ends declarative (statement) and imperative (command) sentences. The **QUESTION MARK** (?) terminates interrogative sentences (questions). Lastly, **EXCLAMATION POINTS** end exclamatory sentences, in which the writer or speaker is exhibiting intense emotion or energy.

> Sarah and I are attending a concert.
> How many people are attending the concert?
> What a great show that was!

The colon and the semicolon, though often confused, each have a unique set of rules for their use. While both punctuation marks are used to join clauses, the construction of the clauses and the relationship between them is different. The **SEMICOLON** (;) is used to join two independent clauses (IC; IC) that are closely related.

> I need to buy a new car soon; my old car broke down last month.

The **COLON** (:) is used to introduce a list, definition, or clarification. The clause preceding the colon has to be independent, but what follows the colon can be an independent clause, a dependent clause, or a phrase.

> The buffet offers three choices: ham, turkey, or roast beef.
> He decided to drive instead of taking the train: he didn't think the train would arrive in time.

COMMAS show pauses in the text or set information apart from the main text. There are lots of rules for comma usage, so only the most common are summarized below.

1. Commas separate two independent clauses along with a coordinating conjunction.
   George ordered the steak, <u>but</u> Bruce preferred the ham.

2. Commas separate coordinate adjectives.
   She made herself a big bowl of <u>cold, delicious</u> ice cream.

3. Commas separate items in a series.
   The list of groceries included <u>cream, coffee, donuts, and tea.</u>

4. Commas separate introductory words and phrases from the rest of the sentence.
   <u>For example</u>, we have thirty students who demand a change.

5. Commas set off non-essential information and appositives.
   Estelle, <u>our newly elected chairperson</u>, will be in attendance.

6. Commas set off the day and month of a date within a text.
   I was born on February <u>16, 1988</u>.

7. Commas set up numbers in a text of more than four digits.
   We expect <u>25,000</u> visitors to the new museum.

8. Commas set off the names of cities from their states, territories, or provinces.
   She lives in <u>Houston, Texas</u>.

QUOTATION MARKS have a number of different purposes. They enclose titles of short, or relatively short, literary works such as short stories, chapters, and poems. (The titles of longer works, like novels and anthologies, are italicized.) Additionally, quotation marks are used to enclose direct quotations within the text of a document where the quotation is integrated into the text. Writers also use quotation marks to set off dialogue.

> We will be reading the poem "Bright Star" in class today.
> The poem opens with the line "Bright star, would I were steadfast as thou art."

APOSTROPHES, sometimes referred to as single quotation marks, have several different purposes.

1. They show possession.
   boy's watch, Ronald and Maria's house

2. They replace missing letters, numerals, and signs.
   do not = don't, 1989 = '89

3. They form plurals of letters, numerals, and signs.
   A's, 10's

Less commonly used punctuation marks include:

▶ EN DASH (–): indicates a range

▶ EM DASH (—): shows an abrupt break in a sentence and emphasizes the words within the em dashes

▶ PARENTHESES ( ): enclose nonessential information

▶ BRACKETS [ ]: enclose added words to a quotation and add insignificant information within parentheses

▶ SLASH (/): separates lines of poetry within a text or indicates interchangeable terminology

▶ ELLIPSES (…): indicate that information has been removed from a quotation or create a reflective pause

13. Which sentence includes an improperly placed comma?
    A) Ella, Cassie, and Cameron drove to South Carolina together.
    B) Trying to impress his friends, Carl ended up totaling his car.
    C) Ice cream is my favorite food, it is so cold and creamy.
    D) Mowing the lawn, Navid discovered a family of baby rabbits.

14. The following sentence contains an error. How should it be rewritten?

    Oak trees—with proper care—can grow taller than thirty feet; providing shade for people, shelter for animals, and perches for birds.
    A) replace the em dashes with commas
    B) remove the comma after *people*
    C) insert an apostrophe at the end of *animals*
    D) replace the semicolon with a comma

Capitalization

CAPITALIZATION is writing the first letter of a word in uppercase and the remaining letters in lowercase. Capitalization is used in three main contexts. The first, and most common, is in the first word after a period or the first word of a text. For example, the first word in each sentence of this paragraph is capitalized.

The second most common usage of capitalization is for proper nouns or adjectives derived from proper nouns. For instance, **F**rance—as the name of a country—is capitalized. Similarly, **F**rench, the adjective derived from the proper noun *France*, is also capitalized. There is an exception to this rule: when the adjective has taken on a meaning independent of the original proper noun. For example, the term *french fries* is not capitalized.

The third usage of capitalization is in a title or honorific that appears before a name: "**P**resident George Washington never lived in the capital." If, however, that same title is used *instead of* the name, or if the name and title are separated by a comma, it remains lowercase. For example, "The first **p**resident, George Washington, never lived in the capital" or "The **p**resident did not originally live in the capital."

EXAMPLE

15. Which sentence CORRECTLY uses capitalization?
    A) Robert and Kelly raced across the River in their small boats.
    B) ducks flying in a V-formation cross the Midwest in the fall.
    C) The chairwoman of the board, Keisha Johnson, will lead today's meeting.
    D) The Senators from Virginia and Louisiana strongly favor the bill.

Common Language Errors
SUBJECT-VERB AGREEMENT

Verbs must agree in number with their subjects. Common rules for subject-verb agreement are given below.

1. Single subjects agree with single verbs; plural subjects agree with plural verbs.
   The <u>girl walks</u> her dog.
   The <u>girls walk</u> their dogs.

2. Ignore words between the subject and the verb: agreement must exist between the subject and verb.
   The new <u>library</u> ~~with its many books and rooms~~ <u>fills</u> a long-felt need.

3. Compound subjects joined by *and* typically take a plural verb unless considered one item.
   <u>Correctness and precision are required</u> for all good writing.
   <u>Macaroni and cheese makes</u> a great snack for children.

4. The linking verbs agree with the subject and not the subject complement (predicate nominative).
   My <u>favorite</u> is strawberries and apples.
   My <u>favorites are</u> strawberries and apples.

5. When a relative pronoun (*who, whom, which, that*) is used as the subject of the clause, the verb will agree with the antecedent of the relative pronoun.
   This is the <u>student who is receiving</u> an award.
   These are the <u>students who are receiving</u> awards.

6. All single, indefinite pronouns agree with single verbs.
   <u>Neither</u> of the students <u>is</u> happy about the play.
   <u>Each</u> of the many cars <u>is</u> on the grass.
   Every <u>one</u> of the administrators <u>speaks</u> highly of Trevor.

EXAMPLE

16. Which sentence in the following list is CORRECT in its subject and verb agreement?

A) My sister and my best friend lives in Chicago.

B) My parents or my brother is going to pick me up from the airport.

C) Neither of the students refuse to take the exam.

D) The team were playing a great game until the rain started.

PRONOUN-ANTECEDENT AGREEMENT

Similarly, pronouns must agree with their antecedents (the words they replaced) in number; however, some pronouns also require gender agreement (*him, her*). **PRONOUN-ANTECEDENT AGREEMENT** rules can be found below:

1. Antecedents joined by *and* typically require a plural pronoun.
   The <u>children and their dogs</u> enjoyed <u>their</u> day at the beach.
   If the two nouns refer to the same person, a singular pronoun is preferable.
   My <u>best friend and confidant</u> still lives in <u>her</u> log cabin.

2. For compound antecedents joined by *or*, the pronoun agrees with the nearer or nearest antecedent.
   Either the resident mice <u>or the manager's cat</u> gets <u>itself</u> a meal of good leftovers.

3. When indefinite pronouns function in a sentence, the pronoun must agree with the number of the indefinite pronoun.
   <u>Neither</u> student finished <u>his or her</u> assignment.
   <u>Both</u> students finished <u>their</u> assignments.

4. When collective nouns function as antecedents, the pronoun choice will be singular or plural depending on the function of the collective.
   The <u>audience</u> was cheering as <u>it</u> rose to <u>its</u> feet in unison.
   Our <u>family</u> are spending <u>their</u> vacations in Maine, Hawaii, and Rome.

5. When *each* and *every* precede the antecedent, the pronoun agreement will be singular.
   <u>Each and every man, woman, and child</u> brings unique qualities to <u>his or her</u> family.
   <u>Every creative writer, technical writer, and research writer</u> is attending <u>his or her</u> assigned lecture.

How would you complete the following sentence? "Every boy and girl should check _____ homework before turning it in." Many people would use the pronoun *their*. But since the antecedent is "every boy and girl," technically, the correct answer would be *his or her*. Using *they* or *their* in similar situations is increasingly accepted in formal speech, however. It is unlikely that you will see questions like this appear on the CHSPE, but if you do, it is safest to use the technically correct response.

EXAMPLE

17. Which sentence in the following list is CORRECT in its pronoun and antecedent agreement?

A) The grandchildren and their cousins enjoyed their day at the park.

B) Most of the grass has lost their deep color.

C) The jury was relieved as their commitment came to a close.

D) Every boy and girl must learn to behave themselves in school.

18. Which sentence in the following list is CORRECT in its pronoun and antecedent agreement?

A) Either my brother or my dad will bring their van to pick us up.

B) The university is having their tenth fundraiser tonight.

C) Alyssa and Jacqueline bought herself a big lunch today.

D) Each dog, cat, and rabbit has its own bowl and blanket.

VERB-TENSE AGREEMENT

In any passage, verb tense should be consistent and make sense in context of other verbs, adverbs, and general meaning. To succeed on verb tense questions, pay attention to the context of the entire passage.

> **INCORRECT:** Deborah <u>was speaking</u> with her colleague when her boss <u>will appear</u>, demanding a meeting.

In this sentence, the subject, *Deborah*, is acting in an ongoing event in the past, so the verb describing this action, *speaking*, is conjugated in the continuous past tense. In the context of the sentence, the appearance of her boss is a completed event that happens during the conversation. The verb describing the boss' appearance should be conjugated in the simple past tense. The corrected sentence reads as follows:

> **CORRECT:** Deborah <u>was speaking</u> with her colleague when her boss <u>appeared</u>, demanding a meeting.

One clue to the correct conjugation of the verb *appeared* is the adverb *when*, which implies that a completed event occurred to interrupt the ongoing event (in this case, Deborah's talk with her colleague).

Pay attention to how verbs are conjugated in the beginning of a sentence or passage, and look for clues to spot any errors in verb tense agreement.

EXAMPLE

19. The following sentence contains an error. How should it be rewritten?

Veronica attended cooking classes, and she goes to yoga classes too.

A) Veronica attends cooking classes, and she went to yoga classes too.

B) Veronica attended cooking classes, and she went to yoga classes too.

C) Veronica attended cooking classes; she goes to yoga classes too.

D) Veronica attended cooking classes. She goes to yoga classes too.

PARALLELISM

Errors in **PARALLELISM** prevent a writer from creating a smooth flow, or coherence, from word to word and sentence to sentence. Writers should create parallel structure in words, phrases, and clauses wherever two or more similar and equally important ideas exist next to each other in a sentence. Errors in parallel structure frequently appear in sentences with verb phrases, prepositional phrases, and correlative conjunctions like *either…or, neither…nor,* and *not only…but also.*

> **INCORRECT**: Adia could <u>program</u> computers, <u>repair</u> cars, and <u>knew how to make</u> croissants.
>
> **CORRECT**: Adia could <u>program</u> computers, <u>repair</u> cars, and <u>bake</u> croissants.

In the corrected sentence, the verbs are aligned in parallel structure. Furthermore, the first sentence contains a verb error. By omitting "program computers, repair cars," the sentence reads "Adia could…knew how to make croissants." Rewriting the sentence in parallel structure corrects the verb error.

In sentences with multiple prepositional phrases in a parallel series, the preposition must be repeated unless the same preposition begins each phrase.

> **INCORRECT**: You can park your car <u>in</u> the garage, the carport, or <u>on</u> the street.
>
> **CORRECT**: You can park your car <u>in</u> the garage, <u>in</u> the carport, or <u>on</u> the street.

EXAMPLE

20. The following sentence contains an error. How should it be rewritten?

Shelly achieved more at nursing school because she was going to bed earlier, eating healthy food, and she started to stay home and study more.

A) Shelly achieved more at nursing school. She was going to bed earlier, eating healthy food, and she started to stay home and study more.

B) Shelly achieved more at nursing school because she was going to bed earlier, eating healthy food, and studying more.

C) Shelly achieved more at nursing school; she was going to bed earlier, eating healthy food, and she started to stay home and study more.

D) Shelly achieved more at nursing school; she was going to bed earlier, and she started to eat healthy food and studying more.

SENTENCE CONSTRUCTION ERRORS

SENTENCE ERRORS fall into three categories: fragments, comma splices (comma fault), and fused sentences (run-on). A **FRAGMENT** occurs when a group of words is not a complete sentence but is punctuated like one. The fragment might be a phrase or a dependent clause. To fix a fragment, an independent clause needs to be created.

> **FRAGMENT (PHRASE):** The girl in my class who asks a lot of questions.
> **CORRECT:** The girl in my class who asks a lot of questions sits in the back row.
> **FRAGMENT (DEPENDENT CLAUSE):** Because of the big storm we had last weekend.
> **CORRECT:** Because of the big storm we had last weekend,
> the park will be closed.

A **COMMA SPLICE** (comma fault) occurs when two independent clauses are joined together in a paragraph with only a comma to "splice" them together. **FUSED** (run-on) sentences occur when two independent clauses are joined with no punctuation whatsoever. To fix a comma splice or fused sentence, add the correct punctuation and/or conjunction.

> **COMMA SPLICE:** My family eats turkey at Thanksgiving, we
> eat ham at Christmas.
> **CORRECT:** My family eats turkey at Thanksgiving, and we
> eat ham at Christmas.
> **CORRECT:** My family eats turkey at Thanksgiving. We eat ham at Christmas.
> **CORRECT:** My family eats turkey at Thanksgiving; we eat ham at Christmas.
> **FUSED SENTENCE:** I bought a chocolate pie from the bakery it was delicious.
> **CORRECT:** I bought a chocolate pie from the bakery. It was delicious.
> **CORRECT:** I bought a chocolate pie from the bakery, and it was delicious.
> **CORRECT:** I bought a chocolate pie from the bakery; it was delicious.

EXAMPLE

21. Which of the following is CORRECTLY punctuated?
    A) Since she went to the store.
    B) The football game ended in a tie, the underdog caught up in the fourth quarter.
    C) The mall is closing early today so we'll have to go shopping tomorrow.
    D) When the players dropped their gloves, a fight broke out on the ice hockey rink floor.

EASILY CONFUSED WORDS

A, AN: *a* precedes words beginning with consonants or consonant sounds; *an* precedes words beginning with vowels or vowel sounds.

AFFECT, EFFECT: *affect* is most often a verb; *effect* is usually a noun. (*The experience affected me significantly* OR *The experience had a significant effect on me.*)

AMONG, AMONGST, BETWEEN: *among* is used for a group of more than two people or items; *amongst* is an uncommon, archaic term; *between* distinguishes two people or items.

AMOUNT, NUMBER: *amount* is used for noncountable sums; *number* is used with countable nouns.

CITE, SITE: the verb *cite* credits an author of a quotation, paraphrase, or summary; the noun *site* is a location.

EVERY DAY, EVERYDAY: *every day* is an indefinite adjective modifying a noun; *everyday* is a one-word adjective implying frequent occurrence. (*Our visit to the Minnesota State Fair is an everyday activity during August.*)

FEWER, LESS: *fewer* is used with a countable noun; *less* is used with a noncountable noun. (*Fewer parents are experiencing stress since the new teacher was hired; parents are experiencing less stress since the new teacher was hired.*)

GOOD, WELL: good is always the adjective; *well* is always the adverb except in cases of health. (*He writes well. She felt well after the surgery.*)

IMPLIED, INFERRED: *implied* is something a speaker does; *inferred* is something the listener does after assessing the speaker's message. (*The speaker implied something mysterious, but I inferred the wrong thing.*)

IRREGARDLESS, REGARDLESS: *irregardless* is nonstandard usage and should be avoided; *regardless* is the proper usage of the transitional statement.

ITS, IT'S: *its* is a possessive pronoun; *it's* is a contraction for *it is*.

PRINCIPAL, PRINCIPLE: as a noun, *principal* is an authority figure, often the head of a school; as an adjective, *principal* means *main*; the noun *principle* means idea or belief. (*The principal of the school spoke on the principal meaning of the main principles of the school.*)

QUOTE, QUOTATION: *quote* is a verb; *quotation* is a noun.

SHOULD OF, SHOULD HAVE: *should of* is improper usage—*of* is not a helping verb and therefore cannot complete the verb phrase; *should have* is the proper usage. (*He should have driven.*)

THAN, THEN: *than* sets up a comparison; *then* indicates a reference to a point in time. (*When I said that I liked the hat better than the gloves, my sister laughed; then she bought both for me.*)

THEIR, THERE, THEY'RE: *their* is the possessive case of the pronoun *they*. *There* is the demonstrative pronoun indicating location or place. *They're* is a contraction of the words *they are*.

TO LIE (TO RECLINE), TO LAY (TO PLACE): *to lie* is the intransitive verb meaning *to recline*; *to lay* is the transitive verb meaning *to place something*. (*I lie out in the sun; I lay my towel on the beach.*)

WHO, WHOM: *who* is the subject relative pronoun. (*My son, who is a good student, studies hard.*) Here, the son is carrying out the action of studying, so the pronoun is a subject pronoun (*who*). *Whom* is the object relative pronoun. (*My son, whom the other students admire, studies hard.*) Here, *son* is the object of the other students' admiration, so the pronoun standing in for him, *whom*, is an object pronoun.

YOUR, YOU'RE: *your* is the possessive case of the pronoun *you*. *You're* is a contraction of the words *you are*.

EXAMPLE

22. Which of the following sentences contains an error?

   A) I invited fewer people to my birthday party this year.

   B) The students asked the principle to postpone the meeting.

   C) My sister baked cookies and then asked me to help clean the kitchen.

   D) She paints well even though she has no formal training.

Answer Key

1. **B) is correct.** Nouns are people, places, things, or ideas; they usually act as the subject or object in a sentence.

2. **D) is correct.** The reflexive pronoun *ourselves* refers back to the subject of the sentence. Because it is in the first person plural, the subject should also be in the first person plural (*we*).

3. **A) is correct.** The phrase *By this time tomorrow* describes an action that will take place and be completed in the future, so the future perfect tense (*will have arrived*) should be used.

4. **C) is correct.** *Package* is the direct object of the verb *brought*.

5. **B) is correct.** The speaker is comparing today's run to the norm, not to any additional instances, so the comparative is acceptable here. Furthermore, the word *than* appears, a clue that the comparative is appropriate. *Less* is the irregular comparative form of *little*.

6. **D) is correct.** *Carelessly* is an adverb modifying *sped* and explaining *how* the driving occurred. The subject was not mindful as he drove; he raced through a yellow light when he should have exercised caution.

7. **A) is correct.** This sentence includes two independent clauses: "He liked to cook" and "baking was his specialty." They can be connected with a comma and coordinating conjunction (the

conjunction *and* is appropriate here). The sentence could also be written with a semicolon and no conjunction.

8. **A) is correct.** "While they read the paper" is a dependent clause; the subordinating conjunction *while* connects it to the independent clause "Anne and Peter drank their coffee languidly."

9. **B) is correct.** "Through the tunnel" is a prepositional phrase explaining the relationship between the subjects and the tunnel using the preposition *through* and the object *the tunnel*.

10. **D) is correct.** *Yay* is an expression of emotion and has no other grammatical purpose in the sentence.

11. **D) is correct.** The phrase is a verbal phrase modifying the noun *Rachel*. It begins with the word *dodging*, derived from the verb to *dodge*.

12. **B) is correct.** "Alligators...still" and "they...speed" are two independent clauses connected by a comma and the coordinating conjunction *but*.

13. **C) is correct.** "Ice cream... food" and "it...creamy" are two independent clauses. The writer should include a coordinating conjunction like *for* or separate the clauses with a semicolon.

14. **D) is correct.** "Providing shade..." is not an independent clause;

therefore it cannot be preceded by a semicolon.

15. **C) is correct.** *Keisha Johnson*, as a proper noun, should be capitalized, but "chairwoman of the board" should not be because it is separated from the name by a comma.

16. **B) is correct.** The verb agrees with the closest subject—in this case, the singular *brother*.

17. **A) is correct.** The plural antecedents *grandchildren* and *cousins* match the plural possessive pronoun *their*.

18. **D) is correct.** When *each* precedes the antecedent, the pronoun agreement is singular. The pronoun *its* therefore agrees with the antecedents *Each dog, cat, and rabbit*.

19. **B) is correct.** In this sentence, the verbs *attended* and *went* are both correctly conjugated in the simple past tense.

20. **B) is correct.** In this sentence, three related clauses are written in parallel structure using the participles *going*, *eating*, and *studying*.

21. **D) is correct.** This is a complete sentence that is punctuated properly with a comma between the dependent and independent clauses.

22. **B) is correct.** A principle is a belief; a principal is the head of a school.

CHAPTER SEVEN
The Essay

There is one writing task, or **ESSAY**, on the Language subtest of the English-Language Arts section of the CHSPE. You will be provided with a prompt and asked to take a position on it. To do well on the writing task, take a clear side on the issue put forth in the prompt. Support your perspective with strong arguments and specific examples. An effective essay is clearly organized and structured, displays strong vocabulary, and features complex sentences.

There are two common types of essays:

▶ an expository essay explains an issue without taking sides or promoting a perspective

▶ a persuasive essay argues in favor of or against an issue or perspective

For the CHSPE, you'll be writing a persuasive essay.

Writing a Thesis Statement

A **THESIS STATEMENT** articulates the main argument of the essay. No essay is complete without it: the structure and organization of the essay revolves around the thesis statement. The thesis statement is simply the writer's main idea or argument. It usually appears at the end of the introduction.

In a good thesis statement, the author states his or her idea or argument and why it is correct or true.

EXAMPLE

Take a position on the following topic in your essay. You can choose to write about either of the two viewpoints discussed in the prompt, or you may argue for a third point of view.

Many scientists argue that recent unusual weather patterns, such as powerful hurricanes and droughts, are due to climate change triggered by human activity. They argue that automobiles, oil and gas production, and manufacturing generate carbon emissions that artificially heat the atmosphere, resulting in extreme weather patterns. Others disagree. Some researchers and media pundits argue that climate change is natural, and that extreme weather has always been a feature of Earth's atmosphere.

Around the world more people than ever before are driving cars, and industrial production is at an all-time high: it is obvious that human activity is affecting the atmosphere and causing extreme weather events.

I believe that temperatures and storms are more extreme than ever because of the environmental impact of human activity; not only do scientists have overwhelming evidence that climate change is unnatural, but I can also personally remember when there were fewer storms and variations in temperature.

Society needs cars and manufacturing, but governments should restrict harmful emissions released into the atmosphere so we can slow down climate change and save lives.

Structuring the Essay

On the CHSPE, a strong essay will have an introduction, a body, and a conclusion. While there are many ways to organize an essay, on this exam it is most important that the essay is clearly structured. There is no need to get too complicated: this simple structure will do.

INTRODUCTIONS

DID YOU KNOW?

If you're not sure what to include in your introduction, start your essay with just the thesis statement. You can go back and complete the introduction once the rest of the essay is finished.

Some writers struggle with the introduction, but it is actually an opportunity to present your idea or argument. On the CHSPE, the introduction can be one paragraph that ends with the thesis statement. In the rest of the paragraph, the writer provides some context for his or her argument. This context might include counterarguments, a preview of specific examples to be discussed later on, acknowledgement of the complexities of the issue, or even a reference to personal experience. The writer can reexamine some of these issues in the conclusion.

EXAMPLE

In the example below, the writer has written an introduction that includes context for her argument: background information, a counterargument, and personal experience. As a result, the reader has a better idea of how complex the issue is and why the writer feels the way she does. The thesis statement appears at the end of the paragraph; as a result of the introduction as a whole, the thesis statement has more impact.

A century ago, there were barely any cars on the road. Oil had just been discovered in a few parts of the world. Industrial production existed but had not yet exploded with the introduction of the assembly line. Refineries and factories were not yet churning out the chemical emissions they are today. Certainly, hurricanes and droughts occurred, but the populations and infrastructure affected were far smaller. Now, scientists have evidence that human activity—like pollution from industry and cars—is affecting the atmosphere and making weather more extreme. In 2017, millions of people were affected by hurricanes and wildfires. It is true that some researchers disagree that human activity has caused these and other extreme weather events. But why take the risk? If we can limit destruction now and in the future, we should. Extreme weather events are a danger to people all around the world. Society needs cars and manufacturing, but governments should restrict harmful emissions released into the atmosphere so we can slow down climate change and save lives.

THE BODY PARAGRAPHS

Most writers find the body of the essay the easiest part to write. The body of the essay is simply several paragraphs, each beginning with a topic sentence. Each paragraph usually addresses an example that supports the argument made in the thesis statement or, in the case of an expository essay, explains the writer's reasoning. On the CHSPE, you may use specific examples or personal anecdotes, present problems and solutions, or compare and contrast ideas. You do not need to refer to any outside literature or documentation.

To strengthen the body of the essay, writers will maintain consistency in paragraphs, always beginning with a topic sentence, which introduces the main idea of each paragraph. Each paragraph deals with its own main topic, but writers should use transition words and phrases to link paragraphs with each other. A good essay maintains readability and flow.

EXAMPLE

This example body paragraph is related to the introduction provided above. It provides reasoning and historical evidence for the author's argument that human activity is impacting the earth and causing climate change.

Human industrial activity has been growing exponentially, putting more pollution into the atmosphere than ever. Over the past forty years, large countries like China and India have become industrialized and manufacture many of the world's products. As their populations become more prosperous, demand for automobiles also rises, putting more cars on the road—and exhaust in the air. While industrial development has benefited Asia and other areas, carbon emissions that cause climate change have multiplied. Meanwhile, previously industrialized countries in Europe and North America continue to produce carbon emissions. In the nineteenth century, only a few countries had industrial sectors; today, global industry strains the environment like never before. The past 150 years have seen unprecedented industrial growth. Even if the climate changes naturally over time, it cannot be denied that recent human activity has suddenly generated enormous amounts of carbon emissions that have impacted the atmosphere. Scientists say that the earth is warming as a result.

CONCLUSIONS

The conclusion does not need to be long. Its purpose is to wrap up the essay, reminding the reader why the topic and the writer's argument is important. It is an opportunity for the writer to reexamine the thesis statement and ideas in the introduction. It is a time to reinforce the argument, not just to repeat the introduction.

EXAMPLE

This example is taken from the same essay as the introduction and body paragraph above. It reinforces the writer's argument without simply repeating what she said in the introduction. The writer does address the topics she spoke about in the introduction (climate change and protecting people from extreme weather) but she does not simply rewrite the thesis: she calls for action.

No doubt, scientists, pundits, and politicians will continue to argue over the reasons for extreme weather. Meanwhile, Mother Nature will continue to wreak havoc on vulnerable areas regardless of what we think. Because we have proof that climate change is related to extreme weather and we know that extreme weather threatens people's lives, the time to act is now. We can take steps to mitigate pollution without lowering quality of life. Doing anything else is irresponsible—and for some, deadly.

Providing Supporting Evidence

As discussed above, a good essay should have specific evidence or examples that support the thesis statement. On the CHSPE, a specific example should be something related to the idea of the paragraph and the essay, not a new idea. A specific example can be from your general knowledge; you do not need to know about specific academic issues to do well on the essay. Remember, you are being tested on your reasoning and argumentative skills.

The following are some examples of general statements and specific statements that provide more detailed support:

GENERAL: Human industrial activity has been growing exponentially, putting more pollution into the atmosphere than ever.

SPECIFIC: Over the past forty years, large countries like China and India have become industrialized and manufacture many of the world's products. As their populations become more prosperous, demand for automobiles also rises, putting more cars on the road—and exhaust in the air.

SPECIFIC: Meanwhile, previously industrialized countries in Europe and North America continue to produce carbon emissions. In the nineteenth century, only a few countries had industrial sectors; today, global industry strains the environment like never before.

GENERAL: More people than ever are affected by extreme weather.

SPECIFIC: In 2017, several hurricanes affected the United States and the Caribbean. In Texas, Hurricane Harvey led to historic flooding in Houston and the Texas Coast. Millions of people were affected; thousands lost their homes, jobs, and livelihoods.

SPECIFIC: Hurricane Irma damaged the US Virgin Islands and neighboring Caribbean nations. Soon after, Hurricane Maria catastrophically devastated Puerto Rico. Months later, Puerto Ricans were still without power and basic necessities. It is still not clear how many have died due to the storm and related damage.

EXAMPLE

In the example below, the paragraph is structured with a topic sentence and specific supporting ideas. This paragraph supports the introduction in the example above.

More people than ever are affected by extreme weather. In 2017, several hurricanes affected the United States and the Caribbean. In Texas, Hurricane Harvey led to historic flooding in Houston and the Texas Coast. Millions of people were affected; thousands lost their homes, jobs, and livelihoods. Hurricane Irma damaged Florida, the US Virgin Islands, and neighboring Caribbean nations. Soon after, Hurricane Maria catastrophically devastated Puerto Rico. Months later, Puerto Ricans were still without power and basic necessities. It is still not clear how many have died due to the storm and related damage. In California, severe droughts led to exceptionally large wildfires that threatened Los Angeles and destroyed neighboring communities. Meanwhile, those same areas—Southern California, the Texas Coast, and Florida—continue to grow, putting more people at risk when the next hurricane or fire strikes.

Writing Well

Using transitions, complex sentences, and certain words can turn a good essay into a great one. Transitions, syntax, word choice, and tone all help clarify and amplify a writer's argument or point and improve the flow of an essay.

TRANSITIONS

An essay consists of several paragraphs. **TRANSITIONS** are words and phrases that help connect the paragraphs and ideas of the text. Most commonly, transitions would appear at the beginning of a paragraph, but writers should also use them throughout a text to connect ideas. Common transitions are words like *also, next, still, although, in addition to*, and *in other words*. A transition shows a relationship between ideas, so writers should pay close attention to the transition words and phrases they choose. Transitions may show connections or contrasts between words and ideas.

Table 7.1. Common Transitions	
TRANSITION TYPE	**EXAMPLES**
Addition	additionally, also, as well, further, furthermore, in addition, moreover
Cause and effect	as a result, because, consequently, due to, if/then, so, therefore, thus
Concluding	briefly, finally, in conclusion, in summary, thus, to conclude
Contrast	but, however, in contrast, on the other hand, nevertheless, on the contrary, yet
Examples	in other words, for example, for instance
Similarity	also, likewise, similarly
Time	after, before, currently, later, recently, subsequently, since, then, while

SYNTAX

SYNTAX refers to how words and phrases are arranged in writing or speech. Writing varied sentences is essential to capturing and keeping a reader's interest. A good essay features different types of sentences: simple, complex, compound, and compound-complex. Sentences need not always begin with the subject; they might start with a transition word or phrase, for instance. Variety is key.

Still, writers should keep in mind that the point of an essay is to get an idea across to the reader, so it is most important that writing be clear. They should not sacrifice clarity for the sake of flowery, overly wordy language or confusing syntax.

WORD CHOICE and TONE

Like syntax, word choice makes an impression on readers. The CHSPE does not test on specific vocabulary or require writers to use specific words on the writing sample. However, the essay is a good opportunity to use strong vocabulary pertaining to the prompt or issue under discussion. Writers should be careful, though, that they understand the words they are using. Writers should also avoid vague, imprecise, or generalizing language like *good, bad, a lot, a little, very, normal,* and so on.

EDITING, REVISING, and PROOFREADING

On the CHSPE, you have a limited amount of time to complete the essay. If there is time for editing or proofreading, writers should hunt for grammar, spelling, or punctuation mistakes that could change the meaning of the text or make it difficult to understand. These include sentence fragments, run-on sentences, subject-verb disagreement, and pronoun-antecedent disagreement.

CHAPTER EIGHT
Practice Test

Mathematics

Work the problem, and then choose the most correct answer.

1. Simplify: $(4.71 \times 10^3) - (2.98 \times 10^2)$

   A) 1.73×10

   B) 4.412×10^2

   C) 1.73×10^3

   D) 4.412×10^3

2. The average speed of cars on a highway (s) is inversely proportional to the number of cars on the road (n). If a car drives at 65 mph when there are 250 cars on the road, how fast will a car drive when there are 325 cars on the road?

   A) 50 mph

   B) 55 mph

   C) 60 mph

   D) 85 mph

3. Simplify: $\sqrt[3]{64} + \sqrt[3]{729}$

   A) 13

   B) 17

   C) 31

   D) 35

4. The coordinates of point A are (7,12) and the coordinates of point C are (-3,10). If C is the midpoint of $\overline{AB}$, what are the coordinates of point B?

   A) (2,11)

   B) (-13,8)

   C) (17,14)

   D) (-13,11)

5. Which statement about the following set is true?

   {60, 5, 18, 20, 37, 37, 11, 90, 72}

   A) The median and the mean are equal.

   B) The mean is less than the mode.

   C) The mode is greater than the median.

   D) The median is less than the mean.

6. Which inequality is represented by the following graph?

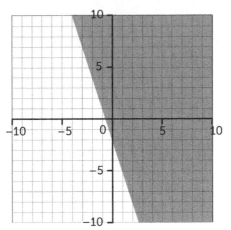

- **A)** $y \geq -3x - 2$
- **B)** $y \geq 3x - 2$
- **C)** $y > -3x - 2$
- **D)** $y \leq -3x - 2$

7. The line of best fit is calculated for a data set that tracks the number of miles that passenger cars traveled annually in the US from 1960 to 2010. In the model, $x = 0$ represents the year 1960, and y is the number of miles traveled in billions. If the line of best fit is $y = 0.0293x + 0.563$, approximately how many additional miles were traveled for every 5 years that passed?

- **A)** 0.0293 billion
- **B)** 0.1465 billion
- **C)** 0.563 billion
- **D)** 0.710 billion

8. If the length of a rectangle is increased by 40% and its width is decreased by 40%, what is the effect on the rectangle's area?

- **A)** The area is the same.
- **B)** It increases by 16%.
- **C)** It increases by 20%.
- **D)** It decreases by 16%.

9. Simplify: $(1.2 \times 10^{-3})(1.13 \times 10^{-4})$

- **A)** 1.356×10^{-7}
- **B)** 1.356×10^{-1}
- **C)** 1.356×10
- **D)** 1.356×10^{12}

10. In the figure below, there are six line segments that terminate at point O. If segment $\overline{DO}$ bisects $\angle AOF$ and segment $\overline{BO}$ bisects $\angle AOD$, what is the value of $\angle AOF$?

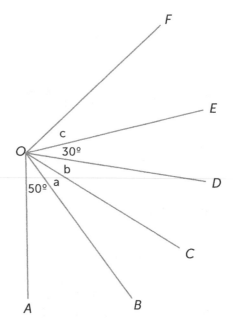

- **A)** 140°
- **B)** 160°
- **C)** 170°
- **D)** 200°

11. Which of the following has the greatest value?

- **A)** $-4(3)(-2)$
- **B)** $-16 - 17 + 31$
- **C)** $18 - 15 + 27$
- **D)** $-20 + 10 + 10$

12. Which of the following is a solution to the inequality $2x + y \leq -10$?

A) $(0,0)$

B) $(10,2)$

C) $(10,10)$

D) $(-10,-10)$

13. Two spheres are tangent to each other. One has a volume of 36π, and the other has a volume of 288π. What is the greatest distance between a point on one of the spheres and a point on the other sphere?

A) 6

B) 9

C) 18

D) 63

14. Which of the following is not a negative value?

A) $(-3)(-1)(2)(-1)$

B) $14 - 7 + (-7)$

C) $7 - 10 + (-8)$

D) $-5(-2)(-3)$

15. Which of the following could be the perimeter of a triangle with two sides that measure 13 and 5?

A) 24.5

B) 26.5

C) 36

D) 37

16. Convert 8 pounds, 8 ounces to kilograms to the nearest tenth of a kilogram.

A) 3.6 kilograms

B) 3.9 kilograms

C) 17.6 kilograms

D) 18.7 kilograms

17. Which of the following is equivalent to:

$54z^4 + 18z^3 + 3z + 3$?

A) $18z^4 + 6z^3 + z + 1$

B) $3z(18z^3 + 6z^2 + 1)$

C) $72z^7 + 3z$

D) $3(18z^4 + 6z^3 + z + 1)$

18. Which of the following is listed in order from least to greatest?

A) $-0.95, 0, \frac{2}{5}, 0.35, \frac{3}{4}$

B) $-1, -\frac{1}{10}, -0.11, \frac{5}{6}, 0.75$

C) $-\frac{3}{4}, -0.2, 0, \frac{2}{3}, 0.55$

D) $-1.1, -\frac{4}{5}, -0.13, 0.7, \frac{9}{11}$

19. The pie graph below shows how a state's government plans to spend its annual budget of \$3 billion. How much more money does the state plan to spend on infrastructure than education?

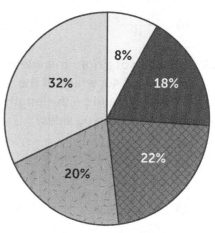

A) \$60,000,000

B) \$120,000,000

C) \$300,000,000

D) \$600,000,000

20. Simplify: $\left(\dfrac{4x^{-3}y^4z}{8x^{-5}y^3z^{-2}}\right)^2$

A) $\dfrac{x^4yz^3}{2}$

B) $\dfrac{x^4y^2z^6}{2}$

C) $\dfrac{x^4y^2z^6}{4}$

D) $\dfrac{x^4yz^3}{4}$

21. What is the axis of symmetry for the given parabola?

$y = -2(x + 3)^2 + 5$

A) $y = 3$

B) $x = -3$

C) $y = -3$

D) $x = 3$

22. Simplify: $\dfrac{3 + \sqrt{3}}{4 - \sqrt{3}}$

A) $\dfrac{13}{15}$

B) $\dfrac{15 + 7\sqrt{3}}{13}$

C) $\dfrac{15}{19}$

D) $\dfrac{15 + 7\sqrt{3}}{19}$

23. If one leg of a right triangle has a length of 40, which of the following could be the lengths of the two remaining sides?

A) 50 and 41

B) 9 and 41

C) 9 and 30

D) 50 and 63

24. The population of a town was 7,250 in 2014 and 7,375 in 2015. What was the percent increase from 2014 to 2015 to the nearest tenth of a percent?

A) 1.5%

B) 1.6%

C) 1.7%

D) 1.8%

25. Which of the following is a solution of the given equation?

$4(m + 4)^2 - 4m^2 + 20 = 276$

A) 3

B) 6

C) 12

D) 24

26. In the following graph of $f(x) = y$, for how many values of x does $|f(x)| = 1$?

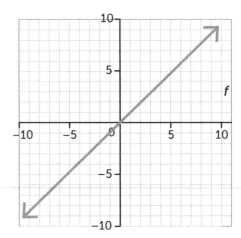

A) 0

B) 1

C) 2

D) ∞

27. If $y = 2x^2 + 12x - 3$ is written in the form $y = a(x - h)^2 + k$, what is the value of k?

A) -3

B) -15

C) -18

D) -21

28. Simplify: $\dfrac{7.2 \times 10^6}{1.6 \times 10^{-3}}$

A) 4.5×10^{-9}

B) 4.5×10^{-3}

C) 4.5×10^3

D) 4.5×10^9

29. 600 people between the ages of 15 and 45 were polled regarding their use of social media. 200 people from each age group were part of the study. The results are listed in the relative frequency table below.

	Hours Per Day Spent on Social Media			
AGE (YEARS)	LESS THAN 2 HOURS	2 TO 4 HOURS	MORE THAN 4 HOURS	TOTAL
15 – 24	0.15	0.40	0.45	1.0
25 – 34	0.52	0.28	0.20	1.0
35 – 45	0.85	0.10	0.05	1.0
Total	**0.51**	**0.26**	**0.23**	**1.0**

Which of the statements are true?

I.   Of people 25 to 34 years old, 20% spend more than 4 hours per day on social media.

II. Of the population of 15- to 45-year-olds, 26% spend 2 – 4 hours a day on social media.

III. Of people between the ages of 15 and 34, 67% spend 0 – 2 hours per day on social media.

IV. 5 people who reported using social media more than 4 hours per week were 35 to 45 years old.

A)   II only

B)   I and II

C)   I, II, and IV

D)   I, II, and III

Use the following graph for questions 30 and 31.

Number of Months with 3 or Fewer Than 3 Inches of Rain

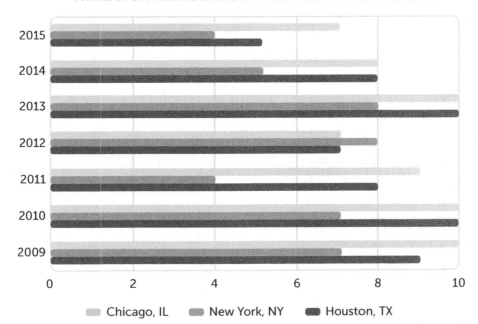

30. New York had the fewest months with less than 3 inches of rain in every year except:

A) 2012

B) 2013

C) 2014

D) 2015

31. From 2009 to 2015, what is the average number of months that Chicago had 3 or less inches of rain?

A) 6

B) 7

C) 8

D) 9

32. Simplify: $(3^2 \div 1^3) - (4 - 8^2) + 2^4$

A) −35

B) −4

C) 28

D) 85

33. A bag contains 6 blue, 8 silver, and 4 green marbles. Two marbles are drawn from the bag. What is the probability that the second marble drawn will be green if replacement is not allowed?

A) $\frac{2}{9}$

B) $\frac{4}{17}$

C) $\frac{11}{17}$

D) $\frac{7}{9}$

34. What is the solution set for the inequality $2x^2 - 4x - 6 < 0$?

A) $(-1, 3)$

B) $(-\infty, \infty)$

C) $\varnothing$

D) $(-\infty, -1) \cup (3, \infty)$

35. Which of the angles in the figure below are congruent?

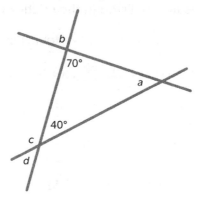

A) a and d

B) b and d

C) a and b

D) c and b

36. Which of the following is equivalent to $z^3(z + 2)^2 - 4z^3 + 2$?

A) 2

B) $z^5 + 4z^4 + 4z^3 + 2$

C) $z^6 + 4z^3 + 2$

D) $z^5 + 4z^4 + 2$

37. In a theater, there are 4,500 lower-level seats and 2,000 upper-level seats. What is the ratio of lower-level seats to total seats?

A) $\frac{4}{9}$

B) $\frac{4}{13}$

C) $\frac{9}{13}$

D) $\frac{9}{4}$

38. Which of the following represents a linear equation?

A) $\sqrt[3]{y} = x$

B) $\sqrt[3]{x} = y$

C) $\sqrt[3]{y} = x^2$

D) $y = \sqrt[3]{x^3}$

39. A cube is inscribed in a sphere such that each vertex on the cube touches the sphere. If the volume of the sphere is 972π cm³, what is the approximate volume of the cube in cubic centimeters?

A) 9

B) 10.4

C) 1125

D) 1729

40. If a student answers 42 out of 48 questions correctly on a quiz, what percentage of questions did she answer correctly?

A) 82.5%

B) 85%

C) 87.5%

D) 90%

41. What is the relationship between the mean and the median in a data set that is skewed right?

A) The mean is greater than the median.

B) The mean is less than the median.

C) The mean and median are equal.

D) The mean may be greater than, less than, or equal to the median.

42. Which of the following is the y-intercept of the given equation?

$7y - 42x + 7 = 0$

A) $(0, \frac{1}{6})$

B) $(6,0)$

C) $(0,-1)$

D) $(-1,0)$

43. What are the real zero(s) of the following polynomial?

$2n^2 + 2n - 12 = 0$

A) $\{2\}$

B) $\{-3, 2\}$

C) $\{2, 4\}$

D) There are no real zeros of n.

44. Line a and line b are perpendicular and intersect at the point $(-100,100)$. If $(-95,115)$ is a point on line b, which of the following could be a point on line a?

A) $(104,168)$

B) $(-95,115)$

C) $(-112,104)$

D) $(-112,-104)$

45. In the xy-coordinate plane, how many points have a distance of four from the origin?

A) 0

B) 2

C) 4

D) ∞

46. A worker was paid $15,036 for 7 months of work. If he received the same amount each month, how much was he paid for the first 2 months?

A) $2,148

B) $4,296

C) $6,444

D) $8,592

47. Which value is equivalent to $5^2 \times (-5)^{-2} - (2 + 3)^{-1}$?

A) 0

B) 1

C) $\frac{5}{4}$

D) $\frac{4}{5}$

48. Which of the following sets of shapes are NOT all similar to each other?

A) right triangles

B) spheres

C) 30–60–90 triangles

D) squares

49. Simplify: $\frac{(3x^2y^2)^2}{3^3x^{-2}y^3}$

A) $3x^6y$

B) $\frac{x^6y}{3}$

C) $\frac{x^4}{3y}$

D) $\frac{3x^4}{y}$

50. A pair of 6-sided dice is rolled 10 times. What is the probability that in exactly 3 of those rolls, the sum of the dice will be 5?

A) 0.14%

B) 7.2%

C) 11.1%

D) 60%

English Language Arts

Writing Task

Topic: Driving Age: Is Sixteen Too Young?

Some people believe that sixteen is too young to be driving. Do you agree or disagree? Write an essay to **persuade** readers to accept your opinion on this issue. Be specific and explain your reasons.

Multiple-Choice Questions

Directions: In the following sentences, the underlined portion of the sentence may contain a mistake in punctuation, capitalization, or word usage. If you find a mistake, choose the answer that is the best way to write the underlined section of the sentence. If there is no mistake, choose *Correct as is*.

1. In 1948, the Chicago Tribune published an erroneous headline about the winner of the <u>Presidential election</u>.
    A) presidential Election
    B) Presidential Election
    C) presidential election
    D) *Correct as is*

2. While these incidents sometimes end in funny or heartwarming <u>stories: other</u> times they end in fear and destruction.
    A) stories. Other
    B) stories, other
    C) stories; other
    D) *Correct as is*

3. The artist <u>Prince, was</u> one of the most successful musical artists of the last century.
    A) Prince was
    B) Prince; was
    C) Prince: was
    D) *Correct as is*

4. When determining the conservation status of a species, biologists consider many <u>factors: including population</u> size and rate of reproduction.
    A) factors including, population
    B) factors. Including population
    C) factors, including population
    D) *Correct as is*

5. We celebrate Valentine's day in February, and we celebrate <u>Independence Day in Summer</u>.
    A) Independence day in Summer
    B) Independence Day in summer
    C) independence day in Summer
    D) *Correct as is*

6. Though the term *nomad* is often associated with early <u>populations; nomadic cultures continue to exist</u> even today.
    A) populations nomadic cultures continue to exist
    B) populations: nomadic cultures continue to exist
    C) populations, nomadic cultures continue to exist
    D) *Correct as is*

7. <u>My aunt lives in Canada with her husband</u>; they work in oil and gas in Edmonton, Alberta.
    A) Aunt lives in Canada with her husband
    B) Aunt lives in Canada with her Husband
    C) aunt lives in Canada with her Husband
    D) *Correct as is*

8. The high death toll of the Civil War was not only due to battle losses; <u>in addition,</u> many soldiers and civilians got sick and died because of living conditions during the war.
    A) therefore,
    B) however,
    C) on the other hand,
    D) *Correct as is*

9. An active volcano can destroy <u>it's immediate surroundings, and</u> an eruption can threaten passing aircraft.
    A) its immediate surroundings, and
    B) its immediate surroundings and
    C) it's immediate surroundings; and
    D) *Correct as is*

10. We're going to my <u>Brother's Graduation in Austin, Texas</u>.
   A) Brother's graduation in Austin, Texas
   B) brother's Graduation in Austin, Texas
   C) brother's graduation in Austin, Texas
   D) *Correct as is*

11. Baseball today has strict regulations for the design of bats; in the early days of baseball, <u>in consequence,</u> players often made their own bats.
   A) on the other hand
   B) nevertheless
   C) although
   D) *Correct as is*

12. I used to drink coffee every <u>morning but my office</u> took away the coffee machine.
   A) morning: but my office
   B) morning, but my office
   C) morning; but my office
   D) *Correct as is*

13. The <u>Automobile Industry and Microsoft</u> are collaborating on new technology for cars.
   A) Automobile Industry and microsoft
   B) Automobile industry and Microsoft
   C) automobile industry and Microsoft
   D) *Correct as is*

14. Freediving is sometimes <u>combined of</u> other underwater activities like underwater photography.
   A) combined in
   B) combined with
   C) combined over
   D) *Correct as is*

15. Kiana went to <u>class; but</u> Lara stayed home.
   A) class, but
   B) class but
   C) class: but
   D) *Correct as is*

16. The Pacific and the Atlantic are the <u>Largest Oceans on our Planet</u>.

    A)   largest oceans on our Planet

    B)   largest Oceans on our planet

    C)   largest oceans on our planet

    D)   *Correct as is*

17. Professional dental care is <u>relatively wide available</u> in wealthy countries, but more people have cavities due to high rates of sugar consumption.

    A)   relatively widely available

    B)   relative widely available

    C)   relatively wide availability

    D)   *Correct as is*

18. My <u>sister starts college in August</u>, so I will get to drive her car.

    A)   sister starts College in August

    B)   Sister starts College in August

    C)   sister starts college in august

    D)   *Correct as is*

19. I always buy <u>bread, from</u> the bakery down the street.

    A)   bread from

    B)   bread' from

    C)   bread; from

    D)   *Correct as is*

20. You can <u>taking either the bus or</u> the subway.

    A)   take neither the bus or

    B)   take either the bus or

    C)   take either the bus nor

    D)   *Correct as is*

Directions: The following sentences may contain errors in sentence structure or redundancy. If you find a mistake, choose the answer that is the best way to rewrite the sentence. If there is no mistake, choose *Correct as is*.

21. Javi took his basketball to school one day, and it got stolen by a gang of some mean older boys as he was walking.

    A)   Walking to school, Javi's basketball was stolen by a gang of mean older boys.

B) Walking to school, a gang of mean older boys stole Javi's basketball.

C) As Javi was walking to school, a gang of mean older boys stole his basketball.

D) *Correct as is*

22. Pizza is one of DeQuan's favorite foods but meat toppings make him feel queasy.

A) DeQuan loves eating pizza, but meat toppings make him feel queasy.

B) Though he avoids meat toppings, pizza being one of DeQuan's favorite foods.

C) Meat toppings on pizza makes DeQuan feel queasy.

D) *Correct as is*

23. Realizing that Mario had burned it, the soup stayed on the stove for too long.

A) Mario realized he had burned the soup by leaving it on the stove for too long.

B) Left on the stove for too long, Mario realized he had burned the soup.

C) Burning on the stove, Mario realized he had left the soup on for too long.

D) *Correct as is*

24. In 1977, Jerry R. Ehman detected a signal that seemed to come from a source outside the Earth's atmosphere, using a powerful radio telescope, which played for over a minute.

A) In 1977, Jerry R. Ehman, using a powerful radio telescope, detected a signal that seemed to come from a source outside the Earth's atmosphere, which played for over a minute.

B) In 1977, using a powerful radio telescope, Jerry R. Ehman detected a signal that seemed to come from outside the Earth's atmosphere, which played for over a minute.

C) In 1977, Jerry R. Ehman, using a powerful radio telescope, detected a signal, which played for over a minute, that seemed to come from outside the Earth's atmosphere.

D) *Correct as is*

25. The attorney smiled despite her dearth of courtroom wins, lack of free time she had, and growing list of clients she was helping.

A) The attorney smiled despite the losses she had experienced, the free time she lacked, and her growing client list.

B) The attorney smiled despite her dearth of courtroom wins, lack of free time, and growing list of clients.

C) The attorney smiled despite her dearth of courtroom wins, the free time she lacked, and the list of clients she was growing.

D) *Correct as is*

26. They're is nobody over their. Did you think you saw someone?

    A) Their is nobody over they're. Did you think you saw someone?

    B) They're is nobody over there. Did you think you saw someone?

    C) There is nobody over there. Did you think you saw someone?

    D) *Correct as is*

27. Because we love animals, our family has adopted a rescue dog and four rescue cats.

    A) Our family, because we love animals, we have adopted a rescue dog, and also four rescue cats.

    B) Because we love animals, our family has adopted five animals: four rescue cats and a rescue dog, too.

    C) Our family has adopted a rescue dog and because we love animals, four rescue cats.

    D) *Correct as is*

28. You needing a ride to the party, I can pick you up if I am on my way there.

    A) On my way over there, to the party, I can pick you up, if you need a ride there.

    B) If on my way to the party, you need a ride, I can pick you up.

    C) If you need a ride to the party, I can pick you up on my way over there.

    D) *Correct as is*

29. Before I feed the cats; first I need to finish my essay on responsibility.

    A) Before I feed the cats, I need to finish my essay on responsibility.

    B) I am needing finish my essay on responsibility before I feed the cats.

    C) First, I am going to finish my essay on responsibility, and then, I will feed the cats afterwards.

    D) *Correct as is*

30. In our class, only Pablo, of all the students, was the only one who earned an A grade.

    A) There were many students in our class, and Pablo was the only one of all of them with an A grade.

    B) Of all the students in our class, Pablo was the only one who earned an A grade.

C) Pablo was the only one in our class of all the students who earned an A grade.

D) *Correct as is*

31. She loves shopping only at hardware stores and antique shops.
    A) Only at hardware stores she loves shopping and at antique shops.
    B) She loves shopping; only at hardware stores and antique shops.
    C) At antique shops, and at hardware stores she loves to shop.
    D) *Correct as is*

32. Too busy to study for the test but I offered to help her.
    A) After she was too busy to study, I offered to help her with the test.
    B) She was too busy to study for the test; so I offered to help her.
    C) I offered to help her study for the test, but she was too busy.
    D) *Correct as is*

33. I love thin-crust pizza topped with roasted red peppers and caramelized onions.
    A) Topped with roasted red peppers and caramelized onions, I love thin-crust pizza.
    B) Loving thin-crust pizza, I am topped with roasted red peppers and caramelized onions.
    C) I love thin-crust pizza; topped with roasted red peppers and caramelized onions.
    D) *Correct as is*

34. Having been going to college, Dad had been in his early twenties at the time.
    A) Dad went to college; and he was in his early twenties then.
    B) When Dad was going to college, he was in his early twenties.
    C) In his early twenties, college was where Dad went.
    D) *Correct as is*

35. I will invite you to my birthday party; if you promise to bring your favorite brownies.
    A) Promise me to bring your famous brownies, then I will invite you to my party for my birthday.
    B) If you promise to bring your famous brownies, I will invite you to my birthday party.
    C) I am having a birthday party, and I promise to invite you, if you bring your famous brownies.
    D) *Correct as is*

36. On May nineteenth, it is my brother's college graduation, and my parents and me are flying to see him.

A) My brother's college graduation is on May nineteenth, so my parents and I are flying to see him.

B) My brother is graduating college; and it is on May nineteenth, and so I am flying with my parents to see him.

C) I am flying to see my brother, who is graduating college on May nineteenth, with my parents.

D) *Correct as is*

Directions: Read the passage, then answer the questions that follow.

Passage 1

(1) Artists and philosophers have always debated about the relationship between life and art. (2) While some argue that art is an imitation of life, others believe that life ends up imitating art. (3) The impact of art on our real lives is most visible in science fiction. (4) Science fiction writers like Jules Verne, Gene Roddenberry, H.G. Wells, and Stanley Kubrick have introduced ideas that, though fantastical at the time, eventually became reality. (5) Many of these artists were dead before they ever saw their ideas come to life.

(6) Some of humanity's biggest accomplishments were achieved first in science fiction. (7) Jules Verne wrote about humanity traveling to the moon over a century before it happened. (8) Scientists Robert H. Goddard and Leo Szilard both credit his work—on liquid-fueled rockets and atomic power, respectively—to the futuristic novels of H.G. Wells. (9) Gene Roddenberry, the creator of Star Trek, dreamed up replicators long before 3-D printers were invented.

(10) Jules Verne's work, for example, was the inspiration for the submarine and the helicopter. (11) H.G. Wells wrote about automatic doors long before they appeared in almost every grocery store in America. (12) Roddenberry's Star Trek is even credited as the inspiration for the mobile phone. (13) Kubrick's HAL from 2001: A Space Odyssey represented voice control at its finest, long before virtual assistants were installed in all the new smartphone models.

37. In context, which is the best version of sentence 1 (reproduced below)?

Artists and philosophers have always debated about the relationship between life and art.

A) Artists and philosophers have examined the facts and debated about the relationship between life and art.

B) Artists and philosophers have hemmed and hawed about the relationship between life and art.

C) Artists and philosophers have debated and had controversies about the relationship between life and art.

D) *Correct as is*

38. In context, which revision to sentence 5 (reproduced below) is most needed?

Many of these artists were dead before they ever saw their ideas come to life.

A) delete the sentence

B) change *many* to *most*

C) change *dead* to *deceased*

D) change *saw* to *witnessed*

39. Which of the following introductory phrases should be inserted at the beginning of sentence 6 (reproduced below)?

Some of humanity's biggest accomplishments were achieved first in science fiction.

A) Therefore,

B) In fact,

C) However,

D) In addition,

40. In context, which revision to sentence 8 (reproduced below) is most needed?

Scientists Robert H. Goddard and Leo Szilard both credit his work—on liquid-fueled rockets and atomic power, respectively—to the futuristic novels of H.G. Wells.

A) delete the sentence

B) insert *always* after the word *both*

C) change *his* to *their*

D) delete the phrase inside the dashes

41. In context, which of the following sentences would provide the best introduction to the final paragraph?

A) Transportation was of particular concern to science fiction writers, who dreamed up new ways for humanity to get around the world.

B) These same authors had other interesting ideas as well.

C) Sometimes science fiction is so much like life it is incredible.

D) Many of the ideas life borrows from science fiction have infiltrated our everyday lives and our world to an even greater degree.

42. In context, which of the following would provide the best conclusion to the essay?

   A) Science fiction will, no doubt, continue to influence our technology and our world for many years to come.

   B) These men are important figures in history for their ideas, and they should be respected as such.

   C) It is unfair that these creative individuals did not receive any money or rewards in exchange for their ideas.

   D) Science fiction is really an interesting topic, with many ideas and influential people to study and understand.

Passage 2

(1) Humans and animals have a complicated relationship. (2) Humans stay at the top of the food chain by asserting their control over the animal kingdom. (3) However, things do occasionally go wrong. (4) While these incidents sometimes end in funny or heartwarming stories, other times they end in fear and destruction. (5) One thing is clear: we do not control as much as we think we do.

(6) Sometimes, escaped animal stories end happily and leave us feeling even more affection for our furry neighbors. (7) In the 1980s, for example, the world fell in love with Ken Allen, an orangutan who escaped three times from his enclosure at the San Diego Zoo. (8)When he escaped, Ken Allen would go for peaceful walks around the park because he liked observing the other animals and zoo patrons with fascination. (9) Hercules, a trained grizzly bear who escaped from the set of a television commercial, found similar fame during his twenty-four-days of freedom; news audiences fell in love with the bear who, despite his hunger, refused to hunt and kill the various wildlife he encountered.

(10) Other times, though, escaped animals can pose a threat to safety. (11) Goldie, a male golden eagle, escaped from the London Zoo in 1965 and attacked two terriers who were at a park with their owner; fortunately, the owner was able to drive the predatory bird away, and zookeepers finally caught Goldie. (12) In 2007, a gorilla named Bokito became infamous when he escaped his enclosure at a Netherlands zoo and promptly abducted and injured a zoo visitor. (13) It was reported that the visitor, who visited Bokito at the zoo multiple times each week, ignored numerous warnings by zookeepers to avoid making eye contact and smiling with the large gorilla, nonverbal cues that they worried he would interpret as aggressive. (14) In 1994 during a circus performance, Tyke, a female African elephant, killed her trainer and attacked two other circus employees before escaping the arena and running free for nearly half an hour; police fired numerous shots at the animal, eventually killing her.

43. Should sentences 3 and 4 (reproduced below) be combined at the underlined point? If so, how?

However, things do <u>occasionally go wrong. While these incidents</u> sometimes end in funny or heartwarming stories, other times they end in fear and destruction.

- **A)** occasionally go wrong, while these incidents
- **B)** occasionally go wrong; however, while these incidents
- **C)** occasionally go wrong while these incidents
- **D)** *Correct as is*

44. Which of the following, if added to sentence 5 (reproduced below), would clarify the author's meaning?

One thing is clear: we do not control _____ as much as the think we do.

- **A)** all the time
- **B)** on a regular basis
- **C)** day in and day out
- **D)** the animals around us

45. Which of the following is the best revision of sentence 6 (reproduced below)?

Sometimes, escaped animal stories end happily and leave us feeling even more affection for our furry neighbors.

- **A)** People love animals, especially animals who are smart and crazy.
- **B)** Many animals that are portrayed as aggressive are not as scary as they are made out to be by experts.
- **C)** Some animals just can't get enough fun.
- **D)** *Correct as is*

46. Which is the best revision of the underlined portion of sentence 8 (reproduced below)?

When he escaped, Ken Allen would go for peaceful walks around the <u>park because he liked observing the other animals and zoo patrons with fascination.</u>

- **A)** park, observing the other animals and zoo patrons with fascination.
- **B)** park; observing the other animals and zoo patrons with fascination.
- **C)** park, he observed the other animals and zoo patrons with fascination.
- **D)** *Correct as is*

47. Which is the best revision for sentence 13 (reproduced below)?

It was reported that the visitor, who visited Bokito at the zoo multiple times each week, ignored numerous warnings from zookeepers to avoid making eye contact and smiling with the large gorilla, nonverbal cues that they worried he would interpret as aggressive.

A) delete the sentence

B) change *who* to *whom*

C) change *from* to *through*

D) change *they* to *zookeepers* and *he* to *Bokito*

48. Which of the following provides the best conclusion for this passage?

A) These stories are sad, but they are important moments in history and should be studied as such.

B) Tyke's story, fortunately, has led to many changes in circuses around the world, which have begun to minimize their use of animals in their acts.

C) These stories, both the happy and the sad, should serve as a clear warning to any human who encounters an animal: you are not in control.

D) Today, circus companies like Cirque du Soleil achieve equally stunning effects without the use of animal performers.

Reading Comprehension

Read the passage, and then answer the questions that follow.

The following passage refers to questions 1–6.

Skin coloration and markings have an important role to play in the world of snakes. Those intricate diamonds, stripes, and swirls help the animals hide from predators, but perhaps most importantly (for us humans, anyway), the markings can also indicate whether the snake is venomous. While it might seem counterintuitive for a venomous snake to stand out in bright red or blue, that fancy costume tells any nearby predator that approaching him would be a bad idea.

If you see a flashy-looking snake in the woods, though, those markings don't necessarily mean it's venomous: some snakes have found a way to ward off predators without the actual venom. The scarlet kingsnake, for example, has very similar markings to the venomous coral snake with whom it frequently shares a habitat. However, the kingsnake is actually nonvenomous; it's merely pretending to be dangerous to eat. A predatory hawk or eagle, usually hunting from high in the sky, can't tell the difference between the two species, and so the kingsnake gets passed over and lives another day.

1. What is the author's primary purpose in writing this essay?
   A) to explain how the markings on a snake are related to whether it's venomous
   B) to teach readers the difference between coral snakes and kingsnakes
   C) to illustrate why snakes are dangerous
   D) to demonstrate how animals survive in difficult environments

2. What can the reader conclude from the passage above?
   A) The kingsnake is dangerous to humans.
   B) The coral snake and the kingsnake are both hunted by the same predators.
   C) It's safe to handle snakes in the woods because you can easily tell whether they're poisonous.
   D) The kingsnake changes its markings when hawks or eagles are close by.

3. What is the best summary of this passage?
   A) Humans can use coloration and markings on snakes to determine whether they're venomous.
   B) Animals often use coloration to hide from predators.
   C) The scarlet kingsnake and the coral snake have nearly identical markings.
   D) Venomous snakes often have bright markings, although nonvenomous snakes can also mimic those colors.

4. Which statement is NOT a detail from the passage?

  A) Predators will avoid eating kingsnakes because their markings are similar to those on coral snakes.

  B) Kingsnakes and coral snakes live in the same habitats.

  C) The coral snake uses its coloration to hide from predators.

  D) The kingsnake is not venomous.

5. What is the meaning of the word *intricate* in the first paragraph?

  A) complex

  B) colorful

  C) purposeful

  D) changeable

6. What is the difference between kingsnakes and coral snakes according to the passage?

  A) Both kingsnakes and coral snakes are nonvenomous, but coral snakes have colorful markings.

  B) Both kingsnakes and coral snakes are venomous, but kingsnakes have colorful markings.

  C) Kingsnakes are nonvenomous while coral snakes are venomous.

  D) Coral snakes are nonvenomous while kingsnakes are venomous.

The following passage refers to questions 7–12.

The most important part of brewing coffee is getting the right water. Choose a water that you think has a nice, neutral flavor. Anything with too many minerals or contaminants will change the flavor of the coffee, and water with too few minerals won't do a good job of extracting the flavor from the coffee beans. Water should be heated to between 195 and 205 degrees Fahrenheit. Boiling water (212 degrees Fahrenheit) will burn the beans and give your coffee a scorched flavor.

While the water is heating, grind your beans. Remember, the fresher the grind, the fresher the flavor of the coffee. The number of beans is entirely dependent on your personal taste. Obviously, more beans will result in a more robust flavor, while fewer beans will give your coffee a more subtle taste. The texture of the grind should be not too fine (which can lead to bitter coffee) or too large (which can lead to weak coffee).

Once the beans are ground and the water has reached the perfect temperature, you're ready to brew. A French press (which we recommend), allows you to control brewing time and provide a thorough brew. Pour the grounds into the press, then pour the hot water over the grounds and let it steep. The brew shouldn't require more than five minutes, although those of you who like your coffee a bit harsher can leave it longer. Finally, use the plunger to remove the grounds and pour.

7. What is the author's intent in writing this passage?
   A) to describe how to make hot beverages
   B) to argue that grinding beans makes a better cup of coffee
   C) to claim that coffee is better than tea
   D) to explain how to brew a cup of coffee

8. According to the passage, which of the following lists the steps for brewing coffee in the correct sequence?
   A) Choose a water that doesn't have too many or two few minerals. Then, heat water to boiling and pour over coffee grounds.
   B) Grind the beans to the appropriate texture and pour into the French press. Then, heat water to boiling and pour over the ground beans. Finally, use the plunger to remove the grounds and pour.
   C) Grind beans to the appropriate texture, and then heat water to 195 degrees Fahrenheit. Next, pour water over the grounds and steep for no more than five minutes. Finally, remove the grounds using the plunger.
   D) Choose the right type of water and heat it to the correct temperature. Next, grind the beans and put them in the French press. Then, pour the hot water over the grounds and let the coffee steep.

9. Which of the following best describes the structure of the text?
   A) chronological
   B) cause and effect
   C) problem and solution
   D) contrast

10. Which of the following statements based on the passage should be considered an opinion?
    A) While the water is heating, grind your beans.
    B) A French press (which we recommend), allows you to control brewing time and provide a thorough brew.
    C) Anything with too many minerals or contaminants will change the flavor of the coffee, and water with too few minerals won't do a good job of extracting the flavor from the coffee beans.
    D) Finally, use the plunger to remove the grounds and pour.

11. Which of the following conclusions is best supported by the passage?
    A) Coffee should never be brewed for longer than five minutes.
    B) It's better to use too many coffee beans when making coffee than too few.
    C) Brewing quality coffee at home is too complicated for most people to do well.
    D) The best way to brew coffee is often determined by personal preferences.

12. Which of the following would be an appropriate title for this passage?

- **A)** How to Brew the Perfect Cup of Coffee
- **B)** Why Drinking Coffee Is the Best Way to Start the Day
- **C)** How to Use a French Press to Make Coffee
- **D)** The Importance of Grinding Coffee Beans

The following passage refers to questions 13–18.

Influenza (also called the flu) has historically been one of the most common, and deadliest, human infections. While many people who contract the virus will recover, many others will not. Over the past 150 years, tens of millions of people have died from the flu, and millions more have been left with lingering complications such as secondary infections.

Although it's a common disease, the flu is not actually highly infectious, meaning it's relatively difficult to contract. The flu can only be transmitted when individuals come into direct contact with bodily fluids of people infected with the flu or when they are exposed to expelled aerosol particles (which result from coughing and sneezing). Because the viruses can only travel short distances as aerosol particles and will die within a few hours on hard surfaces, the virus can be contained with fairly simple health measures like hand washing and face masks.

However, the spread of the flu can only be contained when people are aware such measures need to be taken. One of the reasons the flu has historically been so deadly is the amount of time between when people become infectious and when they develop symptoms. Viral shedding—the process by which the body releases viruses that have been successfully reproducing during the infection—takes place two days after infection, while symptoms do not usually develop until the third day of infection. Thus, infected individuals have at least twenty-four hours in which they may unknowingly infect others.

13. What is the main idea of the passage?

- **A)** The flu is a deadly disease that's difficult to control because people become infectious before they show symptoms.
- **B)** For the flu to be transmitted, individuals must come in contact with bodily fluids from infected individuals.
- **C)** The spread of the flu is easy to contain because the viruses do not live long either as aerosol particles or on hard surfaces.
- **D)** The flu has killed tens of millions of people and can often cause deadly secondary infections.

14. Which of the following correctly describes the flu?

- **A)** The flu is easy to contract and always fatal.
- **B)** The flu is difficult to contract and always fatal.

C) The flu is easy to contract and sometimes fatal.

D) The flu is difficult to contract and sometimes fatal.

15. Why is the flu considered to not be highly infectious?

A) Many people who get the flu will recover and have no lasting complications, so only a small number of people who become infected will die.

B) The process of viral shedding takes two days, so infected individuals have enough time to implement simple health measures that stop the spread of the disease.

C) The flu virus cannot travel far or live for long periods of time outside the human body, so its spread can easily be contained.

D) Twenty-four hours is a relatively short period of time for the virus to spread among a population.

16. What is the meaning of the word *measures* in the last paragraph?

A) a plan of action

B) a standard unit

C) an adequate amount

D) a rhythmic movement

17. Which statement is NOT a detail from the passage?

A) Tens of millions of people have been killed by the flu virus.

B) There is typically a twenty-four hour window during which individuals are infectious but not showing flu symptoms.

C) Viral shedding is the process by which people recover from the flu.

D) The flu can be transmitted by direct contact with bodily fluids from infected individuals or by exposure to aerosol particles.

18. What can the reader conclude from the passage?

A) Preemptively implementing health measures like hand washing and face masks could help stop the spread of the flu virus.

B) Doctors are not sure how the flu virus is transmitted, so they are unsure how to stop it from spreading.

C) The flu is dangerous because it is both deadly and highly infectious.

D) Individuals stop being infectious three days after they are infected.

The following passage refers to questions 19–24.

The bacteria, fungi, insects, plants, and animals that live together in a habitat have evolved to share a pool of limited resources. They've competed for water, minerals, nutrients, sunlight, and space—sometimes for thousands or even millions of years. As these communities have evolved, the species in them have developed complex, long-term interspecies interactions known as symbiotic relationships.

Ecologists characterize these interactions based on whether each party benefits. In mutualism, both individuals benefit, while in synnecrosis, both organisms are harmed. A relationship where one individual benefits and the other is harmed is known as parasitism. Examples of these relationships can easily be seen in any ecosystem. Pollination, for example, is mutualistic—pollinators get nutrients from the flower, and the plant is able to reproduce—while tapeworms, which steal nutrients from their host, are parasitic.

There's yet another class of symbiosis that is controversial among scientists. As it's long been defined, commensalism is a relationship where one species benefits and the other is unaffected. But is it possible for two species to interact and for one to remain completely unaffected? Often, relationships described as commensal include one species that feeds on another species' leftovers; remoras, for instance, will attach themselves to sharks and eat the food particles they leave behind. It might seem like the shark gets nothing from the relationship, but a closer look will show that sharks in fact benefit from remoras, which clean the sharks' skin and remove parasites. In fact, many scientists claim that relationships currently described as commensal are just mutualistic or parasitic in ways that haven't been discovered yet.

19. What is the author's primary purpose in writing this essay?

A) to argue that commensalism isn't actually found in nature

B) to describe the many types of symbiotic relationships

C) to explain how competition for resources results in long-term interspecies relationships

D) to provide examples of the many different ways individual organisms interact

20. Epiphytes are plants that attach themselves to trees and derive nutrients from the air and surrounding debris. Sometimes, the weight of epiphytes can damage the trees on which they're growing. The relationship between epiphytes and their hosts would be described as

A) mutualism.

B) commensalism.

C) parasitism.

D) synnecrosis.

21. Which of the following is NOT a fact stated in the passage?

A) Mutualism is an interspecies relationship where both species benefit.

B) Synnecrosis is an interspecies relationship where both species are harmed.

C) The relationship between plants and pollinators is mutualistic.

D) The relationship between remoras and sharks is parasitic.

22. Why is commensalism debated among scientists?

A) Many scientists believe that an interspecies interaction where one species is unaffected does not exist.

B) Some scientists believe that relationships where one species feeds on the leftovers of another should be classified as parasitism.

C) Because remoras and sharks have a mutualistic relationship, no interactions should be classified as commensalism.

D) Only relationships among animal species should be classified as commensalism.

23. What can the reader conclude from this passage about symbiotic relationships?

A) Scientists cannot decide how to classify symbiotic relationships among species.

B) The majority of interspecies interactions are parasitic because most species do not get along.

C) If two species are involved in a parasitic relationship, one of the species will eventually become extinct.

D) Symbiotic relationships evolve as the species that live in a community adapt to their environments and each other.

24. What is the meaning of the word *controversial* in the last paragraph?

A) debatable

B) objectionable

C) confusing

D) upsetting

The following passage refers to questions 25–30.

Hand washing is one of our simplest and most powerful weapons against infection. The idea behind hand washing is deceptively simple. Many illnesses are spread when people touch infected surfaces, such as door handles or other people's hands, and then touch their own eyes, mouths, or noses. So, if pathogens can be removed from the hands before they spread, infections can be prevented. When done correctly, hand washing can prevent the spread of many dangerous bacteria and viruses, including those that cause the flu, the common cold, diarrhea, and many acute respiratory illnesses.

The most basic method of hand washing involves only soap and water. Just twenty seconds of scrubbing with soap and a complete rinsing with water is enough to kill and/ or wash away many pathogens. The process doesn't even require warm water—studies have shown that cold water is just as effective at reducing the number of microbes on the hands. Antibacterial soaps are also available, although several studies have shown that simple soap and cold water is just as effective.

In recent years, hand sanitizers have become popular as an alternative to hand washing. These gels, liquids, and foams contain a high concentration of alcohol (usually at least 60 percent) that kills most bacteria and fungi; they can also be effective against

C) Simple hand washing with soap and cold water is an effective way to reduce the spread of disease. Antibacterial soaps and hand sanitizers may also be used but are not significantly more effective.

D) Using hand sanitizer will kill many pathogens but will not remove organic matter. Hand washing with soap and water is a better option when available.

27. What is the meaning of the word *harbor* in the last paragraph?

A) to disguise

B) to hide

C) to wash away

D) to give a home

28. Knowing that the temperature of the water does not affect the efficacy of hand washing, one can conclude that water plays an important role in hand washing because it

A) has antibacterial properties.

B) physically removes pathogens from hands.

C) cools hands to make them inhospitable to dangerous bacteria.

D) is hot enough to kill bacteria.

29. What is the author's primary purpose in writing this essay?

A) to persuade readers of the importance and effectiveness of hand washing with soap and cold water

B) to dissuade readers from using hand sanitizer

C) to explain how many common diseases are spread through daily interaction

D) to describe the many ways hand washing and hand sanitizer provide health benefits

30. What can the reader conclude from the passage above?

A) Hand washing would do little to limit infections that spread through particles in the air.

B) Hand washing is not necessary for people who do not touch their eyes, mouths, or noses with their hands.

C) Hand sanitizer serves no purpose and should not be used as an alternative to hand washing.

D) Hand sanitizer will likely soon replace hand washing as the preferred method of removing pathogens from hands.

The following passage refers to questions 31–35.

Taking a person's temperature is one of the most basic and common health care tasks. Everyone from nurses to emergency medical technicians to concerned parents should be able to grab a thermometer to take a patient or loved one's temperature. But what's the best way to get an accurate reading? The answer depends on the situation.

The most common way people measure body temperature is orally. A simple digital or disposable thermometer is placed under the tongue for a few minutes, and the task is some, but not all, viruses. There is a downside to hand sanitizer, however. Because the sanitizer isn't rinsed from hands, it only kills pathogens and does nothing to remove organic matter. So, hands "cleaned" with hand sanitizer may still harbor pathogens. Thus, while hand sanitizer can be helpful in situations where soap and clean water isn't available, a simple hand washing is still the best option.

25. Which of the following is NOT a fact stated in the passage?

    A) Many infections occur because people get pathogens on their hands and then touch their own eyes, mouths, or noses.

    B) Antibacterial soaps and warm water are the best way to remove pathogens from hands.

    C) Most hand sanitizers have a concentration of at least 60 percent alcohol.

    D) Hand sanitizer can be an acceptable alternative to hand washing when soap and water aren't available.

26. What is the best summary of this passage?

    A) Many diseases are spread by pathogens that can live on the hands. Hand washing is the best way to remove these pathogens and prevent disease.

    B) Simple hand washing can prevent the spread of many common illnesses, including the flu, the common cold, diarrhea, and many acute respiratory illnesses. Hand sanitizer can also kill the pathogens that cause these diseases.

    C) Simple hand washing with soap and cold water is an effective way to reduce the spread of disease. Antibacterial soaps and hand sanitizers may also be used but are not significantly more effective.

    D) Using hand sanitizer will kill many pathogens but will not remove organic matter. Hand washing with soap and water is a better option when available.

27. What is the meaning of the word *harbor* in the last paragraph?

    A) to disguise

    B) to hide

    C) to wash away

    D) to give a home

28. Knowing that the temperature of the water does not affect the efficacy of hand washing, one can conclude that water plays an important role in hand washing because it

    A) has antibacterial properties.

    B) physically removes pathogens from hands.

    C) cools hands to make them inhospitable to dangerous bacteria.

    D) is hot enough to kill bacteria.

29. What is the author's primary purpose in writing this essay?

   A) to persuade readers of the importance and effectiveness of hand washing with soap and cold water

   B) to dissuade readers from using hand sanitizer

   C) to explain how many common diseases are spread through daily interaction

   D) to describe the many ways hand washing and hand sanitizer provide health benefits

30. What can the reader conclude from the passage above?

   A) Hand washing would do little to limit infections that spread through particles in the air.

   B) Hand washing is not necessary for people who do not touch their eyes, mouths, or noses with their hands.

   C) Hand sanitizer serves no purpose and should not be used as an alternative to hand washing.

   D) Hand sanitizer will likely soon replace hand washing as the preferred method of removing pathogens from hands.

The following passage refers to questions 31–35.

Taking a person's temperature is one of the most basic and common health care tasks. Everyone from nurses to emergency medical technicians to concerned parents should be able to grab a thermometer to take a patient or loved one's temperature. But what's the best way to get an accurate reading? The answer depends on the situation.

The most common way people measure body temperature is orally. A simple digital or disposable thermometer is placed under the tongue for a few minutes, and the task is done. There are many situations, however, when measuring temperature orally isn't an option. For example, when a person can't breathe through his nose, he won't be able to keep his mouth closed long enough to get an accurate reading. In these situations, it's often preferable to place the thermometer in the rectum or armpit. Using the rectum also has the added benefit of providing a much more accurate reading than other locations can provide.

It's also often the case that certain people, like agitated patients or fussy babies, won't be able to sit still long enough for an accurate reading. In these situations, it's best to use a thermometer that works much more quickly, such as one that measures temperature in the ear or at the temporal artery. No matter which method is chosen, however, it's important to check the average temperature for each region, as it can vary by several degrees.

31. Which statement is NOT a detail from the passage?

A) Taking a temperature in the ear or at the temporal artery is more accurate than taking it orally.

B) If an individual cannot breathe through the nose, taking his or her temperature orally will likely give an inaccurate reading.

C) The standard human body temperature varies depending on whether it's measured in the mouth, rectum, armpit, ear, or at the temporal artery.

D) The most common way to measure temperature is by placing a thermometer in the mouth.

32. What is the author's primary purpose in writing this essay?

A) to advocate for the use of thermometers that measure temperature in the ear or at the temporal artery

B) to explain the methods available to measure a person's temperature and the situation where each method is appropriate

C) to warn readers that the average temperature of the human body varies by region

D) to discuss how nurses use different types of thermometers depending on the type of patient they are examining

33. What is the best summary of this passage?

A) It's important that everyone knows the best way to take a person's temperature in any given situation.

B) The most common method of taking a person's temperature—orally— isn't appropriate in some situations.

C) The most accurate way to take a temperature is placing a digital thermometer in the rectum.

D) There are many different ways to take a person's temperature, and which is appropriate will depend on the situation.

34. What is the meaning of the word "agitated" in the last paragraph?

A) obviously upset

B) quickly moving

C) violently ill

D) slightly dirty

35. According to the passage, why is it sometimes preferable to take a person's temperature rectally?

A) Rectal readings are more accurate than oral readings.

B) Many people cannot sit still long enough to have their temperatures taken orally.

C) Temperature readings can vary widely between regions of the body.

D) Many people do not have access to quick-acting thermometers.

The following passage refers to questions 36–41.

Popcorn is often associated with fun and festivities, both in and out of the home. It's eaten in theaters, usually after being salted and smothered in butter, and in homes, fresh from the microwave. But popcorn isn't just for fun—it's also a multimillion-dollar-a-year industry with a long and fascinating history.

While popcorn might seem like a modern invention, its history actually dates back thousands of years, making it one of the oldest snack foods enjoyed around the world. Popcorn is believed by food historians to be one of the earliest uses of cultivated corn. In 1948, Herbert Dick and Earle Smith discovered old popcorn dating back 4000 years in the New Mexico Bat Cave. For the Aztec Indians who called the caves home, popcorn (or *momochitl*) played an important role in society, both as a food staple and in ceremonies. The Aztecs cooked popcorn by heating sand in a fire; when it was heated, kernels were added and would pop when exposed to the heat of the sand.

The American love affair with popcorn began in 1912, when popcorn was first sold in theaters. The popcorn industry flourished during the Great Depression when it was advertised as a wholesome and economical food. Selling for five to ten cents a bag, it was a luxury that the downtrodden could afford. With the introduction of mobile popcorn machines at the World's Columbian Exposition, popcorn moved from the theater into fairs and parks. Popcorn continued to rule the snack food kingdom until the rise in popularity of home televisions during the 1950s.

The popcorn industry reacted to the decline in sales quickly by introducing pre-popped and unpopped popcorn for home consumption. However, it wasn't until microwave popcorn became commercially available in 1981 that at-home popcorn consumption began to grow exponentially. With the wide availability of microwaves in the United States, popcorn also began popping up in offices and hotel rooms. However, the home still remains the most popular popcorn eating spot: today, 70 percent of the 16 billion quarts of popcorn consumed annually in the United States are eaten at home.

36. What can the reader conclude from the passage above?

   A) People ate less popcorn in the 1950s than in previous decades because they went to the movies less.

   B) Without mobile popcorn machines, people would not have been able to eat popcorn during the Great Depression.

   C) People enjoyed popcorn during the Great Depression because it was a luxury food.

   D) During the 1800s, people began abandoning theaters to go to fairs and festivals.

37. What is the meaning of the word *staple* in the second paragraph?

   A) something produced only for special occasions

   B) something produced regularly in large quantities

   C) something produced by cooking

   D) something fastened together securely

38. What is the author's primary purpose in writing this essay?

- **A)** to explain how microwaves affected the popcorn industry
- **B)** to show that popcorn is older than many people realize
- **C)** to illustrate the history of popcorn from ancient cultures to modern times
- **D)** to demonstrate the importance of popcorn in various cultures

39. Which factor does the author of the passage credit for the growth of the popcorn industry in the United States?

- **A)** the use of popcorn in ancient Aztec ceremonies
- **B)** the growth of the home television industry
- **C)** the marketing of popcorn during the Great Depression
- **D)** the nutritional value of popcorn

40. What is the best summary of this passage?

- **A)** Popcorn is a popular snack food that dates back thousands of years. Its popularity in the United States has been tied to the growth of theaters and the availability of microwaves.
- **B)** Popcorn has been a popular snack food for thousands of years. Archaeologists have found evidence that many ancient cultures used popcorn as a food staple and in ceremonies.
- **C)** Popcorn was first introduced to America in 1912, and its popularity has grown exponentially since then. Today, over 16 billion quarts of popcorn are consumed in the United States annually.
- **D)** Popcorn is a versatile snack food that can be eaten with butter or other toppings. It can also be cooked in a number of different ways, including in microwaves.

41. Which of the following is NOT a fact stated in the passage?

- **A)** Archaeologists have found popcorn dating back 4000 years.
- **B)** Popcorn was first sold in theaters in 1912.
- **C)** Consumption of popcorn dropped in 1981 with the growing popularity of home televisions.
- **D)** Seventy percent of the popcorn consumed in the United States is eaten in homes.

The following passage refers to questions 42–48.

Credit scores, which range from 300 to 850, are a single value that summarizes an individual's credit history. Pay your bills late? Your credit score will be lower than someone who gets that electric bill filed on the first of every month. Just paid off your massive student loans? You can expect your credit score to shoot up. The companies that compile credit scores actually keep track of all the loans, credit cards, and bill payments in your name. This massive amount of information is summed up in a credit report, which is then distilled to a single value: your credit score.

Credit scores are used by many institutions that need to evaluate the risk of providing loans, rentals, or services to individuals. Banks use credit scores when deciding whether to hand out loans; they can also use them to determine the terms of the loan itself. Similarly, car dealers, landlords, and credit card companies will likely all access your credit report before agreeing to do business with you. Even your employer can access a modified version of your credit report (although it will not have your actual credit score on it).

When it comes to credit, everyone begins with a clean slate. The first time you access any credit—be it a credit card, student loan, or rental agreement—information begins to accumulate in your credit report. Thus, having no credit score can often be just as bad as having a low one. Lenders want to know that you have a history of borrowing money and paying it back on time. After all, if you've never taken out a loan, how can a bank know that you'll pay back its money? So, having nothing on your credit report can result in low credit limits and high interest rates.

With time, though, credit scores can be raised. With every payment, your credit report improves and banks will be more likely to loan you money. These new loans will in turn raise your score even further (as long as you keep making payments, of course).

In general, you can take a number of basic steps to raise your credit score. First, ensure that payments are made on time. When payments are past due, it not only has a negative impact on your score, but new creditors will be reluctant to lend while you are delinquent on other accounts.

Being smart about taking on debt is another key factor in keeping your credit score high. As someone who is just starting off in the financial world, there will be multiple offers to open accounts, say, for an introductory credit card or short-term loan. You may also find that as your score increases, you will receive offers for larger and larger loans. (Predatory lenders are a scourge on the young as well as the old.) But just because banks are offering you those loans doesn't make them a good idea. Instead, you should only take on debt you know you can pay back in a reasonable amount of time.

Lastly, keep an eye on unpaid student loans, medical bills, and parking tickets, all of which can take a negative toll on your credit score. In fact, your credit score will take a major hit from any bill that's sent to a collection agency, so it's in your best interest to avoid letting bills get to that point. Many organizations will agree to keep bills away from collection agencies if you set up a fee payment system.

42. What is the author's primary purpose in writing this essay?

   A) to help readers understand and improve their credit scores

   B) to warn banks about the dangers of lending to people with no credit score

   C) to persuade readers to take out large loans to improve their credit scores

   D) to explain to readers how the process of taking out a bank loan works

43. According to the passage, which individual is likely to have the highest credit score?

   A) someone who has had medical bills sent to a collection agency

   B) someone who is in the process of paying back his student loans

   C) someone who has never borrowed any money but pays his bills on time

   D) someone who has borrowed a large amount of money and paid it back on time

44. What is the best summary of this passage?

   A) Individuals with low credit scores will likely have trouble getting credit cards and loans. However, they can improve their credit scores over time.

   B) Having no credit score can often be worse than having a low credit score, so it's important to sign up for credit cards and loans early in life.

   C) Credit scores summarize an individual's credit history and are used by many businesses. They can be improved by making smart financial decisions.

   D) Credit scores can be raised by paying bills on time, taking out reasonably sized loans, and avoiding collection agencies.

45. What is the meaning of the word *distilled* in the first paragraph?

   A) to refine to its essence

   B) to explain at length

   C) to keep records of

   D) to undergo substantial change

46. Which of the following is an opinion stated in the passage?

A) Credit scores, which range from 300 to 850, are a single value that summarizes an individual's credit history.

B) Many organizations will agree to keep bills away from collection agencies if you set up a fee payment system.

C) After all, if you've never taken out a loan, how can a bank know that you'll pay back its money?

D) Predatory lenders are a scourge on the young as well as the old.

47. What can the reader conclude from the passage?

A) It's possible to wipe your credit report clean and start over with a blank slate.

B) People with a large amount of debt can likely get a loan with a low interest rate because they have demonstrated they are trustworthy.

C) Someone who has borrowed and paid back large sums of money will get a loan with more favorable terms than someone who has never borrowed money before.

D) A college student with no credit cards or debt likely has a high credit score.

48. Which statement is NOT a detail from the passage?

A) In general, you can take a number of basic steps to raise your credit score.

B) When it comes to credit, everyone begins with a clean slate.

C) Employers can access your credit score before hiring you.

D) Predatory lenders are a scourge on the young as well as the old.

The following passage refers to questions 49–54.

Have you ever devoured a tasty snow cone only to experience the agony of "brain freeze"? Have you ever wondered why or how that happens? Well, scientists now believe they understand the mechanism of these so-called ice cream headaches.

It begins with the icy temperature of the snow cone (or any cold food, or sometimes even exposure to cold air). When a cold substance (delicious or otherwise) presses against the roof of your mouth, it causes blood vessels there to begin to constrict, and your body starts to sense that something is awry. In response, blood is pumped to the affected region to try to warm it up, causing rapid dilation of the same vessels. This causes the neighboring trigeminal nerve to send rapid signals to your brain. Because the trigeminal nerve also serves the face, the brain misinterprets these signals as coming from your forehead. The duration of the pain varies from a few seconds up to about a minute.

Regardless of the time spent wincing, the danger of the ice cream headache certainly will not stop people for screaming for their favorite frozen treat in the future.

49. Readers can infer from the passage that the author is trying to _____ us.
    A) inform and persuade
    B) inform and entertain
    C) warn and persuade
    D) amuse and entertain

50. Why does the author use the word *screaming* in the last sentence?
    A) to show how painful *brain freeze* can be
    B) to show that ice cream headaches are dangerous
    C) to jokingly refer to a play on words: "I scream for ice cream"
    D) to rhyme with the word *creaming* in a traditional poem

51. Which sentence best summarizes the passage's main idea?
    A) "Have you ever devoured a tasty snow cone only to experience the agony of *brain freeze*?"
    B) "Well, scientists now believe they understand the mechanism of these so-called ice cream headaches."
    C) "When a cold substance (delicious or otherwise) presses against the roof of your mouth, it causes blood vessels there to begin to constrict, and your body starts to sense that something is awry."

D) "Because the trigeminal nerve also serves the face, the brain misinterprets these signals as coming from your forehead."

52. According to the passage, what happens immediately after the roof of the mouth grows cold?
    A) Blood vessels on the roof of the mouth begin to expand.
    B) The body pumps blood to the roof of the mouth to warm it up.
    C) The trigeminal nerve sends rapid signals to the brain.
    D) Blood vessels on the roof of the mouth begin to narrow.

53. Which body part is NOT mentioned in the passage?
    A) the roof of the mouth
    B) the tongue
    C) the face
    D) the forehead

54. In the last sentence of the second paragraph, what does the word *duration* mean?
    A) time period
    B) skin surface
    C) intensity
    D) strength

Vocabulary

Read the sentence, and use the other words in the sentence to determine what the underlined word means.

1. Omari felt <u>apathetic</u> in his employment, so he decided to quit his job and go to nursing school. *Apathetic* means
   A) motivated.
   B) furious.
   C) indifferent.
   D) understanding.

2. The man was angry and <u>belligerent</u> when he found his car had been broken into. *Belligerent* means
   A) hostile.
   B) sad.
   C) worried.
   D) alert.

3. When the boy laughed at the girl who fell down, her friends felt he was being <u>callous</u> and unkind. *Callous* means
   A) lively.
   B) insensitive.
   C) annoyed.
   D) friendly.

4. Cheryl was nervous, but she did not want to <u>hinder</u> her daughter's dream of becoming a police officer. *Hinder* means
   A) encourage.
   B) expedite.
   C) crush.
   D) impede.

5. When Clyde woke up after the accident, he was <u>lucid</u> enough to remember where he had been the night before. *Lucid* means
   A) confused.
   B) rational.
   C) emotional.
   D) boring.

6. Larry thought his neighbor was <u>pilfering</u> his morning newspaper because it was missing for several days in a row. *Pilfering* means
   A) stealing.
   B) borrowing.
   C) moving.
   D) returning.

7. Blanca had an <u>inconspicuous</u> scar on her arm that only she could see. *Inconspicuous* means
   A) revealing.
   B) large.
   C) unnoticeable.
   D) oversized.

8. Julian became <u>frantic</u> when he realized his wallet was missing. *Frantic* means
   A) frenzied.
   B) calm.
   C) frustrated.
   D) alert.

9. Henry only <u>exacerbated</u> the problem when he poured water on a grease fire. *Exacerbated* means

   A) put out.
   B) picked up.
   C) made worse.
   D) looked over.

10. The hospital administrator writes very long, <u>verbose</u> reports with lots of words that are confusing. *Verbose* means

    A) concise.
    B) clear.
    C) confusing.
    D) wordy.

11. Teachers try to <u>foster</u> positive relationships between students and their coursework. *Foster* means

    A) show.
    B) instruct.
    C) discourage.
    D) promote.

12. It is impossible to <u>quantify</u> how much ice cream we ate last night—we lost count after three cones. *Quantify* means

    A) measure.
    B) understand.
    C) extend.
    D) improve.

Choose the word or group of words that means the same as the underlined word.

13. <u>Hydration</u> means the same as
   A) measuring temperature.
   B) maintaining cleanliness.
   C) consuming fluids.
   D) taking vitamins.

14. <u>Asymmetric</u> means the same as
   A) patterned.
   B) unbalanced.
   C) circular.
   D) aligned.

15. <u>Precaution</u> means the same as
   A) warning.
   B) detriment.
   C) prevention.
   D) diagnosis.

16. <u>Adversely</u> means the same as
   A) consequently.
   B) harmfully.
   C) helpfully.
   D) expectedly.

17. <u>Excessive</u> means the same as
   A) too many.
   B) a variety of.
   C) quickly.
   D) taken orally.

18. <u>Sensible</u> means the same as
   A) confusing.
   B) prohibited.
   C) necessary.
   D) wise.

19. Justify means the same as
- **A)** understand.
- **B)** explain.
- **C)** organize.
- **D)** introduce.

20. Progress means the same as
- **A)** agreement.
- **B)** improvement.
- **C)** decision.
- **D)** description.

21. Priority means the same as
- **A)** historical.
- **B)** transportation.
- **C)** precedence.
- **D)** community.

22. Absorb means the same as
- **A)** respond to.
- **B)** take in.
- **C)** forget about.
- **D)** add to.

23. Consistency means the same as
- **A)** irregularity.
- **B)** precision.
- **C)** mistakes.
- **D)** uniformity.

24. Access means the same as
- **A)** enter.
- **B)** exit.
- **C)** escape.
- **D)** find.

25. Fatigue means the same as
- **A)** weariness.
- **B)** stress.
- **C)** pain.
- **D)** lightheadedness.

26. Abbreviate means the same as
- **A)** lengthen.
- **B)** avoid.
- **C)** extend.
- **D)** shorten.

27. Hygiene means the same as
- **A)** feeding.
- **B)** exercise.
- **C)** cleanliness.
- **D)** clothing.

28. Collaborate means the same as
- **A)** debate with.
- **B)** work with.
- **C)** talk to.
- **D)** discuss with.

29. Subtle means the same as
- **A)** valued.
- **B)** understated.
- **C)** overwhelmed.
- **D)** excited.

30. Deficiency means the same as
- **A)** foundation
- **B)** solution
- **C)** injury
- **D)** shortage

Answer Key
MATHEMATICS

1. **D) is correct.**

    Make the exponents the same and subtract the digit parts of each term.

    $(4.71 \times 10^3) - (2.98 \times 10^2)$

    $4.71 \times 10 \times 10^2 = 47.1 \times 10^2$

    $47.1 - 2.98 = 44.12$

    $44.12 \times 10^2 = \mathbf{4.412 \times 10^3}$

2. **A) is correct.**

    Use the formula for inversely proportional relationships to find k and then solve for s.

    $sn = k$

    $(65)(250) = k$

    $k = 16{,}250$

    $s(325) = 16{,}250$

    $s = \mathbf{50}$

3. **A) is correct.**

    Simplify each root and add.

    $\sqrt[3]{64} = 4 \quad \sqrt[3]{729} = 9$

    $4 + 9 = \mathbf{13}$

4. **B) is correct.**

    Use the midpoint formula to find point B.

    $M_x: \dfrac{(7 + x)}{2} = -3$

    $x = -13$

    $M_y: \dfrac{(12 + y)}{2} = 10$

    $y = 8$

    $B = \mathbf{(-13, 8)}$

5. **D) is correct.**

    $\{5, 11, 18, 20, \mathbf{37}, 37, 60, 72, 90\}$

    $median = 37$

    $mode = 37$

    $mean =$

    $\dfrac{60 + 5 + 18 + 20 + 37 + 37 + 11 + 90 + 72}{9} = 38.89$

    The median is less than the mean.

6. **A) is correct.** Eliminate answer choices that don't match the graph.

    B) is incorrect. The graph has a negative slope while this inequality has a positive slope.

    C) is incorrect. The line on the graph is solid, so the inequality should include the "or equal to" symbol.

    D) is incorrect. The shading is above the line, meaning the inequality should be "y is greater than."

7. **B) is correct.**

    The slope 0.0293 gives the increase in passenger car miles (in billions) for each year that passes. Multiply this value by 5 to find the increase that occurs over 5 years: 5(0.0293) = **0.1465 billion miles**.

8. **D) is correct.**

    Use the formula for the area of a rectangle to find the increase in its size.

    $A = lw$

    $A = (1.4l)(0.6w)$

    $A = 0.84lw$

    The new area will be 84% of the original area, a **decrease of 16%**.

9. **A) is correct.**

    Multiply the digits and add the exponents.

    $(1.2 \times 10^{-3}) (1.13 \times 10^{-4})$

    $1.2 \times 1.13 = 1.356$

    $-3 + (-4) = -7$

    1.356×10^{-7}

10. **D) is correct.**

    Set up a system of equations.

    $\overline{OD}$ bisects $\angle AOF$:

    $50 + a + b = 30 + c$

    $\overline{BO}$ bisects $\angle AOD$: $50 = a + b$

    Substitute and solve.

    $50 + 50 = 30 + c$

    $c = 70$

    Add each angle to find m$\angle AOF$.

    $\angle AOF = 50° + a° + b° + 30° + c°$

    $\angle AOF = 50° + 50° + 30° + 70°$

    $\angle AOF = \mathbf{200°}$

11. **C) is correct.**

Evaluate to find greatest.

$-4(3)(-2) = 24$

$-16 - 17 + 31 = -2$

$18 - 15 + 27 = $ **30**

$-20 + 10 + 10 = 0$

12. **D) is correct.**

Plug in each set of values and determine if the inequality is true.

$2(0) + 0 \leq -10$ FALSE

$2(10) + 2 \leq -10$ FALSE

$2(10) + 10 \leq -10$ FALSE

$2(-10) + (-10) \leq -10$ TRUE

13. **C) is correct.**

The greatest distance will be between two points at opposite ends of each sphere's diameters. Find the diameter of each sphere and add them.

$36\pi = \frac{4}{3}\pi r_1^{3}$

$r_1 = 3$

$d_1 = 2(3) = 6$

$288\pi = \frac{4}{3}\pi r_2^{3}$

$r_2 = 6$

$d_2 = 2(6) = 12$

$d_1 + d_1 = 6 + 12 = $ **18**

14. **B) is correct.**

Evaluate to find non-negative.

$(-3)(-1)(2)(-1) = -6$

$14 - 7 + (-7) = $ **0**

$7 - 10 + (-8) = -11$

$-5(-2)(-3) = -30$

15. **B) is correct.**

Use the triangle inequality theorem to find the possible values for the third side, then calculate the possible perimeters.

$13 - 5 < s < 13 + 5$

$8 < s < 18$

$13 + 5 + 8 < P < 13 + 5 + 18$

$26 < P < 36$

26.5 is the only answer choice in this range.

16. **B) is correct.**

Multiply by the converstion factor to get from pounds to kilograms.

8 pounds, 8 ounces = 8.5 pounds

8.5 lb. $\left(\dfrac{1\text{ kg}}{2.2\text{ lb.}}\right)$ = **3.9 kg**

17. D) is correct.

Factor the expression using the greatest common factor of 3.

$54z^4 + 18z^3 + 3z + 3 =$

$3(18z^4 + 6z^3 + z + 1)$

18. D) is correct.

Write each value in decimal form and compare.

$-0.95 < 0 < 0.4 < 0.35 < 0.75$ FALSE

$-1 < -0.1 < -0.11 < 0.8\overline{3} < 0.75$ FALSE

$-0.75 < -0.2 < 0 < 0.\overline{66} < 0.55$ FALSE

$-1.1 < -0.8 < -0.13 < 0.7 < 0.\overline{81}$ TRUE

19. A) is correct.

Find the amount the state will spend on infrastructure and education, and then find the difference.

infrastructure = $0.2(3,000,000,000) = 600,000,000$

education = $0.18(3,000,000,000) = 540,000,000$

$600,000,000 - 540,000,000 =$ **$60,000,000**

20. C) is correct.

Use the rules of exponents to simplify the expression.

$$\left(\dfrac{4x^{-3}y^4z}{8x^{-5}y^3z^{-2}}\right)^2 = \left(\dfrac{x^2yz^3}{2}\right)^2$$

$$= \dfrac{x^4y^2z^6}{4}$$

21. B) is correct.

The axis of symmetry will be a vertical line that runs through the vertex, which is the point $(-3,5)$. The line of symmetry is **$x = -3$**.

22. B) is correct.

Multiply by the complex conjugate and simplify.

$$\dfrac{3 + \sqrt{3}}{4 - \sqrt{3}}\left(\dfrac{4 + \sqrt{3}}{4 + \sqrt{3}}\right) = \dfrac{12 + 4\sqrt{3} + 3\sqrt{3} + 3}{16 - 4\sqrt{3} + 4\sqrt{3} - 3}$$

$$= \dfrac{15 + 7\sqrt{3}}{13}$$

23. B) is correct.

Use the Pythagorean theorem to determine which set of values forms a right triangle.

$40^2 + 41^2 = 50^2$

$3{,}281 \neq 2{,}500$

$9^2 + 40^2 = 41^2$

$1{,}681 = 1{,}681$

$9^2 + 30^2 = 40^2$

$981 \neq 1{,}600$

$40^2 + 50^2 = 63^2$

$4{,}100 \neq 3{,}969$

24. C) is correct.

Use the formula for percent change.

$$\text{percent change} = \frac{\text{amount of change}}{\text{original amount}}$$

$$= \frac{(7{,}375 - 7{,}250)}{7{,}250} = 0.017 = \textbf{1.7\%}$$

25. B) is correct.

Plug each value into the equation.

$4(3 + 4)^2 - 4(3)^2 + 20 = 180 \neq 276$

$4(6 + 4)2 - 4(6)2 + 20 = 276$

$4(12 + 4)^2 - 4(12)^2 + 20 = 468 \neq 276$

$4(24 + 4)^2 - 4(24)^2 + 20 = 852 \neq 276$

26. C) is correct.

The absolute value of $f(x)$ equals 1 twice: once in quadrant I and once in quadrant III.

27. D) is correct.

Complete the square to put the quadratic equation in vertex form.

$y = 2x^2 + 12x - 3$

$y = 2(x^2 + 6x + \underline{\quad}) - 3 + \underline{\quad}$

$y = 2(x^2 + 6x + 9) - 3 - 18$

$y = 2(x + 3)^2 - 21$

28. D) is correct.

Divide the digits and subtract the exponents.

$$\frac{7.2 \times 10^6}{1.6 \times 10^{-3}}$$

$7.2 \div 1.6 = 4.5$

$6 - (-3) = 9$

4.5×10^9

29. B) is correct.

I. True: The row "25 – 34 years old" and the column "more than 4 hours" show a relative frequency of 0.20 or 20%.

II. True: The total relative frequency of participants who spend 2 to 4 hours on social media a day is 0.26 or 26%.

III. False: These percentages cannot be added because the "whole" is not the same. To calculate the percentage of people aged 15 – 34 who use social media less than 2 hours a day, find the total number of people in each category and divide by the total number of people in both categories.

people 15 – 24 years old spending < 2 hrs. = 0.15(200) = 30

people 25 – 34 years old spending < 2 hrs. = 0.52(200) = 104

percentage of people 15 – 34 years old spending < 2 hrs. = $\frac{30 + 104}{400}$ = 0.34 = 34%

IV. False: The number of people aged 35 – 45 who used social media more than 4 hours a day is 0.05(200) = 10.

30. **A) is correct.** In 2012, New York had more months with less than 3 inches of rain than either Chicago or Houston.

31. **D) is correct.** Use the graph to find the number of months Chicago had less than 3 inches of rain in a year, and then find the average.

months with < 3 inches rain in Chicago: {7, 8, 10, 7, 9, 10, 10}

$\frac{(7 + 8 + 10 + 7 + 9 + 10 + 10)}{7}$ = 8.7 ≈ **9**

32. **D) is correct.**

Simplify using PEMDAS.

$(3^2 \div 1^3) - (4 - 8^2) + 2^4$

$= (9 \div 1) - (4 - 64) + 16$

$= 9 - (-60) + 16 = \mathbf{85}$

33. **A) is correct.** Find the probability that the second marble will be green if the first marble is blue, silver, or green, and then add these probabilities together.

$P(\text{first blue and second green}) = P(\text{blue}) \times P(\text{green|first blue}) =$

$\frac{6}{18} \times \frac{4}{17} = \frac{4}{51}$

$P(\text{first silver and second green}) = P(\text{silver}) \times P(\text{green|first silver}) =$

$\frac{8}{18} \times \frac{4}{17} = \frac{16}{153}$

$P(\text{first green and second green}) = P(\text{green}) \times P(\text{green|first green}) = \frac{4}{18} \times \frac{3}{17}$

$= \frac{2}{51}$

$P(\text{second green}) = \frac{4}{51} + \frac{16}{153} + \frac{2}{51} = \mathbf{\frac{2}{9}}$

34. **A) is correct.** Use the zeros of the function to find the intervals where it is less than 0.

$2x^2 - 4x - 6 = 0$

$(2x - 6)(x + 1) = 0$

$x = 3 \text{ and } x = -1$

$(-\infty, -1) \rightarrow 2x^2 - 4x - 6 > 0$

$(-1, 3) \rightarrow 2x^2 - 4x - 6 < 0$

$(3, \infty) \rightarrow 2x^2 - 4x - 6 > 0$

The function is less than 0 on the interval **(−1,3)**.

35. **C) is correct.** Find the measure of each angle.

$m\angle a = 180 - (70 + 40) = 70°$

$m\angle b = 70°$

$m\angle c = 180 - 40 = 140°$

$m\angle d = 40°$

$\angle \mathbf{a} \cong \angle \mathbf{b}$

36. **D) is correct.** Simplify using PEMDAS.

$z^3(z + 2)^2 - 4z^3 + 2$

$z^3(z^2 + 4z + 4) - 4z^3 + 2$

$z^5 + 4z^4 + 4z^3 - 4z^3 + 2$

$\mathbf{z^5 + 4z^4 + 2}$

37. **C) is correct.**

total seats = 4,500 + 2,000

$$\frac{\text{lower seats}}{\text{all seats}} = \frac{4,500}{6,500} = \mathbf{\frac{9}{13}}$$

38. **D) is correct.** Solve each equation for y and find the equation with a power of 1.

$$\sqrt[3]{y} = x \rightarrow y = x^3$$

$$\sqrt[3]{x} = y \rightarrow y = \sqrt[3]{x}$$

$$\sqrt[3]{y} = x^2 \rightarrow y = x^6$$

$$y = \sqrt[3]{x^3} \rightarrow \mathbf{y = x}$$

39. **C) is correct.** Use the formula for the volume of a sphere to find its radius.

$$V = \frac{4}{3}\pi r^3$$

$$972\pi = \frac{4}{3}\pi r^3$$

$$r = 9$$

Use the super Pythagorean theorem to find the side of the cube.

$$d^2 = a^2 + b^2 + c^2$$

$$18^2 = 3s^2$$

$$s \approx 10.4$$

Use the length of the side to find the volume of the cube.

$$V = s^3$$

$$V \approx (10.4)^3$$

$$\mathbf{V \approx 1,125}$$

40. **C) is correct.**

Use the formula for percentages.

$$\text{percent} = \frac{\text{part}}{\text{whole}} = \frac{42}{48}$$

$$= 0.875 = \mathbf{87.5\%}$$

41. **A) is correct.** If the data is skewed right, the set includes extremes values that are to the right, or high. The median is unaffected by these high values, but the mean includes these high values and would therefore be greater.

42. **C) is correct.** Plug 0 in for x and solve for y.

$$7y - 42x + 7 = 0$$

$$7y - 42(0) + 7 = 0$$

$$y = -1$$

The y-intercept is at **(0,−1)**.

43. **B) is correct.** Factor the trinomial and set each factor equal to 0.

$$2n^2 + 2n - 12 = 0$$

$$2(n^2 + n - 6) = 0$$

$2(n + 3)(n - 2) = 0$

$n = -3$ and $n = 2$

44. **C) is correct.** Find the slope of line b, take the negative reciprocal to find the slope of a, and test each point.

$(x_1, y_1) = (-100,100)$

$(x_2, y_2) = (-95,115)$

$m_b = \dfrac{115 - 100}{-95 - (-100)} = \dfrac{15}{5} = 3$

$m_a = -\dfrac{1}{3}$

$(104,168): \ -\dfrac{100 - 168}{-100 - (104)} = \dfrac{1}{3}$

$(-95,115): \ -\dfrac{100 - 115}{-100 - (-95)} = 3$

$(-112,104): \ -\dfrac{100 - 104}{-100 - (-112)} = -\dfrac{1}{3}$

$(-112,-104): \ \dfrac{100 - (-104)}{-100 - (-112)} = 17$

45. **D) is correct.** There are an infinite number of points with distance four from the origin, all of which lie on a circle centered at the origin with a radius of 4.

46. **B) is correct.**

Write a proportion and then solve for x.

$$\frac{15{,}036}{7} = \frac{x}{2}$$

$$7x = 30{,}072$$

$$x = 4{,}296$$

47. **D) is correct.** Simplify using PEMDAS.

$$5^2 \times (-5)^{-2} - 5^{-1}$$

$$= 25 \times \frac{1}{25} - \frac{1}{5}$$

$$= 1 - \frac{1}{5} = \frac{4}{5}$$

48. **A) is correct.** Corresponding angles in right triangles are not necessarily the same, so they do not have to be similar.

B) All spheres are similar.

C) Corresponding angles in 30−60−90 triangles are the same, so all 30−60−90 triangles are similar.

D) Corresponding angles in a square are all the same (90°), so all squares are similar.

49. **B) is correct.**

Use the rules of exponents to simplify the expression.

$$\frac{(3x^2y^2)^2}{3^3x^{-2}y^3} = \frac{3^2x^4y^4}{3^3x^{-2}y^3} = \frac{x^6y}{3}$$

50. **B) is correct.** Use the equation for Bernoulli trials (binomial distribution).

$$P = {}_nC_r(p^r)(q^{n-r})$$

$$n = 10$$

$$r = 3$$

$$p = \frac{4}{36} = \frac{1}{9}$$

$$q = \frac{8}{9}$$

$$P = {}_{10}C_3\left(\frac{1}{9}\right)^3\left(\frac{8}{9}\right)^7 = 0.072 = 7.2\%$$

ENGLISH LANGUAGE ARTS

Writing Task:

Some people have argued that states should raise the driving age for teens from sixteen to seventeen or even eighteen. They are wrong.

Many people worry about young, impulsive, inexperienced drivers on the road harming themselves and others. But what about the hardships this change would impose on parents and teens? For example, some teens provide income to their families by working a part-time job that they need a car for. Other families depend on their teens to pick up younger siblings from school and take them to doctor's appointments or other obligations using a car.

Instead of restricting teen driving and possibly harming families, we should find solutions to the issue. Some states already have graduated licensing and improved driver's education courses to reduce teen fatalities and road accidents. Teen drivers are not denied licenses; instead, they have stricter rules for driving. The rules become more relaxed as drivers get more experienced. Teenage drivers also face harsher penalties for traffic offenses. Other rules like increasing the amount of supervised driving time and limiting the number of passengers a teen driver can carry will improve that teen's skills on the road.

Car accidents are a major cause of death for teens, but raising the driving age will not automatically improve young drivers when they do get behind the wheel. Instead, states should experiment with licensing requirements and improved driver's ed. Before eliminating a beloved rite of passage for American teens, inconveniencing families, and demonstrating to teens that that they cannot be trusted, states should address dangers and problems with solutions that work.

Multiple-Choice Questions:

1. **C)** The adjective *presidential* modifies the common noun *election*; neither word should be capitalized.

2. **B)** The first clause is a dependent clause, so it must be connected to the second (independent) clause with a comma.

3. **A)** There are no modifying phrases requiring commas, so there should be no punctuation between the subject and verb.

4. **C)** This choice creates a complete, uninterrupted sentence because the content that follows *factors* is grammatically nonessential. That is, the sentence make sense without listing the factors. The phrase "including population size and rate of reproduction" cannot exist on its own as an independent clause.

5. **B)** As a proper noun, *Independence Day* should be capitalized. The common noun *summer* should not be capitalized.

6. **C)** The first clause ("Though the term...") is a dependent clause, so it must be connected to the second (independent) clause with a comma.

7. **D)** Capitalization is properly used in this sentence. The common noun *aunt* should not be capitalized unless it is used as part of someone's name.

8. **D)** The phrase "in addition" is the appropriate transitional phrase to signify the additive relationship between the two clauses.

9. **A)** This compound sentence requires a comma after *surroundings* to connect the independent clauses using the coordinating conjunction *and*. Furthermore, an apostrophe is not needed in *its* because it is a possessive pronoun, not a contraction.

10. **C)** The only proper nouns in this sentence are *Austin* and *Texas*, so they are the only underlined words that must be capitalized.

11. **A)** The transitional phrase "on the other hand" appropriately signifies the opposing ideas in the two pieces of information.

12. **B)** This compound sentence requires a comma before the coordinating conjunction *but*.

13. **C)** The only proper noun in the underlined portion is *Microsoft*, so it is the only word that should be capitalized.

14. **B)** The preposition *with* correctly completes the prepositional idiom "combined with" to communicate the intended meaning (that two things are combined with each other).

15. **A)** These two independent clauses must be connected with a comma because they include the conjunction *but*.

16. **C)** All the underlined words are common nouns, so they should not be capitalized.

17. **A)** *Relatively* is an adverb that modifies *widely*, an adverb that modifies the adjective *available*.

18. **D)** The only proper noun in the underlined portion is *August*, so it is the only word that should be capitalized.

19. **A)** No punctuation is needed in this sentence, for there are no dependent clauses. "From the bakery down the street" is a combination of two prepositional phrases.

20. **B)** In this choice, the verb *take* is correctly conjugated and correlating conjunctions "either...or" are correctly paired.

21. **C)** This is the best way to rewrite the sentence. The other choices are wordy or create dangling modifiers.

22. **A)** Choice A correctly connects two independent clauses, "DeQuan loves eating pizza" and "meat toppings make him feel queasy," using a comma and the coordinating conjunction *but*.

23. **A)** Choice A has no misplaced modifiers; this choice makes it clear who burned the soup (Mario) and how he did so (by leaving it on the stove for too long).

24. **C)** Modifying relationships are clear in this sentence: "which played for over a minute" correctly modifies *signal*.

25. **B)** This version maintains parallel structure. All items in the list are nouns (dearth, lack, and list), followed by prepositions (of) and objects of the prepositions (wins, time, and clients).

26. **C)** The word *there* is an indefinite pronoun that indicates a place, as called for in the sentence context. The contraction *they're* means "they are," and *their* is a plural possessive pronoun.

27. **D)** This sentence begins with a dependent clause modifying *our family*. Its original form is the most concise version.

28. **C)** The clearest and most concise version is choice C.

29. **A)** This choice is most concise and contains no errors in usage or grammar.

30. **B)** This sentence is the clearest and most concise, with no grammatical or usage errors.

31. **D)** The original version of the sentence is the most clear and concise, with no errors.

32. **C)** This version correctly uses a coordinating conjunction (but) and a comma to connect two independent clauses.

33. **D)** The original version of this simple sentence is the most concise with no errors.

34. **B)** This sentence begins with a dependent clause attached to the main clause with a comma. It contains no errors and is the most concise version.

35. **B)** A dependent clause is correctly connected to an independent clause with a comma in this version, which is more concise than the other choices.

36. A) This version correctly combines two independent clauses with a coordinating conjunction and a comma, does not contain any grammatical errors, has no dangling modifiers, and is the most concise.

37. D) The current version of the sentence is the clearest, most concise choice.

38. A) This information is unnecessary and detracts from the point of the passage.

39. B) The phrase "in fact" draws attention to interesting information that builds on the previous sentence.

40. C) *His* should become *their* because the work belongs to two people (Goddard and Szilard).

41. D) This choice provides a brief but interesting overview of the information to come.

42. A) This sentence relates directly to the overall idea of the passage—that science fiction has a natural influence on real life.

43. D) The information in the two clauses is equally significant and both ideas require stand-alone sentences.

44. D) The phrase "the animals around us" provides the reader with specific information about what "we do not control."

45. D) The introductory sentence as it is written is appropriately specific in introducing the topic of the paragraph.

46. A) *Observing*, preceded by a comma, correctly sets off the participial phrase that gives more information about Ken Allen.

47. A) Though it is interesting information, the details in this sentence are unnecessary, and they detract from the overall meaning of the paragraph.

48. C) This sentence provides an appropriate amount of detail and reminds the audience of the author's overall purpose—to communicate that humans are not in control of animals.

READING COMPREHENSION

1. **A) is correct.** The passage indicates that a snake's "intricate diamonds, stripes, and swirls help the animals hide from predators, but perhaps most importantly (for us humans, anyway), the markings can also indicate whether the snake is venomous."

2. **B) is correct.** The final paragraph of the passage states that the two species "frequently [share] a habitat" and that a "predatory hawk or eagle, usually hunting from high in the sky, can't tell the difference between the two species, and so the kingsnake gets passed over and lives another day."

3. **D) is correct.** This summary captures the main ideas of each paragraph.

4. **C) is correct.** The first paragraph states that "[w]hile it might seem counterintuitive for a venomous snake to stand out in bright red or blue, that fancy costume tells any nearby predator that approaching him would be a bad idea." The coral snake's markings do not allow it to hide from predators but rather to "ward [them] off."

5. **A) is correct.** The passage states that "intricate diamonds, stripes, and swirls help the animals hide from predators," implying that these markings are complex enough to allow the animals to blend in with their surroundings.

6. **C) is correct.** The second paragraph states that "[t]he scarlet kingsnake, for example, has very similar markings to the venomous coral snake with whom it frequently shares a habitat. However, the kingsnake is actually nonvenomous."

7. **D) is correct.** This passage is a step-by-step explanation of how to brew a cup of coffee.

8. **D) is correct.** This choice lists the steps for brewing coffee in the same order as the passage.

9. **A) is correct.** The author describes the steps for making coffee in chronological order.

10. **B) is correct.** The writer uses the first person, showing his or her opinion, to recommend a French press as the best way to brew coffee.

11. **D) is correct.** The passage mentions several times that decisions about things like water minerals, ground size, and steep time will depend on the preference of the coffee drinker.

12. **A) is correct.** The passage as a whole describes from start to finish how to make a cup of coffee the drinker will enjoy.

13. **A) is correct.** This choice addresses all of the main ideas of the passage: the flu is potentially deadly, highly infectious, and difficult to contain due to viral shedding.

14. **D) is correct.** According to the passage, "the flu is...relatively difficult to contract," and "[w]hile many people who contract the virus will recover, many others will not."

15. **C) is correct.** The second paragraph states that the flu is "relatively difficult to contract" because it "can only be transmitted when individuals come into direct contact with bodily fluids of people infected with the flu or when they are exposed to expelled aerosol particles."

16. **A) is correct.** The author uses the term *measures* to describe the steps that people take to prevent the spreading of the influenza virus.

17. **C) is correct.** The final paragraph of the passage states that viral shedding is "the process by which the body releases viruses that have been successfully reproducing during the infection."

18. **A) is correct.** The second paragraph of the passage states that "the virus can be contained with fairly simple health measures like hand washing and face masks."

19. **B) is correct.** The author writes that "[a]s these communities have evolved, the species in them have developed complex, long-term interspecies interactions known as symbiotic relationships." She then goes on to describe the different types of symbiotic relationships that exist.

20. **C) is correct.** The author writes, "A relationship where one individual benefits and the other is harmed is known as parasitism."

21. **D) is correct.** The author writes, "Often, relationships described as commensal include one species that feeds on another species' leftovers; remoras, for instance, will attach themselves to sharks and eat the food particles they leave behind. It might seem like the shark gets nothing from the relationship, but a closer look will show that sharks in fact benefit from remoras, which clean the sharks' skin and remove parasites."

22. **A) is correct.** The author writes, "But is it possible for two species to interact and for one to remain completely unaffected?...In fact, many scientists claim that relationships currently described as commensal are just mutualistic or parasitic in ways that haven't been discovered yet."

23. **D) is correct.** The author writes, "The bacteria, fungi, insects, plants, and animals that live together in a habitat have evolved to share a pool of limited resources...As these communities have evolved, the species in them have developed complex, long-term interspecies interactions known as symbiotic relationships."

24. **A) is correct.** The author writes that "[t]here's yet another class of symbiosis that is controversial among scientists" and goes on to say that "many scientists claim the relationships currently described as commensal are just mutualistic or parasitic in ways that haven't been discovered yet." This implies that scientists debate about the topic of commensalism.

25. **B) is correct.** In the second paragraph, the author writes, "The [hand washing] process doesn't even require warm water—studies have shown that cold water is just as effective at reducing the number of microbes on the hands. Antibacterial soaps are also available, although several studies have shown that simple soap and cold water is just as effective."

26. **C) is correct.** Together, these sentences provide an adequate summary of the passage overall.

27. **D) is correct.** The author writes that "hands 'cleaned' with hand sanitizer may still harbor pathogens" because sanitizer "does nothing to remove organic matter" from the hands. The bacteria are not completely washed off, and therefore some are able to continue living on the surface of the hands.

28. **B) is correct.** The author writes that because hand sanitizer "isn't rinsed from hands" like water is, "it only kills pathogens and does nothing to remove organic matter."

29. **A) is correct.** Each paragraph examines hand washing from a different angle.

30. **A) is correct.** In the first paragraph, the author writes, "Many illnesses are spread when people touch infected surfaces, such as door handles or other people's hands, and then touch their own eyes, mouths, or noses." The reader can infer from this sentence that hand washing prevents the spread of surface-borne illnesses.

31. **A) is correct.** This detail is not stated in the passage.

32. **B) is correct.** In the first paragraph, the author writes, "But what's the best way to get an accurate reading? The answer depends on the situation." She then goes on to describe various options and their applications.

33. **B) is correct.** The author indicates that "[t]he most common way people measure body temperature is orally" but that "[t]here are many situations... when measuring temperature orally isn't an option." She then goes on to describe these situations in the second and third paragraphs.

34. **A) is correct.** The final paragraph states that "agitated patients...won't be able to sit still long enough for an accurate reading." The reader can infer that an agitated patient is a patient who is visibly upset, annoyed, or uncomfortable.

35. **A) is correct.** The second paragraph of the passage states that "[u]sing the rectum also has the added benefit of providing a much more accurate reading than other locations can provide."

36. **A) is correct.** The author states that "[p]opcorn continued to rule the snack food kingdom until the rise in popularity of home televisions during the 1950s" when the industry saw a "decline in sales" as a result of the changing pastimes of the American people.

37. **B) is correct.** The author states, "For the Aztec Indians who called the caves home, popcorn (or *momochitl*) played an important role in society, both as a food staple and in ceremonies." This implies that the Aztec people popped popcorn both for special occasions ("in ceremonies") and for regular consumption ("as a food staple").

38. **C) is correct.** In the opening paragraph the author writes, "But popcorn isn't just for fun—it's also a multimillion-dollar-a-year industry with a long and fascinating history." The author then goes on to illustrate the history of popcorn from the ancient Aztecs, to early twentieth century America, to the present day.

39. **C) is correct.** The author writes, "The popcorn industry flourished during the Great Depression when it was advertised as a wholesome and economical food."

40. **A) is correct.** This statement summarizes the entire passage, including the brief history of popcorn in ancient cultures and the growth in the popularity of popcorn in America.

41. **C) is correct.** The author writes, "However, it wasn't until microwave popcorn became commercially available in 1981 that at-home popcorn consumption began to grow exponentially. With the wide availability of microwaves in the United States, popcorn also began popping up in offices and hotel rooms."

42. **A) is correct.** The author provides an overview of the various elements that affect credit scores and offers suggestions about how to improve credit scores.

43. **D) is correct.** The author writes that "[w]ith every payment, your credit report improves and banks will be more likely to loan you money. These new loans will in turn raise your score even further (as long as you keep making payments, of course)." Thus, it can be inferred that someone who has paid off a large amount of money and paid it back in time will have a high credit score.

44. **C) is correct.** This statement provides an adequate summary of the passage, as it explains what a credit score is and how individuals can raise their credit scores.

45. **A) is correct.** In this context, *distilled* refers to the process of creditors taking the "massive amount of information [that] is summed up in a credit report" and converting it into a single value that represents the overall reliability of the potential borrower or renter.

46. **D) is correct.** The word *scourge* is emotional and representative of the author's personal opinion about predatory lenders.

47. **C) is correct.** The author writes that "having nothing on your credit report can result in low credit limits and high interest rates." This implies that someone who has borrowed and paid back a loan on time will likely have higher limits and lower interest rates than someone who has no credit history.

48. **C) is correct.** The author writes that "[e]ven your employer can access a modified version of your credit report (although it will not have your actual credit score on it)."

49. **B) is correct.** The passage is primarily informative. However, the author uses jokes like the one in the last paragraph to entertain readers.

50. **C) is correct.** To entertain readers, the author is referring to the following rhyme: "I scream, you scream, we all scream for ice cream."

51. **B) is correct.** As the title shows, the passage is mainly about the causes of brain freeze. The other sentences provide details that support the main idea.

52. **D) is correct.** In paragraph 2, the author writes, "When a cold substance … presses against the roof of your mouth, it causes blood vessels there to begin to constrict." *Constrict* is a synonym for narrow or shrink.

53. **B) is correct.** Readers can infer that when the tongue grows cold due to contact with cold substances such as ice cream, snow cones, or iced drinks, it does not trigger brain freeze.

54. **A) is correct.** In the last sentence, the author writes, "The duration of the pain varies from a few seconds up to about a minute." Readers can infer that "duration of the pain" means "how long the pain lasts." An ice cream headache is short, luckily.

VOCABULARY

1. **C) is correct.** *Apathetic* means "indifferent."

2. **A) is correct.** *Belligerent* means "hostile."

3. **B) is correct.** *Callous* means "insensitive."

4. **D) is correct.** *Hinder* means "impede" or "get in the way of" something.

5. **B) is correct.** *Lucid* means "rational" or "clear."

6. **A) is correct.** *Pilfering* means "stealing."

7. **C) is correct.** *Inconspicuous* means "unnoticeable" or "hard to see."

8. **A) is correct.** *Frantic* means "frenzied" or "panicked."

9. **C) is correct.** *Exacerbated* means "to make something worse" or "aggravate."

10. **D) is correct.** *Verbose* means "wordy."

11. **D) is correct.** Here, *to foster* means "to promote." It can also mean "to take care of."

12. **A) is correct.** *To quantify* is "to measure" or "count the value of something."

13. **C) is correct.** *Hydration* refers to "the act of meeting body fluid demands."

14. **B) is correct.** *Asymmetric* means "lacking symmetry or unbalanced."

15. **C) is correct.** *Precaution* means "an act done in advance to ensure safety or benefit" or "protection against something or someone."

16. **B) is correct.** *Adversely* means "harmful to one's interest; unfortunate."

17. **A) is correct.** *Excessive* means "exceeding what is normal or necessary."

18. **D) is correct.** *Sensible* means having "good sense or reason."

19. **B) is correct.** *Justify* means "to show to be just or right."

20. **B) is correct.** *Progress* means "gradual improvement."

21. **C) is correct.** *Priority* means "first in order of importance" or "precedence"; the one who goes first.

22. **B) is correct.** *Absorb* means "to take in" information or a substance (a sponge absorbs water; a brain absorbs information).

23. **D) is correct.** *Consistency* means "conforming to regular patterns, habits, principles," and so on.

24. **A) is correct.** *Access* means "to enter or gain admission."

25. **A) is correct.** *Fatigue* means "weariness from physical or mental exertion."

26. **D) is correct.** *Abbreviate* means "to shorten or abridge."

27. **C) is correct.** *Hygiene* refers to "habits and conditions, like cleanliness, that promote health."

28. **B) is correct.** *Collaborate* means to "work together on a common project."

29. **B) is correct.** *Subtle* means "understated."

30. **D) is correct.** *Deficiency* means "an amount that is lacking or inadequate."

To take your second CHSPE practice test, follow the link below:

www.acceptedinc.com/chspe-online-resources